CW01083026

COSMIC INFLUENCES
ON HUMAN BEHAVIOR

'Until the beginning of this century, science believed that man was in isolation on earth, separated from the rest of the universe. Now we know that the biological clocks of our brain and our body are attuned to the movement of cosmic forces. . . . This new conception should have not only scientific but also philosophical and even poetic implications for modern thought."

Also published by Aurora Press
How Cosmic and Atmospheric Conditions Affect Your Health
—Dr. Michel Gauquelin

Other titles by Dr. Michel Gauquelin include:
Cosmic Clocks
Planetary Heredity
The Gauquelin Book of American Charts
Written In The Stars

COSMIC INFLUENCES ON HUMAN BEHAVIOR

The Planetary Factors in Personality

by
Dr. Michel Gauquelin

*Translated from the French by
Joyce E. Clemow*

AURORA PRESS

© Aurora Press Inc. 1994

Aurora Press
P.O. Box 573
Santa Fe, NM 87504

Library of Congress Cataloging in Publication Data
Gauquelin, Michel.
    Cosmic influences on human behavior.

    Translation of Le dossier des influences cosmiques.
    1. Astrology. I. Title.
BF1708.2.G3813   1978   133.5   77–28405
ISBN 0–943358–23–X

Contents

Contents

DR. MICHEL GAUQUELIN
Nov. 13, 1928 — May 20, 1991

I first met Michel when he spoke at the January 1969 National Astrological Society conference in New York City that I had organized. Having read his *L'Influence des Astres*, which established the "Mars effect," I expected to meet a dry statistician. Instead I found him warm, with an original sense of humor. He was open and accessible to anyone seeking information. He surprised me with his uncanny ability to guess people's rising planets.

An accomplished tennis player he was ranked among the 50 leading French tennis players. Trained at the Sorbonne in psychology and statistics, he devoted his career to investigating a subject that caused his academic colleagues to attack him. Michel demonstrated courage in confronting and debating his often vicious critics. He provided the *first* significant validation of the astrological hypothesis that man is connected to the cosmos and that planetary positions correlate to specific personality traits. Ironically, while his ground-breaking work provided scientific proof for correlations of planetary effects, his research gave little support to many long-held astrological beliefs. His initial work correlated Mars in the "zones of power" with famous sportsmen. He later connected the Moon in "zones of power" with writers, Saturn with scientists, and Jupiter with actors and politicians.

Michel possessed enormous discipline, impartiality and integrity, always presenting both his positive and negative results. All his initial research (before computers) was undertaken by gathering and calculating extensive horoscope data by hand: he would canvas Europe to collect this data personally paying the requisite fees to registries. During a visit to his laboratory I was overwhelmed viewing thousands of 3 x 5 cards which contained all the data.

In 1989, He was awarded the National Astrological Society's *Marc Edmund Jones Award*, in recognition for his lifelong achievements, which provided astrologers with significant data to communicate to a skeptical scientific establishment.

His untimely death is a tragedy for the whole astrological community. Astrologers owe Michel Gauquelin an enormous debt. His pioneering research laid the scientific foundation for validating planetary effects.   —*Barbara Somerfield*

"General impressions are never to be trusted. Unfortunately when they are of long standing they become fixed rules of life and assume a prescriptive right not to be questioned. Consequently those who are not accustomed to original inquiry entertain a hatred and a horror of statistics. They cannot endure the idea of submitting their sacred impressions to cold-blooded verification. But it is the triumph of scientific men to rise superior to such superstition, to desire tests by which the value of beliefs may be ascertained, and to feel sufficiently masters of themselves to discard contemptuously whatever may be found untrue."

—FRANCIS GALTON

Foreword

No man should hold it to be incredible that
out of the astrologer's foolishness and blasphemies some useful and sacred knowledge may
come . . .

JOHANNES KEPLER

KEPLER'S WORDS might well apply to the results of the
life's work of the Gauquelins. For a quarter of a century
or so they have worked in a "scientifically forbidden" field
and have succeeded not only in demonstrating the "astrologer's foolishness and blasphemies" but, what is far
more important, have demonstrated through discovery
that something of great potential usefulness is inherent in
it. There is a parallel between the labors of Kepler and
those of the Gauquelins. Kepler is known today for his
laws of planetary motion, but the devious and mystical
paths he took in their discovery are rarely recalled. These
laws had a strange history aborning. They truly "fell out"
of the mystical maze of Kepler's seeking for a correspondence between planetary orbits and the five perfect geometric solids, and for relations between the orbits of the
planets and the harmonious combinations of the musical
scale (he was overjoyed when he found that the ratio of
the perihelion and aphelion distances of the planets corresponded roughly to harmonious intervals on the musical
scale). There is no such correspondence or such relations,

but the search for them produced scientific results of monumental value. Out of such mystical musings came modern astronomy!

It is legitimate to wonder whether there might also be scientific fallout from Kepler's astrological musings as there was in astronomy.

Kepler's astrological thinking could no more be separated from his world view than could his ideas about perfect solids and the harmony between planetary orbits and the musical scales. But his "astrology" was not the popular superstition of the day. He warned certain theologians and philosophers that, "while justly rejecting the stargazer's superstition, they should not throw out the child with the bath water . . . For nothing exists nor happens in the visible sky that is not sensed in some hidden manner by the faculties of earth and nature."

The present book is a popular presentation of the results of a long and serious study, the data and results of which are embodied in thirteen volumes.* While not always in sympathy with the manner of presentation and style in this present book, I feel it a duty as an astronomer to call attention to the work of the Gauquelins as popularly summarized here. It is an even greater duty to call attention to the dedicated and tedious work embodied in the previously mentioned thirteen volumes.

This book deals with birth times and horoscopes, but the Gauquelins have *not* proved "astrology" any more than Kepler's laws proved that planets' orbits are based on the five perfect solids. They have, rather, disproved and disposed of much of the "astrologer's foolishness." Indeed, they have quite effectively *disproved* the "astrology of the masses"—the superstitious pap we find, for example, in many of our daily newspapers. Thus in chap-

---

*Currently 21 volumes have been published. See last page for details. Ed.

ter XIX ("The Three Astrological Roulette Wheels"), Gauquelin presents the results of tests on thousands of military men, sports champions, etc., in whose horoscopes, according to the rules of popular astrology, the zodiacal signs of Aries and Scorpio should figure prominently (since they are "governed" by the "planet of physical energy, combativeness, and aggressiveness," Mars), but found that only chance governed the distribution of births of this large group among the zodiacal signs. All down the line Gauquelin found *no basis* for popular astrology whatever.

Nor have I. Even though an astronomer, I am not a stranger to astrology. Many years ago, as a member of Professor Bart Bok's Harvard Committee on Astrology, I cast twenty thousand "horoscopes" of American scientists (sufficiently complete to determine the sign position and the aspects of the planet Mercury, which is touted in most astrological manuals as the "planet of the mind," and found no correlation whatever). (The director of the observatory of which I was a staff member at the time refused permission to publish even this negative result lest it be thought that his staff spent any time in matters of this sort!)

It is important that the claims of astrology be examined scientifically. I cannot agree with those scientists who proclaim the falseness of astrology on purely authoritarian grounds. Appeal solely to authority is not a part of the scientific method, and the public should not be taught that it is. The scientific method in this instance can be demonstrated to the public by applying it to popular astrology and proving that it does not work. With such documentation, garnered by empirical tests, the dignity of science is upheld and the word of the scientist supported by facts, not authority.

It is with considerable hesitancy nonetheless that I write this foreword, because for an astronomer to have anything whatsoever to do with anything remotely related to astrology seems enough to rule him out of the scientific fraternity. I do so, however, because as an astronomer I must discharge my duty to support any valid test of astrology, but more importantly because, quite surprisingly, the work of the Gauquelins has not thrown the baby out with the bath water, but rather has revealed an infant that may grow into a giant. This infant is "planetary heredity" and the demonstrated preferred planetary positions in the births of exceptional people. Kepler stressed the importance of the geometrical positions of the planets in the sky. The Gauquelins have found that two positions in the sky seem to be of prime importance, to the virtual exclusion of all others: the region immediately above the eastern horizon and that immediately past the meridian. This was a totally unexpected result and in astrological lore this result was not foreshadowed. Indeed, these results (which have since been independently confirmed by a group of Belgian investigators) should therefore not be called popular astrology, even though Gauquelin shows that the imagery and symbolism ascribed to Saturn, Mars, Jupiter, and the moon by ancient lore are extremely useful. Thus, through the centuries Mars has been the "planet of energy, aggressiveness, combativeness, etc.," and it is precisely Mars, and not any other planet, which most frequently holds these two critical positions in the horoscopes of outstanding sports champions and military men, in whom these qualities play an obvious part.

It is also a part of my scientific duty, however, to point out that there are parts of Gauquelin's presentation of the material with which I am not totally in sympathy. Its many allusions to astrological lore, which he uses for illustration and analogy, are in sharp contrast to his statistical results on "planetary heredity" and on the amazing preference for certain planetary positions at the time of the birth of *exceptional* people. In the latter he is on firm ground (for a full demonstration of this, however, the reader must refer to the scientific presentation in the aforementioned thirteen volumes). His statistical methods are sound, and one of the most convincing results of his statistical methods is that his findings on "planetary heredity" and on preferential positions of planets at the time of birth applies only to *natural* births, for he shows that births forced to suit the convenience of the obstetrician or of the hospital schedule *do not* show these planetary affinities.

We have thus a phenomenon perhaps much akin to the cosmic biological clocks of Frank Brown, and to the demonstrated influence of the lunar phases on rainfall, and on the mating and reactions of, particularly, the lower animal forms. Both Gauquelin and Brown theorize that their findings bespeak the influence on living matter of subtle changes in the magnetic fields surrounding it. Only time and much further experiment can render final judgment in these matters; the observational facts, however, stand on their own merit. They seem to signal a domain of nature of which science heretofore has been totally unaware.

J. ALLEN HYNEK
Chairman
Department of Astronomy
Northwestern University

Confession in the Form of a Prologue

As FAR BACK as I can go in my childhood, not to my earliest memories but to my first rational experiences, I have always known that I would be interested in astrology. Why? I do not know. Initially, chance played a role. No one in my family was an astrologer. They regarded horoscopes as a parlor game, nothing more. By the age of seven, I was asking my classmates their birth dates to tell them triumphantly the zodiac sign under which they were born.

By the age of ten, I was begging my father to show me how to calculate the ascendant of an astrological theme. This was during the "disaster" of 1940; my family, fleeing from the Germans, had taken refuge in the south of France for several months, leaving everything they owned behind them. However, I eagerly learned the laws of horoscope.

At the age of fifteen, together with a boy who has remained my best and most trusted friend, I cut classes at the Lycée Charlemagne to cross over the Seine and ferret through old Mr. Chacornac's astrological bookstore opposite Notre Dame de Paris. We had no money to buy books, so we read them there in the store. By the age of seventeen, I had devoured more than a hundred works on astrology and I was drafting my own "Treatise" during the tedious hours of French-Latin classes. One day the teacher caught me at it. He read my youthful compendium and was quite disconcerted by it. Shrugging his shoulders, he returned my work to me and predicted that I would fail the baccalaureat examination, which was rapidly approaching. I have kept this notebook with its hard gray cover, my first "Treatise." Even this year, my friend and I were still laughing about his embarrassment. Yet basically, I had absorbed all the mysteries of the horoscope. A childish game, a waste of time—who knows?

Until then, I had never asked myself this question: is all of this true? The limited success my predictions had earned me among my classmates, who had nicknamed me Nostradamus, and the small prestige which my specialty bestowed on me from very young persons of the opposite sex, were an ample reward. But the insatiable intellectual hunger that compelled me to read everything published about astrology was soon overcome by my desire to gather so many horoscopes that all skepticism would crumble under the weight of this proof.

I had discovered skepticism, not only in others, but also deep within myself. I could quote Descartes' first principle: Never accept anything as true unless I clearly and obviously know it to be true. But this would be deluding my readers and myself. One tends to rationalize afterward what has happened. I had at the very most a feeling that perhaps the astrological tree was concealing a forest of emptiness. Assurances from the astrologers I met were unrelated to the complex nature of the problem. It is true that for them there was no problem, and I found it increasingly difficult to tolerate their palaver. Was their proof only in their imaginations?

I decided to look for proofs and, if possible, to collect them. I began to frequent the Seine Archives, researching dates of birth. I filled notebook after notebook with figures, working as assiduously as a Benedictine monk. My head was full of such astrological aphorisms as: "Death occurs more frequently under the influence of Saturn;" "Professional soldiers are often born under the sign of Aries." I would find out if they were true or false. The little pocket money that I had was spent on stamps so that I could write to the many registry offices of France for records of hours of birth.

I was not the first to have this idea. Some astrologers, also claiming to be mathematicians, had believed that there was only one way to establish the validity of astrology: this was to provide statistics on a large number of births. Their books had convinced no one. Had they been mistaken? They had been mistaken, for mere enumerations are not sufficient. One must know the laws of chance. I enrolled at the Sorbonne to learn them.

A feeling of hopelessness, at first vague, crept into my thoughts. It seemed that astrological laws were quite incompatible with modern scientific knowledge. This realization was reinforced by the very unencouraging results obtained from the columns of figures I had tabulated in my large notebooks. No, death does not occur more frequently under the influence of Saturn. No, professional soldiers are not born any more frequently than poets under the sign of Aries.

Yet the passion did not desert me for a single moment. I examined the most obscure aspects of horoscopes to drain the astrological abscess and burst the zodiacal bubble, but also perhaps with the secret hope of being that "hard-working hen" referred to by Kepler, which "in the stinking dung-heap of astrology may find a grain of corn, indeed a pearl or nugget of gold, if it searches and scratches long enough."

I scratched for a long time and eventually I found the gold nugget. At least I believed I had. But at the same time, I was very much aware how unlikely it was that this was true. Could my pearl be an artificial one, a slip of my thoughts, or a mirage conjured up by my subconscious? I was alone with my problem.

But fate was watching over me. On the university benches I met Françoise, my future wife. She was my first listener, my first reader and above all, my first critic. She advised me to write a book setting forth all the labor I had performed in secret. It was to be the "antiastrological" summary of my statistics and the nugget of gold. "And so," she said, "people will read you and criticize you. Then you will know if you have truly found something and if it is worth the trouble of continuing." At the age of twenty-five I wrote that book and I found that it was worth the effort to continue.

This new book reveals how that time has been spent.

CHAPTER ONE

Is the Universe Astrological?

"You know that I believe in a disymmetric cosmic influence which naturally and constantly controls the molecular organization of those principles immediately necessary for life, and that, as a consequence, the types of controls of life are, in their structures, forms, and nuclear arrangements, in a relation with the motions of the universe."

—LOUIS PASTEUR, *letter to his friend Raulin, April 4, 1871*

AS EXPLORERS OF THE COSMOS, astronauts are the pioneer voyagers of distant worlds in the immensity of space. But who is exploring the inner cosmos of our souls and our destiny? The answer is: the astrologers. As early as the fifteenth century, Paracelsus said: "The planets are within us."

Astrology has always been popular. The mass media all assign time and space to it. It has even been incorporated into computer technology. In fact, it has become a daily consumer product.[1] Jean Porte, an administrator at the French National Institute of Statistics, noted, "If astrology's place in society is to be assessed by the number of printed words devoted to it, then it is certainly more important than that allotted by our society to astronomy and mathematics."[2] Yet can we really believe in horoscopes today?

Man in Isolation

From a scientific point of view, scientists claim, astrology is dead. Is it?

At the beginning of the twentieth century, science was categorically dogmatic in its theories. It had totally rejected its very old astrological past and was claiming that an impenetrable gulf existed between man and the sky. Astronomers were engrossed in a cosmos which was constantly becoming more vast, out of all proportion with humanity.

However, one factor distinguished the planet earth from the rest of the universe in the eyes of these early-twentieth-century scientists: earth was the only planet bearing life. The appearance of life on earth was considered an unpredictable, extremely improbable, almost impossible accident. The great English physicist Eddington serenely calculated the probability of life developing on earth at less than one chance in billions of billions. No voices opposing this point of view could be heard among his contemporaries. Man occupied an exceptional place in the universe. Was he the result of pure chance or design?

Biologists, however, saw no reason why life should be related to the cosmos. And this was their right since they believed that life was a strange, unique marvel at the heart of this cosmos. Scientists believed in a chemistry, biology, and psychology of isolation. Man was a prisoner on earth. The sky and the universe were present only through the transparent barrier of the atmosphere. Astronomers and physicists were examining the form of distant galaxies completely indifferent to the minute, improbable phenomenon called life.

The old doctrine that man is a microcosm, the sky a macrocosm, and that there are intimate sympathetic currents between them no longer predominated. It was simply forgotten.

But, as Claude Bernard said in 1856: "If one believes too strongly, the mind finds itself bound and limited by the consequences of its own reasoning. It no longer has freedom of action and thus lacks the initiative of those who know how to free themselves of this blind faith in theories which basically is nothing more than a scientific superstition."[3]

Man in Infinity

A new generation of scientists has replaced the preceding one. A new concept of the relationship between man and the universe has developed. Yesterday's truths have become fallacies. Life did not develop on earth by a stroke of luck. It had to develop here, because all the cosmic conditions necessary for the creation of life were present. The origin of life is now regarded as an unavoidable physico-chemical phenomenon. Oparin in the U.S.S.R. and Miller in the U.S.A. have proved that life was formed from the energy of ultraviolet rays from the sun acting on the waters in the primeval oceans.[4]

In this "primordial soup," to use Haldane's expression, cosmic forces transformed amino acids into proteins, proteins into the first cells, which, three billion years later, with the help of evolution, have produced man. Contemporary chemists and biologists, or at least those at the head of the scientific progress, believe life is primarily a cosmic phenomenon. Astronomers support this idea when, like Fred Hoyle, they claim that life is everywhere in the universe, in the countless galaxies of the universe where the conditions necessary to create life inevitably occur from time to time.[5] Life has a new dimension, the extraterrestrial dimension.

Cosmic Clocks

The path of the researcher appears established. He must not work in isolation any longer, but should describe the bonds uniting life and the universe and try to discover the unknown influences coming from space. A whole new train of thought has spread like wildfire throughout the scientific world.[6]

Professor G. Piccardi of Florence has founded an original science: cosmic chemistry. In the test tubes in his laboratory he has shown that chemical reactions are influenced by the action of the cosmos surrounding us. Professor Frank A. Brown and his colleagues at Northwestern University have demonstrated that numerous animal species "pick up" the mysterious messages emanating from the sun and the moon. Both the Russian biologist N. Schultz and the Japanese professor M. Takata have noted strange relationships, hitherto unknown, between solar activity and human blood.

Stone by stone, a new branch of knowledge is developing, that of cosmic clocks. Nature has woven a network of invisible threads between the cosmos and us. The theory of the "empty" cosmos and biology "in isolation" is disappearing from the scene. The cosmos is much more "present" and the sensitivity of living creatures to this cosmos is infinitely greater than was once believed. Man's biological clocks are dependent on the sky's clocks.

The age-old question can be asked again: Is our universe astrological? But there is an immediate objection. To absorb this recently discovered dimension of man into astrology is a crude conjuring trick similar to the antics of charlatans.

An Old Subject of Scientific Study

There have always been charlatans.[7] In this book, we are not going to discuss the "pop astrology" of the twentieth century with all of its ramifications. According to the surrealist poet André Breton, it is nothing but a prostituted form of astrology. Franz Boll, a German historian, has written: "Regardless of how strange astrology often is for modern man, for several thousands of years it has been one of the spiritual assets shared by all humanity. The literature written on it can be classified as worldwide. It probably represents the only domain where East and West, Christians, Muslims, and Buddhists alike can understand each other without difficulty."[8]

Astrology is a belief on a planetary scale, an interrogation of destiny. Astrology is also a very old subject of scientific study. It was the first doctrine to maintain that man's life is not divorced from the movements of the heavens.

Chaldean priests crystallized the doctrine four thousand years ago. After long hours of observation up in their towers, far from the dust of the cities and the demands of the populace, they accurately described the movements of the planets.

In classical antiquity, astrology was studied by philosophers like Plato and Aristotle and astronomers like the famous Ptolemy of Alexandria, whose *Tetrabiblos*, an astrological work, is a sequel to the *Almagest*, his book on astronomy explaining the systems of the world. In the Middle Ages, alchemists and astrologers were usually doctors and physicists rather than "fortunetellers." During the Renaissance, almost all the great minds studied astrology: Cardan, Paracelsus, Tycho Brahe, Kepler.[9] Apparently, nothing has remained of their astrological studies. They wandered through the undergrowth of astral influences without discovering any laws. The results of this ineffectiveness were not long in being felt. Men of science who, until the seventeenth century, had considered the study of astrology to be as worthy of interest as that of astronomy, decided they were being deluded.

Astronomy was making great progress and discoveries were being recorded. The geocentric system of the world proposed by Ptolemy was supplanted by the heliocentric theory of Copernicus. But after sixteen centuries, nothing had been proposed to replace the famous astrological text written by the same Ptolemy. Practitioners were still blindly applying the same dogma. Astrology was banished from the universities, sometimes even forcibly, as in France, where the Academy of Sciences expressly forbade the study of it. The influence of the stars was outlawed from "official" scientific pursuits. And for three centuries, the serious study of astrology was merely a Sleeping Beauty waiting for a Prince Charming to awaken it.

A Difficult Crossing

Astrology is dead, says the scientist. It has never been so alive, says the horoscope reader. Let us try to chart a course between the astrologer's faith and the scientist's skepticism. We must try to discover *proof* that there is something of value in astrology for the world today. If we do not succeed, the historian Bouché-Leclercq's definition will remain true: "Astrology is a faith which speaks the language of science, and a science which can only find a justification for its principles in faith."

Who will make the scientists aware that the study of astrology can be a serious occupation? Who will convince the astrologers to abandon their faith in the stars' influence and question the value of horoscopes? Who will attempt to bridge these two distant shores?

Shortly before his death, C. G. Jung wrote: "The cultural Philistines believed until recently that astrology had been disposed of long since and was something that could safely be laughed at. But today, rising out of the social deeps, it knocks at the doors of the universities from which it was banished some three hundred years ago."

The moment awaited for so long seems to have arrived—that is, if Kepler was right in maintaining: "No one should regard it as impossible that, from the follies and blasphemies of astrologers, may emerge a sound and useful body of knowledge."

CHAPTER TWO

The Return of the Planets

WILL WE SOME DAY SPEAK of the "physiology" of the solar system?

In ten years, technology has revolutionized astrophysical theories and now the solar system seems like a great cosmos in which the planets play the role of dependent celestial bodies. They have a mutual influence on each other, and even the sun which is the core of our system can be affected by them. Our globe feels the effects of the movements of other planets, of their mass, of their radio emissions, and of their "magnetic tails." The satellites which revolve around these planets are also affected. This "physiological" vision of our cosmic environment succeeds age-old concepts of the universe in which the planets were the principal heroes.

"In the course of the centuries, the scientific study of the planets has presented high points and low points. Today, interest in these heavenly bodies is at its highest. Two factors are the cause of this: the advent of the space age and an improved knowledge of our own planet, earth." So wrote Professor S. K. Runkorn, director of the School of Physics at the University of Newcastle.[1]

After the sun and moon, the planets were the first heavenly bodies to capture the imaginations of observers in antiquity. The Chaldean priests called these planets "wild goats" because they were constantly moving about among the tame and placid herds of the fixed stars. From their observations astronomy was born, along with the entire mythology based on the appearance of the planets. Glowing Mars became the god of war, and Saturn, which climbs slowly over the icy fringe of the horizon, was the dwelling place of Kronos, the fallen god.

In those days, according to the first sky-watchers, the planets were considered the masters of the universe. As centuries passed, Copernicus reduced the planets to the rank of "subjects" of the sun, and Kepler explained the reasons for their apparently capricious journeys. Then, with Newton's celestial mechanics, their occult charm finally disappeared.

At the beginning of this century, the never-ending planetary ballet had been recorded down to the slightest fraction of an arc by astronomers, and the planets appeared to be nothing more than docile servants. These bodies "without knowledge," of which Voltaire spoke, were also believed to be uninfluential. In this mechanical universe, only the fixed course of the planets around the sun gave slight animation to a world surrounded by an interstellar void. But man-made satellites have shown that this "void" is not mere empty space. It is furrowed with numerous energy fields with which the planets and their satellites are strongly associated.

Pirate Emissions

In the spring of 1955, Burke and Franklin intercepted a "pirate" radio emission coming from Jupiter. Why "pirate"? Because it can not be explained as the result of the heating of this planet by the sun. Jupiter was definitely the source. At first, it was discovered that short waves were being emitted in a series of rapid bursts. Then, in 1958, Sloanaker discovered that Jupiter was also emitting long waves.[2]

These emissions were termed "superthermic" and later, scientists traced them to the radiation belts surrounding the planet. Since then, with the aid of much more sensitive receiving equipment, radioastronomers have intercepted radio waves from all the planets, from Mercury to Saturn.

But let us return to Jupiter. The observers were very quick to note variations in the intensity of the radio waves coming from this planet. Jupiter's activity varied with time. From 1954 to 1958, this activity diminished and then increased again. A. Smith, G. Lebo, and T. Carr discovered that the fluctuation was inversely related to activity on the sun.[3]

Far from being an unchangeable sphere, as the ancients believed, the sun has variable moods which are related to the appearance of sunspots. The number of spots follows an eleven-year cycle. For five and a half years the number of spots increases, then over the next five and a half years it decreases. In 1954, the sun had very few spots and was in a calm period. In 1958, it was passing through a period of agitation. Jupiter's radiation seems to be strongest when sunspot activity on the sun is quietest. It is as if the sun will only allow Jupiter to manifest itself during its own relatively quiet periods. According to the scientists, the radio waves emitted by Jupiter meet a magnetic screen caused by solar activity.

We can compare Jupiter and the sun to two antagonistic cogwheels. The acceleration of one brakes the other and vice versa. But a grain of sand can get caught in the wheels. In this instance, the grain of sand takes the giant form of Io, Jupiter's main satellite. Io disturbs the "pirate" emission from Jupiter which we receive. According to the astrophysicist E. K. Bigg, of Sydney, who made this discovery in 1964, the disturbance is controlled by the angle formed by Jupiter and its satellite Io, as viewed from the earth.

At what angle, viewed from earth, will Io allow Jupiter's radio emissions to reach the earth? To answer this, we must measure the distances from the conjunction of the satellite with the planet. (There is conjunction when the two stars appear to us to be aligned with each other.) A sudden increase in Jupiter's activity can be observed when Io, as viewed from earth, is as far away as possible from Jupiter, either to the right or the left. (In scientific terms, this is when Io is located at its maximum east or west elongation. Elongation is the greatest angular distance at which two heavenly bodies can be observed from earth.) Bigg's conclusion: "By revolving around Jupiter, the satellite imposes a modulation on the planet's radio wave activity."[4]

The influence exercised by Io is gravitational. This seems to be confirmed by the presence of another influence on Jupiter's activity by Jupiter's second and third satellites, Europe and Ganymede, but this modulation is of lesser amplitude and so is their gravitational tide.

Indeed, the solar system truly appears like an organic entity. In the interstellar ex-void, the sun, planets, and satellites are constantly exchanging energy and matter.

That the activity of a planet is dependent on the sun is a relatively easy concept to understand. But there are instances where the reverse occurs and the sun, in turn, is affected by the planets. Just as a tidal effect of Jupiter's satellites influences its activity, so a planetary tidal effect can influence the sun's activity.

The Planetary Tides

In 1966, the astronomer Michel Trellis, of the Nice Observatory, presented three scientific reports on this topic to the Academy of Sciences.[5] By computation, Trellis first measured the effect of gravitation which the planets exercise on the sun and in particular the effect exercised by Venus, relatively close to it, and the effect exercised by Jupiter, whose mass is very large. His calculations showed that the sun, a gigantic and gaseous mass and therefore able to be distorted, is subject to the influence of planetary tides. These tides are actually of extremely small magnitude; if we calculate the sum of the action of the six planets, the tide's magnitude is at most one millimeter. However, this is sufficient to establish that the surface area of the sunspots seems to depend on the planets' positions. This surface area is greater when the tide is high than when it is low. The effect has been studied over a very long period of time, from 1879 to 1954.

Trellis has also demonstrated a relationship between the number of active centers on the sun's surface and the position of the planets. An active center is a region of the sun where intense activity can be observed. The number of active centers increases when the planetary tide gains in amplitude. Trellis is not implying by this that planetary positions are the cause of the sun's activity, because this activity is no doubt produced by modifications in the internal magnetism of this star. But, he wrote, "We can consider that planetary influences introduce a modulation of activity which is specifically solar in origin."

Radio Disturbances

Another example of planetary influence on the sun actually stems from our globe. In 1951, J. H. Nelson, an engineer with RCA, was asked to study the quality of reception of the radio broadcasts transmitted by this company. For a long time, it had been noted that this quality depended on the activity of sunspots. An examination of the correlation between solar activity and radio broadcasts appeared, however, to leave certain factors unexplained.

Nelson thought that these might be explained by the *heliocentric* positions of the planets, that is, by their relation to the sun. After various studies, he concluded his work as follows: "Research carried out in this observatory since 1946 clearly has shown that sunspots are not the only answer to the problem raised about the quality of radio reception. It is very clear that other forces are involved in addition to the sunspots. It is therefore necessary to find a new approach. The study of the planets as a new approach to the analysis of the propagation of radio waves has revealed encouraging results and a more detailed examination is indicated. A highly developed technique of forecasting radio interference based on the motions of the planets would have the advantage of making possible long-range calculations since the motions of the planets are well known."[6]

According to Nelson, the days when interference is worst are those when the planets are in the following relation to the sun: either at right angles to one another (90 degrees), or in conjunction (0 degrees), or in opposition (180 degrees).

Magnetic Tails

What is the explanation for these close interactions between planets, sun, and satellites? For a long time the planets were regarded as minute spheres of relatively dense matter in comparison to the infinity of space. The area of a planet seemed limited to its atmosphere. Beyond that, there was the so-called void. We now know that there is no interplanetary void. It is filled with minute particles and electromagnetic waves. Some of these come from the galactic spaces, but most emanate from the celestial bodies of the solar system. The sun, in addition to its intense and sporadic activity, regularly emits beams of protons and electrons. This has been termed a solar wind. This solar wind, a sort of gaseous continuation of the solar atmosphere to which very precise limits cannot be assigned, extends beyond the earth's orbit, so that the earth is, in a way, situated inside the solar atmosphere.

Around 1950, the astrophysicist I. Biermann discovered the solar wind while studying the mystery of comets' tails. These tails always extend in a direction opposite to the sun. Biermann has proved that the solar wind is responsible for this phenomenon, which results in the gases of the comets being pushed behind their nuclei.

Artificial satellites have shown that the planets also leave a trail behind them called magnetic tails. These are attributed to the meeting of the solar wind with the magnetic fields of the planets. The magnetic lines of force are compressed on the sun's side but not on the opposite side. Hence there is a long magnetic tail following all the planets, especially earth, on the side opposite the sun.

Dessler has calculated that the earth's magnetic tail extends at least twenty times the distance between earth and the moon. The magnetic tails of the other planets may also extend just as far into space. According to Norman Ness of the Goddard Space Flight Center, every planet, and earth in particular, can be likened to a comet with the earth as the nucleus of the comet and the magnetic tail as the comet's tail.[7] The moon also has a magnetic tail. This was recorded for the first time on December 4, 1963, via the artificial satellite IMP1. The tail extends over at least 150 lunar rays.[8]

The discovery of magnetic tails may perhaps provide a "physiological" explanation for a large number of recent puzzling observations. G. Atkinson has registered the relative decline of our globe's magnetism during periods of a full moon. One possible explanation is that at this time the moon is crossing the earth's magnetic tail. There is also a similar period of relative calm on the days when Venus is in lower conjunction. During this period, this star is perfectly aligned between the sun and earth.[9] J. Houtgast's plausible theory is that Venus screens the solar wind.[10] There is another relatively calm period during the opposition of Mars and Jupiter. (That is, when the earth is, in relation to these stars, in the same position as the moon is to the earth during a solar eclipse.)[11]

The silent ballet of the planets around the sun and the satellites around the planets is complex and alive. Through this "cosmic" concept of the solar system, we perceive a new dialogue which has always existed but which, until now, we had no means of understanding. As yet, we comprehend only a few words of this language; many surprises await the investigators.

FIRST INTERLUDE

Louis XIV, the "Sun King"

WE KNOW THE EXACT TIME of birth of the man who was
the greatest French monarch. In the castle at Saint-Ger-
main-en-Laye, while Anne of Austria was having labor
pains, the official astrologer, Morin de Villefranche, was
waiting on the castle terrace for the proclamation of the
royal child's first cry. The delivery was long and painful.
This was the queen's first child. Finally Morin was told
that the child had just uttered his first sound. The date was
September 5, 1638, and the time was exactly eleven minutes after eleven in the morning.

This child was to reign for more than a half century
with absolute power. Born to be king, he had a royal
temperament—a fortunate combination of destiny and
character. "There is in him the stuff of four kings," said his
minister Mazarin. A few days before his death, Louis XIII
called the dauphin, then aged five, into his room and
asked him his name. "I am Louis XIV," replied the child.
"Not yet, my son, not yet," said the dying man. This
prince was anxious to wear the crown and exercise, as he
wrote in his memoirs, "the profession of King which is a
great, noble, and delightful profession." As soon as he took

power, Louis XIV affirmed his authority. "I had to take care that I was the sole master; that people should expect favors only from me . . . without allowing my authority to be affected in any way." Hugues de Lionne, the Secretary of Foreign Affairs, wrote in 1669: "As soon as our emperor was old enough to govern by himself, he assumed complete authority, sharing none of it with anyone." Louis XIV wrote, "it was not in my interest to consult men of high quality. Above all, I had to establish my own reputation and make known to the public by the very ranks from which I chose these men that it was not my intention to share my authority with them."[1]

What was the dominant trait of this king "of merely average or even mediocre intelligence who received an elementary education"? Pride, a pharonic pride. "My Glory, my Greatness, my Repute" are the words which recur most often in his Memoirs. . . . This pride, heightened by his foreign victories, was boundless and the king, believing himself to be infallible, lost considerable power in Europe through his excessive self-confidence. But no one has disputed his intentions, his capacity for work or, as we say today, his professional conscience.

From 1671 onward, the king resided at the Palace of Versailles, which he had built at great expense. The court and courtesans also lived at Versailles. "There is nothing so curious or artificial than the cycle of court life. . . . Since the state is incarnate in the royal person, the sovereign's residence becomes an essential instrument of government. Its role is to dazzle men, both to arouse their ambition and to give them hope of satisfying it. It serves to gather around the king, under his surveillance, the most powerful and dangerous men and to provide him with agents to perform his will."

At the court, the king rigorously maintained and enforced strict etiquette. This emphasized the sacred character of the king. At eight o'clock in the morning, when the monarch awoke, the family members, doctors, and valets were ushered into the bedroom. A quarter of an hour later, the "grand admissions," namely, the grand chamberlain and first gentlemen of the chamber, were called. After the king had read the prayer of the Holy Spirit, the "second admissions" arrived. These were the princes of royal blood and the lords, and they watched the king put on his shoes. But it was still considered a privilege to be among the sixth admissions and, with about one hundred other people, watch the king finish dressing.

The king always arranged to be on display. "The king dined around ten o'clock with the queen surrounded by a great gathering of ladies and courtiers, some seated, others standing. When he retired to bed, it was with the same ceremony which accompanied his rising and this event took place very late in the presence of a privileged few. Naturally, some days and hours were set aside for official duties, hunting parties, concerts, games and feasts. These latter were held quite frequently and were dazzling. Hugues de Lionne remarked: "The king sees everything, hears everything, resolves everything, directs everything, and works continually eight hours a day at his affairs of state."

A great eater and great hunter, with countless adoring mistresses who gave him about twenty illegitimate offspring, he identified himself with the state: "I am the state." Everything about him was solemn and majestic, even the way he held his head. His bearing and his every gesture were deliberate. In addition, he was vain. He had hundreds of portraits painted and busts sculptured for his own glory. There is Louis XIV in his royal robes, Louis XIV as a Roman emperor and as the "Sun King," a nickname which has survived him. When he died on September 1, 1715, at eight o'clock in the morning, he had ruled for seventy-two years.

"No prince could have better suited the role of a majestic and glorious king than this descendant of the

Habsbourgs and Capetians. A natural feeling for dignity, the art of uttering fine phrases, a real sense of choosing the right words, a great ability to act, a certain lack of sensitivity, a suspicion which was always aroused, an absolute conviction of his own right, excellent health, and an insatiable appetite are the traits attributed to this monarch, whom Paris officially named Louis the Great and for whom the intellectuals filling his academies coined the motto: 'Nec pluribus impar' (Unequaled in all things)."

A Fine Example of Professional Success

Can the hour of the birth of Louis XIV provide an explanation for this "royal" character filled with ambition, pride, and authority—all qualities necessary for a great head of state, regardless of his political views and family background?

When the future Louis the Great uttered his first cry on September 5, 1638, at eleven minutes past eleven in the morning, the planet Jupiter was just rising on the horizon at the Saint-Germain castle. We have collected more than one thousand dates and hours of birth of known politicians, and we have found that they were born more often than ordinary men when Jupiter was just rising over the horizon. In short, the future Louis XIV was born at an hour favorable for those who are to participate in the leadership of state affairs.

We would like to show in this book that this man, the Sun King, was in fact King Jupiter. But what mysterious powers does this planet exercise to assist those who hope to occupy important positions in the affairs of state? Or, in simpler terms, what leads us to believe in the interference of a planet in the lives of men? The example of Louis XIV poses these questions. His case is of no scientific value by itself because, as we shall see, the facts are not so simple.

CHAPTER THREE

The Gold Nugget

LET US IMAGINE that we are strolling on the upper deck of a ship. It is a clear night and the sea is calm. Above us are the constellations, which are made up of stars and bear names that are familiar to us: the Big Dipper, the little Dipper, the Dragon, Hercules, Orion . . . Often too, among these stars, we can distinguish the moon and the planets. The planets generally appear brighter than most of the fixed stars even though they are much smaller because they are considerably closer to earth.

If we look south, it is easy to recognize the planets, which constantly revolve in an area of the firmament called the zodiac. The appearance of the planets, with their characteristic glow, helps us to identify them. Thus Venus is a beautiful star with a blueish, almost white light which is always very bright. Mars is a reddish or rust color and its brightness varies according to its distance from earth. Jupiter always shines with a bright glow, while Saturn, which is farther from us and smaller, seems to have a veiled yellow or ashen appearance. This is why the earliest observers were unfavorably impressed with this planet and felt that it was responsible for most of the evil events on earth.

Stellar Movements

It is just midnight and we are observing the sky. We see Jupiter rising on the eastern horizon, just as it did at the hour when Louis XIV was born. Mars is directly above us, and far down in the sky, opposite Jupiter, and the moon is about to set in the haze of the western horizon. Naturally, we cannot see all of the planets on any given night. Some of them are below the horizon and therefore will not appear in this particular nocturnal sky.

If we study the sky again four hours later on the same night, the configurations will have changed. The moon and the planets will all have moved in the same direction and the same apparent distance in space. For example, the Big Dipper will have moved toward the west. Jupiter, which has just risen at midnight, will now be high in the sky. Mars, which was directly above our heads, will have descended toward the horizon. The moon will have disappeared and will be continuing its journey below the earth. Venus will have risen over the horizon, heralding the rising of the sun.

What we have observed affects all the stars. In fact, these are only apparent movements, for it is earth that is rotating on its own axis every twenty-four hours in a uniform motion. We all know that this rotation is responsible for the alternation of day and night. Every day, the same phenomenon occurs among all the stars. The moon, planets, and constellations rise, reach their highest point in the sky, and set, like the sun. But each follows its own schedule in time and space.

From earliest times, observers have noted that from one day to the next, the bodies in the solar system do not rise at exactly the same hour. The variation is gradual and slow, but constant. The sun does not rise at the same moment every day, which is why the days and nights vary in length throughout the year. What happens to the other stars? The moon, if it rises one day at 11 P.M., will rise the next day at around midnight, and the following day at about 1 A.M. As far as the planets are concerned, the variation in the time at which they rise from one day to the next is much less than for the moon. For example, if Mars rises one day at 11 A.M., it will rise the next day at 10:56 A.M.

Thanks to celestial mechanics, astronomers have for a long time been able to calculate in advance the exact time the stars will rise, culminate at the meridian, and set. Their reckonings are published in the astronomical almanacs of each country. For example, suppose we wish to know the comportment of Mars when viewed from Paris on May 24, 1956. We simply have to refer to a French astronomical almanac of that year to learn that, on that day, Mars rose at 12:44 A.M., that it reached its culmination (the highest point in its path across the sky) at 5:33 A.M., and that it set at 10:22 A.M. It is therefore possible to take a given point on earth at a given time and locate very precisely the positions of the moon and planets in the sky.

Now, supposing that on May 24, 1956, a certain child was born in Paris. What was the position of Mars in the heavens at the time of his birth? If the infant was born at 1 A.M. on that day, he was born just after Mars had risen above the horizon. If the birth occurred at 6 A.M., Mars would have just reached its culmination point at the Paris meridian and would be starting to descend toward the horizon.

In scientific matters we cannot be satisfied with vague definitions of Mars' position in the sky at a certain hour. In order to apply the calculation of probabilities to the positions of this star, we must divide the circle of its daily movement into a certain number of sectors which will serve as reference points. Thus, to pursue our research, we have divided the diurnal motion of each planet into 36 sectors,[1] forming a sort of cosmic roulette wheel, numbered from 1 to 36 starting from the star's point of rising.

At the moment when an infant is delivered into the world, every star of the solar system is situated in one of the 36 sectors of this celestial dial. If we study a group of 100 or 1000 births, we can then count the number of times a planet is situated in each sector—for example, the number of times Mars appears in sector number 1, number 2, up to number 36, just as we would at a gambling table by noting the successive showings of the numbers at each spin of the roulette wheel.

An Astronomical Roulette Wheel

What is the normal frequency of a star in each sector? If we select an ordinary group of births, taken for example at random from a voting register, how will Mars be distributed throughout all the sectors of its diurnal motion at the time of these births? The calculation of probabilities has taught us to differentiate between possible and impossible distributions, for chance follows certain laws. The example of the roulette wheel helps us understand how these laws work.

If we spin the roulette wheel 3600 times, noting each time which number emerges, the 36 numbers of the wheel will each appear almost the same number of times. "Almost" means that there are likely to be slight variations in the number of times each number appears, but these variations will be within a normal range. If number 1 emerges 110 times, and number 2 only 90 times, we cannot interpret this as significant or expect that it will occur regularly. We must simply say that number 2 has not been as fortunate as number 1 but that this situation is not fixed.

If, however, the "luck" of number 1 should persist for several days, beyond all probable expectations, there would have to be a reason for this consistency. It would probably be necessary to service the roulette

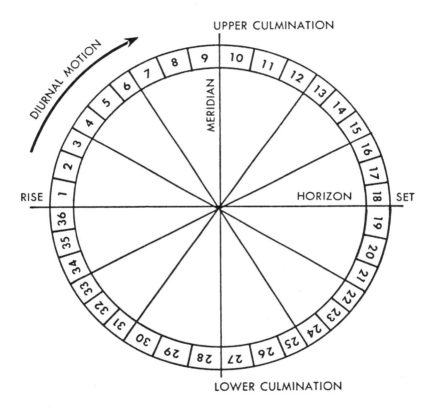

Figure 1. Astronomical roulette wheel of diurnal motion

This roulette wheel is used in the statistical study of the influence of the stars at birth. The daily motion of the star is divided into thirty-six sectors, with the first sector situated at the horizon, where the star rises.

wheel, for this is an apparent malfunction. This is why, in casinos, every number spun from a wheel is recorded in order to check if the wheel is working properly, for the game depends on pure chance.

To know if a piece of apparatus, an event, or a star "is playing the game" and not cheating, very complete tables must be recorded. If the statistics are unusual, the cause must be established. Obviously, there are precise mathematical laws to tell us when a critical point has been reached and what the magnitude of the problem is.[2]

Let us return to our planet Mars and imagine that the 36 sectors of the diurnal motion are comparable to the 36 numbers on the roulette wheel, with the planet Mars represented by the ball. Then we shall choose 3600 birth hours at random from the voting register. Corresponding with these births are 3600 positions of Mars, which are like 3600 spins of the wheel with the ball falling by chance into any one of the 36 sectors each time. When we conducted an experiment of this kind,[3] each sector was not occupied exactly 100 times by Mars. But no sector was unusally high or low in the number of times it was occupied by the planet. We conducted similar experiments with the other planets of the solar system and each time obtained "normal" results.

These results reassured us that the method we were using was reliable. Then we switched from individuals chosen at random and selected certain specific births from the general population—those of people who had achieved brilliant success in their chosen professions. And then the situation began to change.

The Roulette Wheel Deviates

When we examined the planetary positions at the time of birth of 576 academicians of French medicine, we were confronted by a strange anomaly.[4] In the group of academicians, the frequency of certain positions of the stars was suddenly far from normal. The results could not be attributed to chance, for any statistician would have regarded them as highly significant.

There seemed to be an odd preference among people who were later to become eminent doctors to be born at a moment when Mars and Saturn had just risen over the horizon or culminated at the meridian. What differentiated the medical academicians from ordinary men seemed to have an incidence on the frequency with which Mars and Saturn were situated in these sectors. The wheel of destiny was no longer functioning by chance. It had gone wild for them, yet it behaved normally in the case of the man in the street.

If, at a gambling table, the numbers located at the base of the wheel turn up more frequently than the others, it is probably because the table on which the wheel rests is slightly inclined. Similarly, when Mars appears so frequently in the rising sector at the birth of medical academicians, this anomaly which refutes the laws of chance had to be closely scrutinized. Perhaps it was due to a simple error on our part. We looked for an error, but found none, nor could the scientists we consulted in this matter. It had to be rechecked. We decided to start the experiment again and see if the phenomenon would recur.

We therefore examined a different group of 508 eminent French doctors. After the astronomical calculations and statistics had been tabulated, the evidence had to be accepted. As in the first group, these famous doctors' births were inexplicably grouped after the rise and culmination of Mars and Saturn. There was an undeniable relationship between a birth time occurring when Mars or Saturn was rising or culminating and the likelihood of becoming a famous doctor.

CHAPTER FOUR

The Stars and Success

"There are no great or small nations: there are only great or small men."

—VICTOR HUGO

THESE SURPRISING CONCLUSIONS demanded a more thorough investigation. Now, after more than twenty years of research, we feel that we have been rewarded for our efforts. The peculiarities observed among the medical academicians have opened the door to an impressive number of other phenomena worthy of study.

The Pursuit of Birth Records

We decided to accumulate records of groups of people in various professions: for example, actors, sportsmen, writers. But to do this we had to devise our own method. The first difficulty: the *hour* of birth was absolutely essential in order to place the stars in their correct sectors. The hour of birth is generally recorded in the registry office of the city hall in the town where the birth took place—at least in some countries.[1] After studying the problem and the requirements, we decided to conduct our study in five countries: France, Italy, Germany, Belgium, and the Netherlands. These are all Common Market countries, and the facilities for research here were the best available for us.

Having thus defined the field of investigation, we looked for biographical works which could provide us with the dates and birth places of the people in various professional groups. We encountered numerous difficulties in this research. My wife and I had to spend endless hours in the libraries of Europe. In some cases, real detective investigations were necessary. As a typical example, in our study on the German military chiefs of the Second World War, we had to "uncover" the little village in the Rhineland where the archives of the Wehrmacht had been deposited, and then use all the powers of persuasion we could muster in order to gain access to them.

We then had to write to the registry offices in many cities for the exact time of birth of our subjects. Even more persuasion was necessary to obtain this information because, for reasons of discretion, it is not imparted to everyone. Anyone who tries to discover the time of birth of Himmler, the Reichführer of the S.S., from the registrar of his home town will be fully aware of the difficulty of this undertaking. But the authorities were very understanding and granted us the appropriate official authorizations.

Finally, we had collected more than 27,000 birth records of which 12,000 were from France, 7000 from Italy, 3000 from Germany, 3000 from Belgium, and 2000 from the Netherlands. These births covered a period extending from 1794 to 1945, but most of them dated from the second half of the nineteenth century and the early years of the twentieth. All this information from the registry offices has been stored in the archives of our laboratory as proof. For every birth, there is a corresponding numbered index card containing all the biographical and astronomical data necessary for a statistical analysis.[2] Of these 27,000 births, 16,000 represent well known personalities. The other 11,000 are those of people who worked at the same professions without such outstanding success. Born during the same periods as the celebrities, they serve as a control group. Our Laboratory for the Study of Relationships Between Cosmic and Psychophysiological Rhythms undertook, in 1970, to publish the birth times of these pople in six volumes.[3]

The information contained in these volumes indicates that the celebrities, unlike the other ordinary men, were born under specific positions of the moon or the planets Mars, Jupiter, and Saturn. The most significant results regularly appeared when each planet had just risen or culminated. According to their various professions, celebrities "choose" or even "avoid" being born when certain planets are in these areas of the sky. Thus there are "busy hours" and "slack hours" which are so evident that they cannot be attributed to chance.

The Busy Hours

Of the 3647 famous doctors and scientists, 724, instead of 626 (the calculated theoretical number), were born after the rise or the culmination of Mars. (See Figure 1.) "After the rise" corresponds to sectors 1, 2, and 3; "after the culmination" to sectors 10, 11, and 12. Each of these sectors more or less represents two hours of the planet's diurnal motion. The probability is only 1 in 500,-000 that chance could be the cause of such an excessive number of births in these sectors. In the same group of scientists, 704 instead of 598 were born after the rise or culmination of Saturn. The probability of chance being the cause is 1 in 300,000.[4, 5]

Some scientists born under these positions are: the Nobel Prize winners for physics Enrico Fermi, born in Rome on September 29, 1901, at 7 P.M. and Henri Becquerel, born on December 15, 1852, in Paris at 3 P.M.; the

Nobel Prize winner for medicine Charles Richet, born on August 26, 1850, at 9:30 P.M. in Paris, and many other great physicians such as Charcot, Babinski, etc.

In the group of 3438 famous soldiers, Jupiter and Mars are frequently found in the sectors following their rise or their culmination: Jupiter 703 times instead of 572 and Mars 680 times instead of 590. The possibility of chance being responsible for this discrepancy is, in both cases, less than 1 in a million.

Examples of soldiers born after Mars has risen or reached its culmination are: in France, Marshal Pétain and Marshal Juin. In Germany, Admiral Canaris, chief of German counterespionage, Sepp Dietrich, commander of the Waffen S.S. Born under Jupiter, Marshal Lyautey, General Jodl (hanged at Nuremberg), and the Italian Marshal Badoglio, etc.

In the group of 2088 sports champions, Mars alone dominates and with a surprising statistical emphasis. It was recorded 452 times instead of 358 rising or at its culmination, which means that the probability of chance being responsible is 1 in 5 million.

Among the 1409 famous actors, Jupiter was recorded 283 times instead of 235 in the same sectors of the sky. Probability of chance being the case: 1 in 1000.

Among the 1003 politicians, Jupiter was recorded 205 times instead of 167 after its rise or culmination, which means that the probability of chance being responsible is 1 in 100.[6]

Among the 1352 writers, the moon appears very frequently after it has risen or reached its culmination for it was recorded in these positions 292 times instead of 225. Statistically, this abundance could happen by chance only one time in every 100,000.

For the 903 journalists, Jupiter was found rising or culminating 185 times instead of 150.5. Probability of chance: 1 in 100.

Finally, among the 202 large industrial managers, Mars is present after the rise or the culmination 49 times instead of 34.6. Probability of chance: 1 in 200.

The Slack Hours

The frequency deviations, however, do not always occur in excess. They also occasionally occur too seldom for chance.

Among the 1473 great painters, Mars and Saturn were rarely observed after their rise or culmination. Mars was recorded only 203 times instead of 253 and Saturn only 188 times instead of 238. The likelihood of this being attributable to chance is, in both instances, less than 1 in 200. The same phenomenon was seen with 866 musicians associated with the planet Mars (120 births instead of 149; likelihood of chance: 1 in 30) and with writers and journalists associated with Saturn (only 287 births instead of 338; probability of chance: 1 in 500).

Similarly, chance cannot explain the unusually low number of scientists and doctors born at the rise or culmination of Jupiter (only 540 instead of 602, or 1 chance in 30 that this low frequency is due to chance).[7]

The "Ideal" Curve

Tables I and II provide two good examples of the "busy" hours and "slack" hours of the planet Saturn. The sectors situated after the setting and lower culmination show the same statistical tendencies as those located at the rise and upper culmination: busy for scientists, slack for artists. Obviously these tendencies are less pronounced and seem like faint echoes of the trends observed after the rise and upper culmination. But they are nevertheless real.

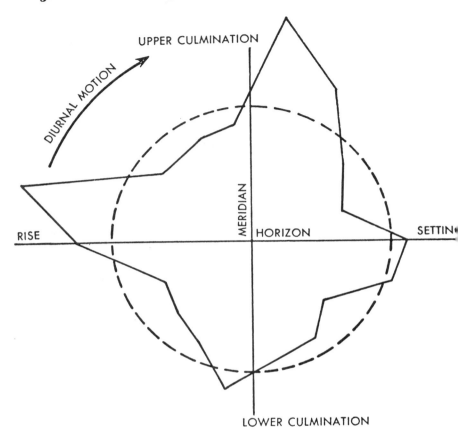

Figure 2. How the star's influence is exercised during its daily movement

This "ideal" schedule was obtained by grouping the observations noted for the births of professional celebrities. There are four moments of maximum intensity: at both horizons and both meridians. However, the moments when the planet has just risen or crossed the upper culmination are more intense than the setting of the lower culmination. We shall see that this law is also valid in the study of temperaments and cosmic heredity.

From M. Gauquelin, *Les Hommes et les astres.*

TABLE I
Saturn at the Birth of 3647 Scientists

SECTOR	1	2	3	4	5	6	7	8	9	10	11	12	Total
OBSERVED	355	292	286	349	284	282	318	290	289	311	267	324	3647
THEORETICAL	299	299	299	299	299	299	309	309	309	309	309	309	3647

TABLE II
Saturn at the Birth of 5100 Artists

SECTOR	1	2	3	4	5	6	7	8	9	10	11	12	Total
OBSERVED	376	434	448	358	421	429	421	444	440	436	444	449	5100
THEORETICAL	414	414	414	414	414	414	436	436	436	436	436	436	5100

Saturn's schedule does not indicate the same hour for scientists and artists.

The first line of each table: number of births observed.

The second line of each table: the theoretical number for each sector.

Scientists are often born when Saturn has just crossed the horizon and the meridian (sectors 1, 4, 7, and 10).

Artists follow an opposite schedule and are born relatively rarely when Saturn is occupying these areas of the sky.

From M. and F. Gauquelin, *Recapitulative Volume, Series A and B.*

What we obesrve in this instance with Saturn also occurs with the moon, Mars, and Jupiter. The general consequence of this observation can be seen by examining Figure 2. The curve has been obtained by adding all the anomalies noted among the 16,000 celebrities.[8] It provides a good indication of a planet's influence during its diurnal path. It is called an ideal curve because the large number of cases examined allows us to predict almost perfectly the planetary tendencies observed when the inevitable fluctuations attributable to chance have been eliminated.

In 1960 we wrote: "Mars, Jupiter, Saturn and the

moon are, at the birth of certain very specific individuals, also at some very specific positions in their diurnal motion. Within their daily twenty-four-hour path, their positions are divided into four six-hour cycles of which the most important are situated after the star has passed the

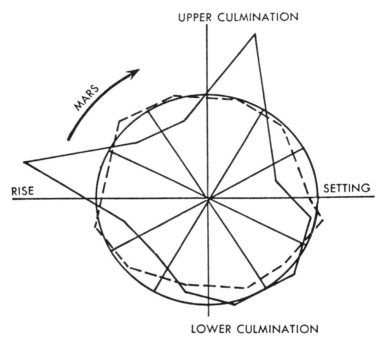

Figure 3. The Mars schedule indicates solely the birth of hours of well-known sports champions

The circle represents the theoretical findings.

The unbroken line represents Mars at the birth of 2088 champions. The "busy periods" after the rise and culmination are evident.

The dotted line represents Mars at the birth of 717 ordinary sportsmen. The "busy periods" after the rise and culmination have disappeared.

From M. Gauquelin, *Les Hommes et les astres.*

horizon or the meridian. The sectors corresponding to the rise and upper culmination of the star are of distinctly greater importance than the other two."[9] The exact astronomical demarcation of the significant zones situated "past the horizon" and "past the meridian" is described in our specialized publications.[9]

Readers should not be discouraged by this somewhat abstract theorem. It expresses both the mystery of planetary influence and the first explanations of this mystery.

Proof from Unknown Persons

Is it really possible that the position of the planets may determine our choice of profession? We do not believe so. We have gathered some groups of individuals as controls who have practiced the same professions as their brilliant colleagues but have not distinguished themselves.

This second series of professional persons did not yield the same remarkable results as the first group. This group was comprised of:

•1458 scientists who have made no important discoveries, have not published much material, or have never won any awards or honors. These unknown control subjects did not tend to be born after Mars or Saturn had passed the horizon. Scientifically "ordinary" men, they were born, cosmically speaking, like the average person.

•717 professional sportsmen who could not be considered champions. They had broken no records, won no major competitions, and had not been selected to represent their countries in their chosen sport. In this group, 124 subjects were born after Mars had risen or culminated. The average frequency for these sectors would be 122, so this is a perfectly normal distribution. (Figure 3.)

•2840 soldiers taken from the ranks. They did not

distinguish themselves either by their rank in the army or by their military exploits. There were no military leaders or heroes among them. The distribution of Mars and Jupiter was perfectly regular.

•2123 congressmen and senators who never advanced to occupy positions of importance in their political parties. There was no noticeably high distribution of Jupiter in any one sector.

•Among artists, the planetary effect disappears when the artists in question are unknown painters. The same results are found among actors by comparing the planets' position with their understudies. The "unknown" groups of artists and actors showed no planetary characteristics to distinguish them from other ordinary people.

It is therefore essential that a certain measure of success be achieved, that a certain threshold of fame be reached, before positive results can be observed. Moreover, the greater the heights reached by an individual in his chosen profession, the more likely he is to have been born in "planetary conformity" with his peers. This tendency has been noted for famous statesmen, sports champions, great war heroes, the "sacred monsters" of the theater and cinema, and the master painters.[10]

The Structure of the Results

Figure 4 enables us to see at a glance the overall structure of the results. "Similar" professions yielded comparable planetary arrangements. "Antagonistic" professions produced opposing planetary arrangements.

For example, the "artists" can be contrasted with the "scientists". The scientists are doctors, physicists, astronomers, chemists, etc. As a group, they enter the world when Mars or Saturn has just passed the horizon and the meridian. The artists are painters, musicians, actors and, to a certain extent, writers. As a group, those who become artists tend not to enter the world when Mars or Saturn is crossing over the horizon or the meridian.

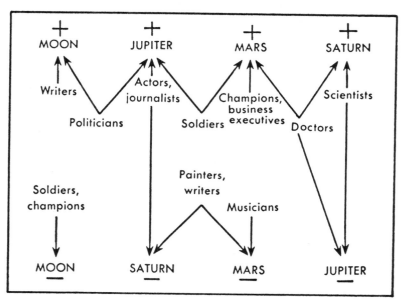

Figure 4.

The + sign means "busy hours," high frequency of births after rise and culmination.

The — sign means "slack hours," low frequency of births after rise and culmination.

The arrows indicate the significant bonds that have been observed between a profession and a planet.

These profession-planet relationships are not distributed randomly, but have an internal structure that must be taken into consideration in order to understand the results.

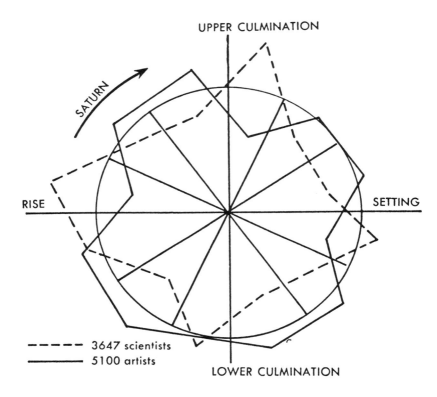

Figure 5. Saturn's schedule does not indicate the same for scientists and artists

The classical antagonism between art and science can be observed by this study of 5100 artists and 3647 scientists, noting the position of Saturn at their respective births. The busy hours of the former (unbroken line) correspond to the slack hours of the latter (dotted line). The circle indicates the theoretical average for each sector.

From M. Gauquelin, *Les Hommes et les astres.*

Studying Figure 5, it is astonishing to see just how rare success is in an artistic or literary career if the individual is born when Mars or Saturn is in the indicated positions.

Other traditionally antagonistic professional groups are soldiers and musicians. In our statistics, there are no two distributions of Mars so distinctly opposed as those of soldiers and musicians. But where does military music fit into this picture? We can answer this question because we investigated a group of 382 leaders of military bands in France.[11] At their birth, we observed that the planet Mars was distributed very regularly along the path of its diurnal motion. In respect to Mars, therefore, the military musicians are situated halfway between pure music and war.

But there are also professional groups which are mutually compatible. This is the case with sports champions and soldiers. In every era, sport has been a sort of preparation for war: boxing, javelin throwing, and archery are still popular evidence of this. Champions and soldiers do enter the world at the same moments of Mars' diurnal course. Similarly, actors and politicians, who both function in a representative capacity, and whose names appear most often in newspaper headlines, have the same Jupiterian birth schedule.

The planetary studies do have a significance. There is nothing anarchic about the statistical features observed: they are structured according to a definite plan. This plan, however, still appears somewhat confused. Now we must examine the mentalities hidden behind the simple professional label.

CHAPTER FIVE

Success and Character

The Two Factors Behind Success

TWO IMPORTANT FACTORS underlie success in life. The first is of a social nature. "The future is decided," wrote Alain Girard, "for almost everyone as soon as he enters life, and it unfolds from childhood and adolescence under the family's influence." The statistics indicate this; most men who have been successful in life came from families in privileged social positions. In general terms, two thirds of famous people originate from 5 percent of the population comprised primarily of the wealthiest and most intellectual people.[1] A professional proclivity is transmitted from generation to generation and there is no doubt that this circumstance creates favorable possibilities.

The planets have no role in this social aspect of success. As far as the movements of the planets are concerned, everyone is socially equal. As the opponents of astrology have remarked, the banker's son and the laborer's son can be born at the same time in the same town.

The social environment surrounding the infant in his crib is irrelevant to our observations.

But there is a second factor behind success. This was also stressed by Alain Girard: "Only a small number of children from the privileged social groups achieve true success. The importance of social factors does not eliminate the role of individual characteristics. In order to succeed, 'a special quality' is necessary. This quality is derived from the individual's natural talents and ambition sustains it. . . . This inner drive, requiring the active participation of the individual, is a basic prerequisite for success and there is no action, environment, or natural talent which can compensate for it. It is tempting to apply what Buffon said about genius to every kind of achievement: 'It is only a greater ability to be patient.' Within every group and particularly in the privileged social groups, the chances of an individual's rising above his peers are also unequal. For there is another selective process which is not as easy to describe or diagnose and which is linked to the most specific character traits of every individual. These are intellectual abilities and the psychological forces capable of putting them to work and they vary greatly from one individual to another."[2]

It is in this second factor behind success, the personal factor, that we have discovered a bond linking man's destiny with the hour of his birth. This is a psychological bond.

The type of success may vary from group to group. "It is quite improbable," wrote Claude Lévy-Leboyer, "that there is a genius-type personality common to all famous men. But it seems more reasonable to study the characteristics of homogenous subgroups performing the same professional activities. For example, successful businessmen have . . . personality traits which will not be found in famous scientists or writers. They have a characteristic rapid judgment, a very strong sense of reality, a need to resolve pressing problems, unusual energy and activity, the constant need for promotion (a new goal is set as soon as the preceding one is reached), and their satisfaction is directly derived from accomplishments even if these are in the form of greater aspirations."[3]

In other words, according to Lévy-Leboyer, there is a business executive's temperament. Our statistics indicate that business executives are usually born when Mars has just risen or culminated. This leads us to the question of whether the preceding description is partially applicable to the "Mars" temperament in general.

Anne Roe, a psychologist, gave projection tests (Thematic Apperception Test, Roschach) to a group of scientists, including biologists and physicists. "All were distinguished researchers . . . all showed a distinct desire to establish and maintain their personal independence. The psycho-social development of the physicists and biologists was characterized by isolation, a restricted social life, and limited associations with other people."[4] More recently, two other psychologists, Cattell and Drevdahl, analyzed the answers of a long personality questionnaire from a group of biologists, physicists, and psychologists. Their results indicated that eminent scientists are stable and enterprising, but they have a tendency to be reserved and rather isolated from the outside world.

According to our statistics, scientists tend to be born after the planet Saturn has risen or culminated. So we must determine whether the Saturnine temperament accounts for the character traits listed above.

We shall first try to determine the personality traits necessary to succeed in each profession. Perhaps a Martian temperament, a Jupiterian temperament, a Saturnine temperament, or a lunar one corresponding to these professions will emerge.

A Questionnaire Containing One Hundred Traits

Following is a questionnaire we prepared and gave to a large number of college educated subjects.

The subjects had to complete the questionnaire, indicating their opinion of the favorable or unfavorable traits they thought necessary to succeed in a given profession. If you wish, you may also give your opinion by answering the questions.

There is a list of one hundred personality traits. Opposite this list, there are ten columns, each corresponding to a profession.

•Make a plus sign (+) opposite each personality trait which you feel is quite common among those who successfully practice that profession.

•Make a minus sign (−) opposite each personality trait which you believe is rarely seen among those people practicing that profession.

	SCIENTISTS	ARTISTS	SOLDIERS	JOURNALISTS	ACTORS	SPORTS CHAMPIONS	POLITICIANS	BUSINESS EXECUTIVES	WRITERS	GREAT DOCTORS
1. well-dressed										
2. eloquent										
3. brilliant										
4. enthusiastic										
5. fearful										
6. hardened										
7. bold										
8. tough										
9. tenacious										
10. scrupulous										
11. argumentative										
12. reserved										
13. witty										
14. sporty										
15. passive										
16. timid										
17. immodest										
18. courageous										
19. punctual										
20. capricious										
21. indecisive										
22. unfashionable										
23. exuberant										
24. dissipated										
25. self-controlled										
26. apprehensive										
27. dreaming										
28. not adventurous										
29. unemotional										
30. attentive										
31. realistic										
32. eager										
33. lively										
34. changeable										

	SCIENTISTS	ARTISTS	SOLDIERS	JOURNALISTS	ACTORS	SPORTS CHAMPIONS	POLITICIANS	BUSINESS EXECUTIVES	WRITERS	GREAT DOCTORS
35. humorous										
36. impulsive										
37. reckless										
38. adventurous										
39. sociable										
40. modest										
41. sensitive										
42. pompous										
43. orderly										
44. bombastic										
45. quiet										
46. composed										
47. studious										
48. discreet										
49. harsh										
50. unpretentious										
51. minutely careful										
52. relaxed										
53. coarse										
54. humorless										
55. quarrelsome										
56. self-assured										
57. indefatigable										
58. precise										
59. scientific										
60. snobbish										
61. pretentious										
62. harsh										
63. enterprising										
64. amusing										
65. domineering										
66. authoritarian										
67. pessimistic										

	SCIENTISTS	ARTISTS	SOLDIERS	JOURNALISTS	ACTORS	SPORTS CHAMPIONS	POLITICIANS	BUSINESS EXECUTIVES	WRITERS	GREAT DOCTORS
68. gentle										
69. vain										
70. sophisticated										
71. nonconformist										
72. spendthrift										
73. undisciplined										
74. fearless										
75. intrepid										
76. audacious										
77. shrewd										
78. cautious										
79. obstinate										
80. rash										
81. inoffensive										
82. methodical										
83. nonchalant										
84. boastful										
85. talkative										
86. driving										
87. headstrong										
88. conservative										
89. aggressive										
90. not sporty										
91. theatrical										
92. impressionable										
93. opportunistic										
94. energetic										
95. verbose										
96. conventional										
97. self-satisfied										
98. eccentric										
99. austere										
100. irresolute										

Psychological Portrait of the Professions

If you have completed this questionnaire, you can compare your opinion with that of the subjects we tested. From the fifty thousand answers they gave, we have compiled a portrait of scientists, artists, soldiers, etc.[5] Now we shall compare these portraits with the corresponding planetary observations. To do this, it is helpful to refer to Table III, (pp. 68–69), which indicates how a planetary temperament can correspond to professional success.

For example: doctors show a preference to be born when Mars or Saturn is crossing the horizon or the meridian. They are scrupulous, unemotional, realistic, attentive, etc. They are not capricious, dreaming, impressionable, eccentric. Painters, on the other hand, choose to enter the world following the opposite schedule of Mars and Saturn. They are capricious, indecisive, dreaming, impressionable. They are not courageous, realistic, attentive, or composed.

Professional "Families"

Previously we noted that similar professions were associated with comparable planetary arrangements. There is also a deeper logic in these psychological portraits, for a similar planetary arrangement indicates certain temperamental similarities.

Some traits, therefore, are common to several professions. The trait of being "courageous," for example, is representative of doctors, sports champions, soldiers, and business executives. As the members of these four groups all tend to be born after Mars has just crossed the horizon or the meridian, courage probably applies to this position of Mars.

TABLE III
Psychological Portrait of Each Profession

PLANETARY RESULTS*	THE MOST REPRESENTATIVE CHARACTER TRAITS OF THE PROFESSION†	THE LEAST REPRESENTATIVE CHARACTER TRAITS OF THE PROFESSION††
SCIENTISTS: Saturn + Jupiter −	tenacious, scrupulous, reserved, timid, unfashionable, dreaming, modest, quiet, studious, discreet, unpretentious, minutely careful, precise, gentle, cautious, obstinate, methodical, austere	well-dressed, immodest, exuberant, changeable, impulsive, pompous, relaxed, self-assured, snobbish, pretentious, harsh, domineering, authoritarian, vain, boastful, talkative, theatrical, opportunistic
ARTISTS: Mars − Saturn −	capricious, indecisive, dissipated, apprehensive, dreaming, changeable, impulsive, sensitive, snobbish, nonconformist, spendthrift, undisciplined, nonchalant, impressionable, eccentric	courageous, punctual, self-controlled, unemotional, attentive, realistic, orderly, composed, discreet, harsh, precise, ethodical, conservative, energetic, conventional
SOLDIERS: Mars + Jupiter + Moon −	hardened, sporty, punctual, unemotional, orderly, composed, harsh, coarse, humorless, enterprising, domineering, authoritarian, fearless, headstrong, energetic, conventional, surly	eloquent, argumentative, witty, capricious, dreaming, not adventuresome, sociable, sensitive, gentle, nonconformist, undisciplined
JOURNALISTS: Jupiter + Saturn −	eloquent, bold, argumentative, witty, exuberant, reckless, adventurous, relaxed, amusing, intrepid, boastful, talkative, verbose	not adventuresome, quiet, discreet, minutely careful, precise, reserved, cautious
ACTORS: Jupiter + Saturn −	well-dressed, immodest, capricious, exuberant, dissipated, changeable, relaxed, snobbish, pretentious, amusing, spendthrift, boastful, talkative, theatrical, eccentric	reserved, unfashionable, modest, orderly, quiet, discreet, scientific, methodical, austere

CHAMPIONS:
Mars +
Moon −

hardened, tenacious, sporty, courageous, reckless, unpretentious, enterprising, energetic

well-dressed, eloquent, witty, dreaming, pompous, snobbish, shrewd, nonchalant, not sporty, theatrical, verbose

POLITICANS:
Jupiter +
Moon +

well-dressed, eloquent, argumentative, immodest, pompous, relaxed, quarrelsome, pretentious, domineering, authoritarian, boastful, talkative, aggressive, theatrical, opportunistic, verbose

scrupulous, timid, modest, sensitive, quiet, discreet, unpretentious, inoffensive

BUSINESS EXECUTIVES:
Mars +

well-dressed, tough, self-controlled, unemotional, realistic, orderly, insensitive, domineering, authoritarian, methodical, driving

timid, dreaming, changeable, sensitive, nonconformist, nonchalant, impressionable, eccentric

WRITERS:
Moon +
Saturn −
Mars −

eloquent, witty, dreaming, sensitive, gentle, shrewd, nonchalant, not sporty, impressionable

tough, tenacious, sporty, self-controlled, unemotional, realistic, composed, harsh, humorless, indefatigable, scientific, enterprising, audacious, methodical, energetic, punctual

DOCTORS:
Mars +
Saturn +
Jupiter −

scrupulous, unemotional, attentive, realistic, modest, orderly, composed, studious, minutely careful, precise, scientific, cautious, methodical, courageous

capricious, dreaming, boastful, talkative, impressionable, self-satisfied, eccentric

* A plus sign (+) after the planet indicates a high frequency of births after the horizon or the meridian of that planet. A minus sign (−) indicates a low frequency of births after the horizon or the meridian.

† These traits had a score of higher than 20 in our study.
‡ These traits had a score of less than 0.

Furthermore, there are *groups of traits* common to several professions. Perhaps the most interesting example is the group of characteristics for the psychological portraits of actors, journalists, and politicians. This is the list of character traits frequently found in all three groups: eloquent, brilliant, argumentative, immodest, exuberant, sociable, relaxed, self-assured, pretentious, pleased with themselves, boastful, talkative, theatrical, opportunistic, verbose, self-satisfied. Moreover, all the members of these professional groups show a preference to be born with Jupiter at the horizon or at the meridian. So, as Figure 6 shows, in our statistics for the distribution of Jupiter, there are no groups as similar as these three.

Naturally, it can be said that this similarity in Jupiter's positions should be associated with a similarity of temperament. If this is so, the traits common to actors, journalists, and politicians would constitute an initial sketch of the "Jupiterian" character.

This would also be valid for Mars, Saturn, and the moon. Obviously, the above conclusion has to be investigated and cross-checked. It can only be valid if the opinions expressed by our test subjects in the questionnaire are accurate. The characterological image which the educated public has of the qualities conducive to professional success may or may not concur with the psychological reality.

We must study *each character separately* using the biographies of great men.

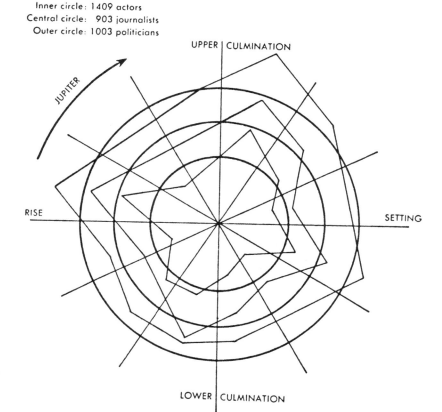

Inner circle: 1409 actors
Central circle: 903 journalists
Outer circle: 1003 politicians

UPPER | CULMINATION

JUPITER

RISE

SETTING

LOWER | CULMINATION

Figure 6. Same schedule for Jupiter-similar temperament?

The Jupiter schedule indicates the same positions for
actors, journalists, and politicians. Moreover, the psychological portraits of these groups show many points in
common.

From M. and F. Gauquelin, *Récapitulative Volume.*

Four Portraits of Men of the Theater

THESE ARE FOUR PORTRAITS of Frenchmen, each of whom has won fame in the theater. Jean-Louis Barrault is an actor and the director of a theatrical company, as is Jean Vilar, director of the Théâtre National Populaire. Marcel Achard is a playwright and member of the French Academy. Gustave Nadaud was one of the most popular *chansonniers* in the last century. All the quotations have been taken from their biographies.

Jean-Louis Barrault

"A sharp face, a very large forehead, a very long nose, a fiery expression which would be harsh if it were not vibrant, unruly hair and above all an air of serenity and complete mastery of his talent without the slightest ostentation: this is Jean-Louis Barrault."

"J.-L. Barrault: a living example of faith, for he believes in the theater with all his heart and with all his soul. He not only believes in it as an actor but as a complete theatrical promoter . . . he loves to give himself over to his demands, mastering them with his impassioned will and all the power of his personality. . . . such a flame has not been seen on the stage for many years, burning so brightly and warming the old hearts of the audience . . . he demands an honest effort from others, but he does not measure his own labor . . . an ardent and generous man who takes risks, loves challenges, and prefers his work to wealth. . . . his entire being emanates an extraordinary power of life so that no one is surprised by the influence he has over his friends. He is the leader who overturns obstacles and triumphs completely. . . . he could have been a dancer, and an excellent one at that. His build, his ideas about movement and his love of movement are those of a dancer. . . . good, generous, kindly, with the natural warmth of a man who has innate enthusiasm, Jean-Louis Barrault is a good, trusting, sincere friend. . . . Passionately enthusiastic is not an adequate description of J.-L. Barrault. Passionate, by itself, suits him better. This passion has no limits. He instils a tremendous peaceful intensity into everything he likes and everything about him, absolutely everything, reflects this same intensity. . . . Everything he does is done sincerely and ardently, with the intention of doing it well and serving Art with a capital A. . . . He stimulates his friends with the enthusiasm he injects into every aspect of his profession and the apprenticeship of this profession. . . ."

Here are some passages of a text by Jean-Louis Barrault entitled "Joy of Effort," in which this great actor's feeling for life and his psychology are clearly illustrated:

"Necessity and joy of effort. At school, we are surprised by the caterpillar's constant compulsion to follow his instincts. Effort of the paper collector or orange and matchbox collector. Effort of the sportsman, effort of the artist. Joy of effort. Pleasure of suffering. The joy of aspiring to have pain, said Baudelaire. Effort is a joy in itself.

. . . No other reason is necessary than the desire to make this effort. And I believe that joy is the basic reason for this desire to expend an effort. Effort in itself directly procures joy. Naturally there is the joy of being first in a sporting competition, of being successful in a role, of producing a play, of having the finest collection in the world, of being the best hunter in the district, etc. But there is this special, subtle pleasure of suddenly having a weight to bear on one's shoulders. There is the pleasant joy of playing the role of Rodrigue on the stage of the Théâtre Français, but there is also the painful, terrible, cruel joy of having to play the role of Rodrigue . . . in fifteen minutes on the stage of the Théâtre Français. I do not know which of these two joys I prefer. I am very much afraid that it is the cruel joy, the joy of effort, the joy which is derived from the application of will. . . . The theater is largely the art of effort and the art of will . . . and what energy must be expended to produce a play! Perhaps it is this effort which must be expended which pleases me the most when I am producing a play. And perhaps it is this desire to expend the effort which often pushes me to try to do the impossible. . . ." Later, Barrault speaks of sport as follows: "Sport is effort in its pure state. The nonsportsman can not imagine what physical and intellectual effort a true sportsman must produce. Muscular effort, effort of isolation, concentration and constant relaxation throughout his endeavor and an amazing effort of will. Just as the true sportsman does not compete in order to be first, but primarily to perform well, I have only undertaken this task through a desire to work well and produce a first-rate effort. Effort is one of the human capabilities which procures the greatest joy."

It is interesting to note that at Jean-Louis Barrault's birth in Vesinet, near Paris, on September 8, 1910, at 6 A.M., only one planet was rising over the horizon and there were no planets at the culmination. Mars was that planet and it is the most predominant planet when sports champions are born.[1]

Jean Vilar

"Last night, by lamplight," wrote Claude Roy, "I listened to the silence of Vilar, after night had fallen. . . . He was quiet in this silence and reverie, where nature holds sway and thoughts seem free. Yes, it is in silence, a certain silence, that I find the former Vilar and Vilar as he is now. A paradox, I know: to describe an actor and producer who speaks and makes others speak through his periods of silence. But Vilar is also a voice; a voice which is controlled and assured, as is characteristic of a man of fine breeding. . . .

"This Vilar gives the impression of having lived for a thousand years. According to the newspapers, he is only thirty . . . a novice producer, he is austere, and even 'Jansenistic'.

"Vilar is timid, rather reserved and clumsy. But his unostentatious zeal, his obstinate passion for theatrical work and his poverty are reminiscent of Dullin.

"Jean Vilar is cool, calm and distant, but I do not think that he is as calm or cool as he tries to be. The distance he maintains is also a precaution and a discipline.

"The young Vilar of Sainte-Barbe Collège and the Collège de l'Atelier was quiet because he was nothing. The Vilar of Avignon and the Théâtre National Populaire became silent because he was too much. He was distant through shyness, provincial pride, awkwardness of a poor young man and uncertainty of himself. He continued to be distant after he became successful, deliberating, conscientiously questioning and reflecting the modesty of the truly strong. Sometimes people even feel he is coldly distant. His cautious, deliberate leadership heightens his naturally distant and reserved character. There is a certain inborn, rugged clumsiness in his personal relationships which makes him seem like an important figure who knows how to remain aloof.

"His natural bearing is slow and deliberate. It is a slow-motion manipulation of obscured issues in which the pros and cons are patiently mingled, confronted and mixed into a personal hodge-podge. Then suddenly, a clear, obvious, inflexible decision is made. He just has to be himself to appear mysterious, because although he may seem confused at first, he is actually patient and sure of his reasoned instincts, difficult though these may be to understand. Exuberance is not one of his characteristics. Vilar is not a showman, but he does have a quiet quality of leadership. He is reserved and not very joyous. When he does force himself to be outgoing, he has the characteristic awkwardness of a very shy introverted person. He is friendly, but not familiar, attentive but always rather distant. Vilar does not need to flatter or cajole his actors to make them aware of his esteem for them and his respect for their work. He treats his friends with gruff tenderness. He is often preoccupied with a silent self-interrogation: probing the depths of his own mind. Vilar's bearing has always reminded me rather disrespectfully of the well-bred Italian who rolls the spaghetti tightly around his fork so that there are no loose ends and then makes the whole bundle disappear in one graceful mouthful. . . . Vilar does not make friends easily, nor is he an easy friend for those who like him. For in order to have friendly relationships with others, one must no doubt start by having a simple relationship with oneself."

Claude Roy's book, which unfortunately we cannot quote in greater detail, concludes with his judgment: "Accomplished worker, actor, citizen, friend, Jean Vilar is a man of exceptional *dignity*."

To complete this portrait of Jean Vilar, we should like

to quote a few lines from a text written by Jean Vilar himself, entitled "Letter to a Young Actress," in which his attitude toward life is clearly expressed: "A theatrical artist must, throughout his life, be sustained by ambition. But in the final analysis, this ambition must be a matter of choice. The actor's desire cannot be: 'I will be first.' It cannot be: 'I will become famous in my art.' Oh dear! It cannot be: 'Me first, even if I have to walk over my friends.' It cannot be: 'Great role first, anywhere and by any means, then immediate wealth!' All of these attitudes and others which we cannot relate in detail here comprise the Bazaar of Theatrical Ambitions which only serves to produce puppets, break characters, and eventually make the actor or actress wealthy, prominent, and very well known. For these are the attitudes of an 'impoverished' person, believe me. This person may be very sought after, courted, and admired, but he is empty, vacant, without substance, and demoralized by the age of fifty. This is a person who by the time he or she has reached middle age has become a famous failure in life. Poorly directed and poorly chosen ambition will gnaw every day at our lives, nerves, and organs. We have to learn to free ourselves of the desire for false glory, as this is the first step toward happiness."

Jean Vilar was born at Sète in the South of France on March 25, 1912, at 3 P.M. At this time, Saturn was the only planet that had just reached its culmination, as is typical at the births of many scientists.[2]

Marcel Achard

"Marcel Achard is sitting quietly smoking in his favorite armchair. He is wearing a mangificent robe which even Balzac would have envied, made of beautiful, soft yellow English wool. Tucked around his neck in a very

Baudelairian style is a white silk scarf and above it his face is as round and open as a circus ring. His mouth is smiling, his glasses sparkle, and he is puffing at his pipe, which has a bowl in the shape of a gambling die because Marcel Achard loves gambling and card playing. Even as a young man, he could play bridge for days on end. . . . Today, Marcel Achard is known as a 'very Parisian writer.' This means that he is given the best table in restaurants, genuine whiskey in bars, and is greeted warmly by many producers and stars. His casual comments are quoted in newspapers and his evening companions are often film stars. These trifles and the air of prosperity they bestow amuse him immensely."

A few years later, another journalist wrote: "As soon as the name Marcel Achard is mentioned, the reporter immediately thinks of all the clichés which have been used to describe him for many years . . . whimsical, very Parisian, a gentle, shrewd clown, etc. . . . (Achard enters): One could say that he has done his utmost this morning to perfect his appearance. He is draped in a sumptuous mustard-colored robe, the collar encircled with a floral silk scarf, and on his feet are a pair of Cheyenne mocassins. . . . When the conversation starts, I can perceive in Achard's sparkling eyes that malicious gleam which indicates that the alert little imp within him has just awakened.

"Marcel Achard is a happy optimist. His latest play, *Auprès de ma blonde,* is also the title of a song. Actually he has always been an optimst, but he has not always been happy. His early years as a writer were filled with difficulties, but he never became discouraged, simply because of his confident faith in the future. As the editorial secretary for a newspaper, he made some bitter enemies, especially among those who did not understand his quips. However, he is not malicious and he does have a good sense of humor. This poses a problem, because not everybody appreciates his humor. . . . In the theater, this humor is exemplified in *Voulez-vous jouer avec moi.* While searching for an actor to play the role of Crockson, the clown, the author, Achard, used to read this role at rehearsals. He did it so well that finally he played the role of the clown himself . . . Achard became a much discussed man."

A beaming face, enormous glasses which only he could wear, always with a witty remark on his lips—this is Marcel Achard, who both in France and abroad is one of the giants of the contemporary theater.

"Paris is not as forsaken and dismal as people claim, because this man whose *mots* circulate around the salons and newspaper offices at lightning speed has not given up his fourth-floor dwelling at Courty, which is two minutes from the Bourbon Palace. In Parisian society, Marcel Achard has, in a way, succeeded Tristan Bernard and because his remarks are both cutting and charming, he is automatically credited with all the witty comments."

And now, this is how Marcel Achard analyzes himself: "It is generally agreed that I am two very different people: a poet and a joker. My friends insist that the comic elements of my plays do an injustice to me as a poet. Others say that I am sometimes so much the poet that I can no longer be a comic. This is the worst thing that can happen to a man of the theater. Obviously it is very nice to be a poet. But for a playwright it is terribly important to be humorous also, because the poet is often a sad fellow who needs to be comforted, supported, and aided by the joker. The poet can only work when inspired by the Muse —otherwise he sits with his arms folded. The joker, on the other hand, can always fill the silence. . . . I strongly insist on the title of entertainer. It is difficult for people to believe that someone can write in a contented frame of mind. Well: Even if my work is never taken seriously, I must confess that I do not agonize over my work. I work cheerfully, but I work."

Marcel Achard was born on July 5, 1899, at 8 P.M. at Sainte-Foy near Lyon, after the culmination of Jupiter, like so many other actors and playwrights.[3]

Gustave Nadaud

A *chansonnier,* he was in demand everywhere. "And, being a good-natured person, he was very accommodating and went wherever he was asked, singing for as long as people wanted to listen. He lived from day to day by this gentle, amiable philosophy of life. His works were always the fruit and image of his thoughts or impressions of the moment. This *chansonnier* was loyal to all his friends and he did so much good because of his gentleness and modesty that he made countless friends. The literary output of Nadaud is quite prolific, even though, as a *chansonnier,* he was as lazy and idle as a house sparrow. He wrote only when inspired, never worrying about making lines rhyme, but waiting until they sprang spontaneously from his mind. Nadaud never sat down at a desk. He composed his songs in the street, at the theater, on the top of double-decked buses or in bed. . . . Gustave Nadaud was extremely successful in the salons. For years people sought and strove for his company. He was the darling of all the beautiful ladies who never tired of listening to him interpret his songs. His humility in the face of fame, which we have mentioned as a characteristic of Nadaud, was apparent throughout his entire life. He wanted to live modestly, but always independently. . . .

"This man personified distinction, simplicity, good humor, devotion and above all, modesty. Moreover, he had friends everywhere and, oddly, no enemies. His unobtrusive popularity blended gently with every aspect of his fame, never causing him to become conceited. And what a witty man! He had wit to spare and he used it lavishly but not maliciously. A poet and gentleman, Nadaud frequented the salons, always friendly, always cheerful, and in spite of his modest finances, he never accepted any payments which could have earned him a fortune!"

Another portrait, more physical: "Small rather than large, plain rather than handsome, neither dark nor fair, neither ordinary nor distinguished, Gustave Nadaud was well dressed, yet not elegant. He appeared like a bourgeois who had lost his way and wandered into an artist's salon. As soon as he had greeted his hostess, he would retire to a corner, even during the height of his success. When relaxing, his face seemed almost square because of the shape of his beard. He had wide prominent eyes and a heavy-lipped mouth which revealed nothing, absolutely nothing, of his talent. . . . When it was his turn to play, he went quietly to the piano, sitting down rather like someone who is about to unfold a napkin and shell hard-boiled eggs. His face was expressionless, but as soon as he started to perform, his whole countenance became illuminated. . . . It was one of the main attractions of our evenings, after Mounet-Sully had finished bellowing his fine verses, to watch this charming *chansonnier* seated at the piano, his head tilted toward his audience, his eyes twinkling, smiling mischievously into his white beard, singing very quietly and confidentially 'L'Ennui du Sultan' or 'L'Epingle sur la Manche.' . . ."

Nadaud, who was very well known and very popular, rarely dined in his own home, because he received so many invitations to dine out. He dined and sang and made his hosts indebted to him. . . . The rest of his spare time, Nadaud spent happily among his friends.

Some of his songs best reveal Gustave Nadaud's sense of life:

> Working alone as you wish,
> Accepting orders from no one,

Taking the praise that is given
And the success which comes to you!

With an income of three thousand francs!
Although four would be even better;
But that is far too ambitious;
I said three, and that will do me.

And also:

The first step to wisdom
Is the scorn of riches . . .
You can do this, because I have done it.

And finally, this description of the perfect woman:

I want this lovely woman
To find me kind, gentle, charming,
Handsome, witty, adorable,
But all of this without complimenting me.

The moon was rising when Gustave Nadaud was born in Roubaix in Northern France on February 20, 1820, at 11 A.M. To be born when the moon is rising is common among poets.[4]

A Planet for Every Temperament

These four men have acquired fame through the theater. They have a certain common destiny, but they do not have similar characters or comportment or the same sense of life. Jean-Louis Barrault is a "sporting" man of the theater. For him, the essentials of happiness are derived from effort. Marcel Achard, with "a face as round as a circus ring," whose rather caustic remarks are often quoted, is an extroverted optimist. Jean Vilar, on the other hand, is shy and reserved. He weighs the advantages and disadvantages of everything and is a declared enemy of all publicity. Finally, there is the quiet, carefree *chansonnier*, Gustave Nadaud, with numerous friends.

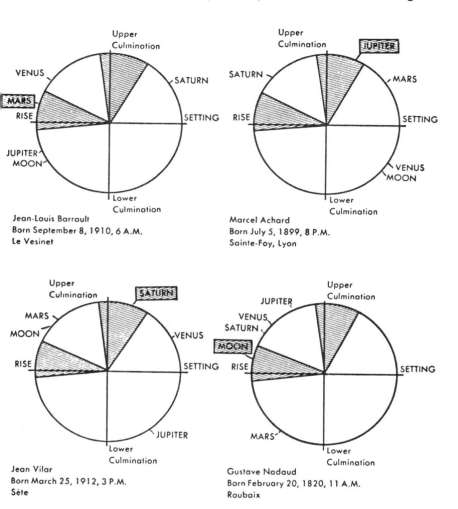

Figure 7. Astronomical birth diagrams of four men of the theater

In each case, only one celestial body is located after the horizon or the meridian. This star is indicated in shaded tones lettering in each of the astronomical diagrams.

He was an honest, modest man, sociable, unselfish and popular—a "good soul" with no real enemies.

Four famous men of the theater, all of different natures and all born under different stars, as can be seen in their astronomical birth charts. (Figure 7.)

In fact, Jean-Louis Barrault spent his theatrical life as a sportsman, Jean Vilar as a scientist, Gustave Nadaud as a poet, and Marcel Achard as a man of the theater. This is very significant for it means that there is no "professional planet"; otherwise all great actors would be born under Jupiter.

There are evidently only "temperamental" planets, so to speak; and actors tend to be born after Jupiter was crossing the horizon and the meridian, because most of them have a temperament corresponding to this planet. The Jupiterian temperament strives for success in the theatrical world, but it is possible to be successful in this domain with a different temperament, as is exemplified by the lives of Jean-Louis Barrault, Jean Vilar, and Gustave Nadaud. That there is a planet for every temperament has yet to be proved scientifically.

CHAPTER SIX

Planets and Character

Need for Biographical Studies

OUR AIM IS TO describe the temperaments associated with each planet, and we hope to do this through individual studies of famous people. It is not sufficient to establish a global relationship between professional personalities and the planets if this relationship cannot be confirmed on an individual basis.

We have already noted that actors, journalists, and politicians show a preference to be born after Jupiter has reached the horizon and the meridian. And we have already concluded that there is a similarity of character between these groups. No doubt, *most* actors, journalists, and politicians are bright, argumentative, fine speakers, and at ease in society, etc. But the most important point has yet to be proved: namely, that the character *of an individual* born under Jupiter may correspond to this description. This seems to be the case in our third portrait, that of the playwright Marcel Achard. Born after the culmination of Jupiter, with no other planets present in the sky, Achard is a bright, argumentative, fine speaker and at ease in society, as expected.

Is this always the case? It is not difficult to find biographies of people whose character corresponds well with the planet under which they were born. But this can constitute evidence only if a large number of biographies are examined objectively. Thus, the correlation evident in a single instance must be confirmed in other instances.[1]

Character Traits: The Basis of the Investigation

We established a work program in 1967. The documents gathered to prove a relationship between the planets and professions were again useful in our attempt to establish a relationship between the planets and character. This collection contained the dates and times of birth of sixteen thousand famous Europeans. But more research was necessary and we had to consult biographical works in which each person would be described in great detail. It was an enormous undertaking to find, record, organize, and analyze several thousand biographical texts. It meant spending many hours in libraries and then innumerable days in our Laboratory. Without the assistance of several collaborators working in our Laboratory we would never have completed all this work, and I should like to take this opportunity to thank them.

The biographical works contained character evaluations, behavioral traits, and anecdotes. The basic purpose of our study was to analyze and correlate the character traits mentioned in all these biographies.[2] The following example, a short biographical account taken from a specialized sporting dictionary, will serve to illustrate what I mean.[3] The text is reproduced in full.

Alfred Nakache

"Of all the champions who have honored competitive swimming in the past fifty years, the most *determined*, the most *courageous*, the swimmer who showed the most

drive, was undoubtedly the North Algerian Alfred Nakache. Between 1932 and 1948, he was one of the best
swimmers in international competitions and terminated
his extraordinary career by adding three European records and two world records to his list of achievements.
Born in 1915 at Constantine, Alfred Nakache succeeded
through his *hard work, determination* and *courage,* in
spite of his rather unorthodox style. He excelled in both
free style and breast stroke and between 1935 and 1948,
he earned thirty-five national titles and had the rare privilege of representing France fifty-five times in international competitions. He was first selected to represent
France in 1934 and was still a member of the team for the
1948 Olympic Games in London, where he even qualified
for the semifinals of the two-hundred-meter breast stroke.

"Alfred Nakache exemplifies, both in his studies and
in his life, certain *moral* and physical qualities necessary
to achieve so many victories. Later he devoted himself to
the teaching of physical education, and in this endeavor
he obtained the necessary qualifications with the highest
honors. During the Second World War, he was deported
to the dreaded Buchenwald camp, but because of his
physical endurance and *determination,* he was able to
return alive from this horrendous experience and continue his remarkable career in sport. His *courage* and
eagerness to compete have become legendary in sporting
circles, and according to his coaches he was never beaten
when he was neck and neck with an opponent twenty-five
meters from the finishing line." (E.-G. Drigny)

We have italicized all the character traits used to describe Nakache by this sports chronicler: determined,
courageous, driving, etc. We recorded each trait on an
index card so that there was one card for his "determination," another for his "courage" and so on. On the front
of each card, we entered his family name, his first name,
and the time, date and place of his birth. On the back of
the card were the planetary positions of the moon, Mars,

Jupiter, and Saturn at the time of his birth. We did not include the purely physical traits contained in the description (for example, "rather unorthodox style") or the traits relating to his intellectual abilities (for example, "obtained the necessary qualifications with the highest honors"). In this study, we were interested only in characterological and behavioral traits.

Nakache is only one example. We proceeded in a similar fashion for all the other celebrities from all walks of life; sports champions, actors, scientists, writers, etc. We soon had thousands of index cards representing the thousands of character traits systematically revealed in the biographies. A statistical analysis of these cards was then performed using an IBM 360 computer. Throughout our entire investigation, we followed three principles which we consider fundamental to our method:

1) Never disregard a subject's biography on the ground that his character does not seem to conform with the "personality" we expected him to have, according to the planet under which he was born.

2) Never disregard a character trait mentioned in a biography which seems out of context with the overall description of the subject.

3) Subject every character trait to a specific statistical analysis before attempting to group them for the purpose of character synthesis.

The results of our investigation of the biographies of four groups—champion sportsmen, actors, scientists, and writers—were the most informative. And since there is a planet to represent each of these groups, our report will review the problem from all aspects. We shall study, respectively, the Mars temperament and champions, Jupiter temperament and actors, Saturn temperament and scientists, and finally, the moon temperament and writers.

Although this research has taught us a great deal, it naturally does not cover all there is to say on the matter.

CHAPTER SEVEN

The Mars Temperament and Sports Champions

> "If you can break through the wall of suffering and reach true agony, then you are a champion."
>
> —DON SCHOLLANDER,
> *Olympic champion*

WE WORKED FOR MORE THAN two years on the biographies of champions, consulting general works like *L'Athlège* and *Le Dictionnaire des Sports*. *Le Miroir des Sports*, a weekly publication, is the oldest French sports paper, with its first issue dating back to 1920. We consulted every issue published between 1920 and 1940. These totaled more than one thousand issues and more than fifty thousand pages to peruse carefully. From this investigation, we obtained a total of five hundred biographies of champion sportsmen. The birth and planetary coordinates of all these champions had already been recorded in the course of our previous project, on planets and professions, published by our Laboratory under the title *Planètes et Profession*.

First we shall give a psychological description of the champion sportsman, as reported by sports journalists and psychologists.[1] This comprehensive but objective description provides the starting point of our analysis.

Sport Examined Microscopically

Quite recently, we heard a well educated person state in a conversation about Eddy Merckx, the four-time winner of the Tour de France cycling race: "Eddy Merckx? He's just a guy who can pedal a bit faster than the others, that's all!" But there is a very important psychological factor linked to the fact that Merckx can pedal a bit faster than the others. Merckx's muscles must be exceptionally strong. But are strong muscles all that a superchampion needs? How does someone become a champion?

"One thing is certain," wrote Dr. Cappon. "It is not only a matter of natural ability, muscle coordination or inborn talent. I know a karate champion who is myopic and subject to neurological disorders. On the other hand, look at all the beautiful muscular bodies uselessly tanning themselves on beaches, or even worse, slouched in armchairs . . . physical perfection is therefore not the indispensable prerequisite. What therefore is the difference between those who have broken the four-minute mile and those who have not? It is basically a psychological difference. In fact, when the body is performing to its greatest capacity, it is the mind which makes the difference." And this same writer adds that in order to give continually good performances, "it is necessary to achieve a delicate balance between the tension which mobilizes all the individual's physical and mental resources and the composure which combats fear and errors. Thus the individual must know how to combat anxiety, stage fright, disappointment, and discouragement. Those who manage to do this can boast of having mental capabilities similar to those of great war leaders or the major captains of industry."[2]

It is not enough to be physically the strongest to be a champion. One must also, and above all, be the strongest mentally. Winning requires a complete mobilization of one's personality.

Evidence

What is the opinion of sports experts, journalists, and coaches? We shall cite some examples taken from the pages of *Le Miroir des Sports*. Paul Hamelle, a journalist, wrote: "A sportsman cannot become a great champion unless he has a fighting spirit, in addition to his natural ability." Ludovic Feuillet, a famous coach, declared, "Determination—and this is not a new thing I am saying—plays an important role in the career of a racing cyclist." Henri Desgrange, founder of the Tour de France cycling race, wrote of Henri Pélissier: "He has all the characteristics of a true champion. He is well built, determined, able to exert himself to his limits and he is bad-tempered." Jean Samazeuilh, a noted critic and former champion himself, wrote about tennis, "What does the expression 'he is better than' mean in tennis? Very often the skill of players is equal but it is the competitive spirit of one player which makes him the winner."

The Motivations of Sportsmen

Psychologists have expressed the following opinions: Michel Bouet, a lecturer in the Faculty of Arts and Human Sciences at Rennes University, France, has described a certain number of basic tendencies in sportsmen: the need for physical activity, self-assertion, sociability, competitive interests, desire to win, desire to be a champion, aggressiveness and combativeness, a love of nature, an enjoyment of risk, and a longing for adventure. Here are some examples to illustrate these motivations:

The need to expend energy: "If, in sport, man seeks to compete, he is primarily trying to enjoy sport," writes Bouet. This need for movement and speed is very intensely felt by those who love sport. Generally speaking, the sportsman does not like to stay in one place. Like Aristotle, he feels that "activity is a source of pleasure." He also needs open spaces. Yvon Goujon, an international football star, states: "I would have made a poor sailor. I would be bored on a boat, I loathe being still and waiting. I am not a dreamer, I love life and action."[3]

We must not forget that the need to expend energy, physical build and character are closely linked. Of the three types established by the American psychologist Sheldon, it is the somatotonic individual, the most muscular of the three, who is the most "sporting." In contrast, the cerebrotonic individual, who is predominantly intellectual, and the viscerotonic individual, who is predominantly social, are relatively uninterested in participating in sports.[4] Moreover, it was noted that the number of somatotonic individuals who competed at the Mexican Olympic Games was very high.

Self-assertion: "All in all, sport seems like a vast ego-promotion system. And it would not be an exaggeration to say that sport fundamentally demands more psychic than physical activity."[5] In sport, the personality "takes shape." For this self-assertion is not only a desire to dominate and a definite search for power and glory, it is the discovery, mastery, and testing of oneself. "The practice of sport has enabled me to forge a character for myself," said one champion. "For me, sport has been a great manifestation of my personality," declared another.

Competitive spirit, desire to win: A competitive spirit in life (commercial competition, rivalry in love, etc.) is one of the basic attitudes of the "true" sportsman that distinguishes him very clearly from the player. Even if the game demands physical expenditure of energy, it does not imply specific demands. To be first—to break records or defeat an opponent—is the goal of a sportsman whenever he plays in competition, regardless of its level.

Baron Pierre de Coubertin's maxim, "The essential aspect of sport is not to win but play the game," is far from true. In actuality, the "noble uncertainty" of sport gives hope to the meekest that he may be able to defeat the strongest. "Your arm is unbeaten, but not unbeatable," he thinks. Naturally this desire to win is more or less firmly ingrained, and it is the determined competitors who are generally the victors. We must recall what the sports journalist wrote about the great swimmer Nakache: "His eagerness to compete has become legendary, and according to his coaches he was never beaten when he was neck and neck with an opponent twenty-five meters from the finishing line."[6]

The need to become a champion is felt from childhood. For some people, sports sometimes becomes both a mental and physical discipline. René Lacoste, in his own opinion, was not very gifted at tennis. But he decided that he would become a champion. His tenacity and perseverance were endless. Every day he would study each of his movements for a long time in front of a mirror. On the court, he would practice the same stroke up to one hundred times to perfect it. He would place a handkerchief on a corner of the court and strive to hit the ball there regularly. He invented a machine to throw the ball to various places in the court and at varying speeds so that he could practice returning it under every possible condition. In a small notebook, he kept detailed records of his progress, the reasons for his wins, and the reasons for his losses. A few years later, Lacoste won the Wimbledon tournament.

The person who wants to become a champion must never yield to discouragement, he must overcome the bitterest disappointments, and train constantly. The athlete Jim Ryun, world record holder for the fifteen hundred meter, trains for an average of three hours a day. He runs at a slower pace in the morning before attending his courses at the university, leaving the most strenuous training session for the late afternoon. "It is easy to see how this type of training demands a will of iron, renunciation of all other pleasures, and even a harshness toward oneself of which few men are capable." Zatopek, an Olympic winner, used to train wearing heavy military boots. Elliot, another Olympic champion, used to run up and down sand dunes every day.

Aggressiveness and combativeness: Michel Bouet wrote: "Sport seems to have been born from the *agon,* a Greek word meaning combat." In ancient times, it served as a preparation for war. Many forms of sport, such as wrestling, boxing, running, javelin throwing, and fencing, have retained this warlike aspect. For in war, victory is primarily a question of speed, strength, and skill. Even in more "civilized" sports like tennis, the players compete in "tournaments" like the knights of old. The racket has supplanted the rapier or the sling, but there still remains a great deal of aggressiveness in the act of smashing a ball out of the opponent's reach with all one's strength. For in sport, there has always been an opponent to defeat or perhaps to punish.

Are great champions more aggressive than other people? Yes, without a doubt. But like Michel Bouet, we must make a distinction between aggressiveness and combativeness. The poorly controlled aggressiveness of criminals, for example, pushes them to commit brutal and reprehensible acts. In life, they are not energetic individuals, but lazy, weak individuals without any sincere aims in life. On the other hand, there are very few cases of delinquency among sportsmen, who are usually very socially minded. They are more combative than aggressive. Moreover, on a sports field, the aggressive individual is rarely the most dynamic, and he will readily cause an infraction against a more skilled opponent, whereas the combative player fights to the end with all his strength. He plays fairly. In football, it is said that the combative player "plays the ball" while the aggressive player has a definite tendency to "play the man." The true sportsman is not content with an easy win. That spoils his pleasure. He is never infatuated by his own success but sensibly evaluates it. The aggressive sportsman believes himself to be superior, acts scornfully, and will cheat if he can. The combative sportsman, on the other hand, views the future dynamically, which is a more wholesome attitude. But it cannot be denied that although all the great champions have exhibited combativeness in the course of their careers, many have not been free of a certain amount of well-controlled and well-chaneled aggressiveness.

The enjoyment of risk also forms part of the sportsman's psychology. This motivation is not found in all sports. The most dangerous sports are car racing, flying, and motorcycling. Furthermore, these sports do not require a very great muscular expenditure. Nevertheless "sport" is always more or less synonymous with brutal contact. For the sportsman, the risk is an added charm, together with his desire to defeat the opponent and his desire to overcome fear. However, daredevils, completely oblivious to danger, are rarer than one would think. Naturally sportsmen take voluntary risks. For example, the skier flies down a slope at breakneck speed. The fullback who is the last line of defense for his team must tackle and stop the opposing forward who is carrying the ball. The football goalkeeper must plunge head first at the feet of his opponent, who is preparing to kick the ball into the goal. So they master their fear, for fear must never be the master if one is to win.

The Sportsman and Life

Contrary to an old popular belief, the sportsman generally shows the same qualities of efficiency and courage in his life as a man as in his life as an athlete. René Lacoste has become an important businessman, like his friend and fellow tennis "musketeer" Jean Borotra and like Louison Bobet, three-time winner of the Tour de France.

During periods of political unrest, champions often act brilliantly and even heroically. Etienne Mattler, a forty-two-time international football player, and captain of the French team, was well known for his courage on the field. Once he played an entire match in tremendous pain because of a sprained ankle and torn ankle ligaments. During the war, his attitude matched his character. He was a member of the Resistance and for months it was rumored that he had been shot. "In fact, after being imprisoned for many days ('I never let myself become disheartened,' he said later, 'and in my cell I did physical exercises and walked around and around the cell, completely wearing out a pair of shoes'), he managed to slip by his guards and cross the Swiss border buried under a cartload of hay."[7]

However, all of these facts do not stop the champion whose career is waning from experiencing certain difficulties in adjusting to "normal life" again. But it is rare that a sportsman does not manage to resolve this problem in a positive way.

Champions with an "Iron Will"

Does our knowledge of the planet Mars give a good picture of this temperament? We had to search through our index card files of thousands of character traits for those traits corresponding to the champion mentality.

Then we checked to see if Mars was often rising or at its culmination when the individuals with these specific traits were born.

Our language is rich in words describing character traits. But everyday language is not "scientific." It is vague and sometimes even contradictory and ambiguous. Furthermore, some expressions are much more common than others. In sports biographies, "courageous" is often used by journalists; "unbeatable" is not as common, and "surly" is much less common. Yet these three words, broadly speaking, reflect varying degrees of the same basic psychological tendency.

We have tried to analyze each trait separately. But many of them occur too infrequently in the biographies to allow a serious statistical study. So we have grouped the characteristics constituting the temperament of a champion. Using our index card file, we have constructed a portrait of champions which is more comprehensive and detailed than if we had included only certain important descriptive words like "courageous" and "determined." For there are several clues to understanding the champion temperament. The choice of these traits, a difficult choice, was not made *a priori*. Using the previous study as a basis, we have followed the opinions of sports experts and the conclusions of psychologists who have examined the temperaments of champions.

The following list of traits taken from our file describes this temperament. Obviously, this list is not final, and, consequently, certain words could be added to it or removed from it.

Portrait of the Champion with an Iron Will

"Tenacious, keen, active, aggressive, lively, eager, bold, adventurous, quarrelsome, rash, rough, brutal, stubborn, spirited, reckless, puts his heart into his work, hard-hitting, quick-tempered, pugnacious, acts courageously, reserved, conquering, grasping, courageous, plucky, reso-lute, determined, seeks difficulty, tough, dynamic, effi-cient, enduring, energetic, well trained, enterprising, fa-natical about his sport, ardent, has faith, driving, fiery, frank, winning, generous, surly, heroic, impetuous, piti-less, relentless, indomitable, untiring, uncompromising, competitive, self-controlled, high-spirited, vigorous, obsti-nate, offensive, headstrong, persevering, afraid of noth-ing, straightforward, passionate, fiery-eyed, inquisitive, resistant, daredevilish, gruff, composed, plays hard, relia-ble, surmounts difficulties, daring, temperate, unyielding, a terror, willful, industrious, valiant, gallant, fierce, manly, full of vitality, nimble, self-willed."

A Good Picture of the Mars Temperament

We now had to prove that champions with an "iron will" possessing traits from the above list are more "Mar-tian" than the others—in other words, that this impres-sionistic portrait of the determined champion reflects the Mars temperament. The results greatly surpassed our ex-pectations.[8] The above list of traits correlates with 1870 births of sports champions listed in our files. We noted the position of Mars at the birth of each of these subjects. Then we compared the distribution of Mars with the dis-tribution obtained from our overall survey of the births of sportsmen. The results indicated that champions who have forged a reputation for courage and determination are *twice as likely* as other champions to be born after Mars had crossed the horizon and the meridian. The dis-tribution of Mars at the births of these iron-willed cham-pions showed statistical anomalies deviating greatly from the distribution curve of the total group of champions (Figure 8).

For example, Yvon Goujon was born as Mars was rising. He once said, "I loathe being still and waiting. I am not a dreamer, I love life and action." Also born when Mars was rising was Etienne Mattler. Eddy Merckx was born after Mars had culminated. So great was his fame that American journalists were stationed along the Tour de France route to cover Merckx's race. He is the best example of the iron-willed champion. Merckx was born in Belgium at Meensel-Kiezegen on June 17, 1945, at 11 A.M., when Mars had just crossed the meridian.

"Weak-willed" Champions

Some champions are described very differently in their biographies. For example, racing cyclist Armand Blanchonnet[9] is quite different from Eddy Merckx in temperament.

"He was called a 'phenomenon' and this was no exaggeration. Blanchonnet, in fact, had absolutely extraordinary physical and physiological endowments which enabled him to perform great exploits with amazing ease. Unfortunately this very talented athlete hated any form of sustained effort and could not adjust to the rigors of training and so did not achieve the career expected of him." (Raymond Huttier)

"An apathetic individual, handsome Blanchonnet was a fine sprinter . . . especially after women. He had an infinite fondness for the fair sex. There is nothing wrong with this, but for a man who should be pedaling, it is not recommended. He was apathetic by nature and moved listlessly. He never became irritable. . . . He had an amazing body, exceptional lungs and an excellent heart. If only Blanchonnet could have followed a strict training schedule, he could have done almost anything." (G. Berretrot)

There are other champions like Blanchonnet who, without necessarily equaling this degree of nonchalance, do not have the soul of "hardened steel" characteristic of the true sportsman. Journalists are quick to point out their slight weaknesses as character judgments in the biographies they write of these men. Understandably, the "unsporting" traits in the biographies of champions are not as numerous as their sporting qualities. However, we discovered 780 cases in our file and grouped them in the following list. They contrast with those attributes listed for iron-willed champions.

Portrait of the Weak-willed Champion

"Amiable, anonymous, anxious, artistic, wise, touching, attentive, not very bold, kind, sensible, sullen, too composed, capricious, good-natured, pleasing, charming, polite, having complexes, intelligent, conciliatory, correct, courteous, fearful, confused, despondent, refined, depressed, disillusioned, distressed, lacking self-consciousness, dilettante, diplomatic, submissive, gentle, unobtrusive, exerts no effort, rarely trains, evasive, excellent nature, weak, whimsical, shrewd, nice, happy, humane, good-humored, impeccable, impressionable, inconspicuous, inefficient, incoherent, undecided, apathetic, indulgent, worried, carefree, unstable, intemperate, intuitive, erratic, lacking self-control, malicious, well-mannered, melomaniac, poor-spirited, naïve, nonchalant, complex, peaceable, pacifist, lazy, timorous, philosophical, quaint, placid, poetic, level-headed, considerate, cautious, soft and kind manner, dreaming, cunning, wise, wordly-wise, calm, timid, quiet, nervous, not diligent, urbane, loves family life, vulnerable."

A Picture Contrary to the Mars Temperament

Now we must prove that champions with character traits from this list are less "Martian" than the others. The results, given in graph form in Figure 8, are clear. "Weak-willed" champions are born significantly less often than "iron-willed" champions when Mars has just passed the horizon and the meridian. Thus the list of personal characteristics describing the "weak-willed" champion depicts a character which is almost the exact opposite of the Mars temperament. This is an interesting proof by contrast of the relationship which exists between the position of Mars and character traits.

It also enlightens us on the psychology of sportsmen. In many instances, it is a character difference which separates the successful athlete from the unsuccessful. Those who want to succeed most are also those who reach the highest levels of success, assuming they have the ability. As we said in the preceding chapter, the relationship between the sportsman and Martian tendencies is particularly strong in the case of ace sportsmen, Olympic champions, and world record holders, and weak in other sportsmen.

Experts in sports psychology have confirmed this characterological aspect of success in sport. William F. Staub, associate professor of physical education at Ithaca College in New York, made a study of the personality traits of football players in relation to the competition grade achieved by each of them. He used the Cattell questionnaire. His results show that the professional players were significantly more often: "tough-minded, forthright, self-assured" etc., and much more rarely "tender-minded, shrewd, apprehensive."[10]

One final statistic should be given. The percentage distribution of Mars after the horizon and the meridian for the births of iron-willed champions is twice the distri-

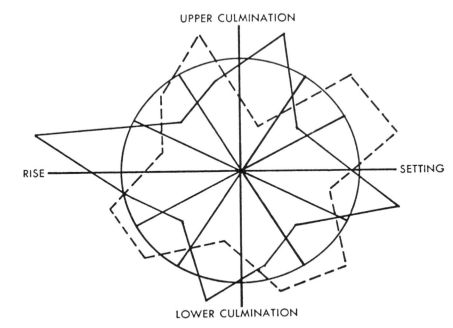

UPPER CULMINATION

RISE

SETTING

LOWER CULMINATION

Figure 8. Mars and "iron-willed" champions versus "weak-willed champions

The circle represents the average number of champions born when Mars is in the various sectors of its diurnal motion.

The unbroken line represents "iron-willed" champions who are born more frequently than the average sportsman when Mars has just passed the horizon and meridian.

The dotted line represents "weak-willed" champions, who are not born as often as iron-willed champions under these same positions of Mars.

From M. and F. Gauquelin, *The Mars Temperament and Sports Champions* bution obtained for ordinary people (64 percent instead of 33 percent). On the other hand, this same percentage among weak-willed champions is less than the distribution recorded for the births of ordinary people (29 percent instead of 33 percent). It is interesting to recall that the percentage distribution of Mars in these two areas of the sky at the birth of artists and musicians is 28 percent. Thus weak-willed champions seem psychologically closer to artists than to their strong-willed teammates. The position of Mars at birth is very much the expression of a temperament and has relatively little to do with one's professional destiny.

CHAPTER EIGHT

The Jupiter Temperament and Actors

> "Being an actor is not a profession, it is an
> adventure and an adventure is more thrilling
> than a profession."
>
> —RENE SIMON,
> *professor of dramatic art*

JUPITER IS THE significant planet for actors. So actors are the best professional group to use in an investigation of the Jupiter temperament.[1]

We started our biographical research on actors by consulting Lyonnet's *Dictionnaire des comédiens français*. This is a remarkable work giving very vivid biographies of the nineteenth-century stage actors. But it provides no information on contemporary actors. So we pursued our investigation on a larger scale. One of the main libraries of Paris, the Arsenal Library, contains a bibliographic treasure on actors, the Rondel collection. Rondel is the name of a very ardent theatrical enthusiast who, over a period of thirty years, collected all the articles, books, and reviews which appeared on French and foreign actors of all periods. We systematically researched this collection. At the present time, we have in our archives more than four thousand photocopies of biographical documents concerning almost five hundred actors. Every type of actor is represented: comic or dramatic actors, stage actors, movie stars, chansonniers, and even cabaret stars. The birth and planetary coordinations of all these celebrities had previously been recorded in the course of our study (*Planètes et professions,* published by our laboratory).

These biographies of actors were analyzed like those of the sports champions. All the characterological or behavioral traits were underlined, then written onto an index card. Each card bears a trait of a specific person. The top of the card lists the actor's civil status and the back contains the planetary coordinates at the time of his birth. For actors alone, we accumulated more than a thousand character traits, each of which is recorded on an index card.

Using the same method, we shall begin by giving a characterological portrait of actors in general.

Psychology of the Actor

How can the psychology of the actor be described? We already know the public's opinion, thanks to the questionnaire that appears on page ••. Let us also examine the opinions of theater experts.

Relatively few works have been published on this subject. We shall try to discover their general opinions using André Villiers's work *La Psychologie du comédien* as a basis.[2]

Generally speaking, actors are extroverts. "You meet a large number of actors who are worldly," wrote Villiers. An actor should love the world, and be at ease in society. People want to see his talent. He must be likable: "Together with a handsome appearance, 'charm' is one of the actor's cardinal virtues." Graceful movements, a pleasant smile, and an ability to mimic allow the actor to communicate easily with the audience and to exercise a power over it. "We love to think the pleasing ease and grace are part of the actor as a person even after he has left the stage and taken off his make-up." In other words, the actor must be very spontaneous both on and off the stage, because "deliberation and reflection, which are the enemies of spontaneity and simplicity, can detract from charm" and the influence exerted on the public.

The acting profession, wrote Louis Jouvet, "does not demand a great knowledge of intellectual matters, it does not require us to be thinkers. It is a question of sensitivity." Nor is too much refinement necessary: "A play with no other merit than that of being lively is better than a very intellectual and cold play." An actor must know how to externalize his feelings.

As a general rule, actors want a dazzling life, full of merriment, with dress rehearsals, opening nights, and parties. "The homes and studios of artists are worldly and witty salons." Actors, in a way, must be very spontaneous. Madame Dussane relates this definition by Dr. Dide on actors: "A vivid imagination, sudden emotions, the ability to create illusions, great character flexibilty." An actor should be colorful, original, and happy. "A traveling troupe does not arouse melancholy. We have mentioned explosions of contagious gaiety before and after performances. The acting instinct is not manifested only in dramatic action. Jokes on the stage are proverbial, even in the most serious forms of theater, and there are countless examples of this type of practical joke. The actor more or less acts in all the facets of his everyday life, and he has a tendency to dramatize the most trivial events of his existence." So it is not by chance that the expression *to play-act* is used of a person who exaggerates his real role in life.

Furthermore, the private lives of some actors and actresses show a morality free of all conventions and "their physical desires are satisfied without any pangs of conscience." A certain disorderliness, tending toward eccentricity, gambling, and exorbitant purchases has appeared to be part and parcel of many actors over the centuries.

Can the "bourgeois" actor be a first-rate actor? Lugné-Poe once wrote about Jules Berry: "What satisfaction to find myself truly face to face with the Actor, the 'excommunicated,' the man whom I esteem the most because, off the stage, he is unreasonable."[3] "Jacques Copeau has often protested against actors' trying to achieve middle-class respectability. For in some theaters, they are changed into a kind of civil-service employee, secure in their professional ability, naturally, but forever alienated from any contact with fantasy, passion, and life."[4]

But actors are also ambitious, opportunistic individuals. To succeed on the stage or on the screen demands boldness, talent, and determination. In a sense, the theater is the worst of professions because time does not automatically bring success or the "big break." Unlike the misunderstood scientist, the actor cannot count on posthumous fame. For the actor, all past time is irrevocably lost. He must constantly struggle to become known while he is still young. The glory aspired to by every actor cannot be attained, in spite of talent, unless the actor manages to catch the public attention at an early age and excel over all the other actors seeking fame. He must never lose his self-confidence.

Two Types of Actors

Not all actors are merely seeking fame, nor are all actors willing to fight for it and submit themselves to the worst excesses of flashy publicity. Louis Jouvet has drawn a distinction between two kinds of actors: the "modest actors" and the "immodest ones." "The actor is an immodest performer. He must flaunt himself. If it is correct to speak of his moral and physical personality, we should also acknowledge that he is proud of it and that he exhibits it shamelessly and with satisfaction, making no attempt to conceal it."[5] He is something of an "exhibitionist." The "immodest" actor acts instinctively and powerfully. His particular personality can be found every time in all the characters he interprets. This constitutes both his strength and his weakness.

The following is a description of the great French romantic actor Mélingue, born on April 16, 1807, at 3 A.M. in Caen, Normandy, after Jupiter had risen. Jules Truffier describes his entrance on the stage as follows: "He began by shouting very loudly, because he felt that a dramatic character should impose himself immediately by uttering some commanding sounds. To someone who expressed surprise at this procedure, he ingenuously answered: 'I have to shout when I appear for the first time; otherwise no one would know that it is Mélingue!' "

This type of actor often has a considerable power over the public. "Some actors do not shine because of their culture, but they find their boldness and spontaneity in their naïveté. Their freedom of action is absolute and unhampered by the surveillance of a stern mind and they are unaware of errors of taste due to their lack of experience and education."

The "modest" actor is quite different. He forgets himself in the role, drawing on his observations, his experience, his intellectual and emotional knowledge, which form a major part of his resources for self-expression. The disadvantage of this second tendency may be "honesty without warmth, technique without soul," and a lack of spontaneity. But what a treat when this refinement and intelligence are coupled with natural gifts of expression! The "modest" actor has a theatrical vocation and is not a ham. Success for him is not only a question of becoming known and being a star, but of developing his personality in his chosen art. It goes without saying that the "modest" actor is less common than the "immodest" one in the list of successful theatrical personalities.

The three examples that follow illustrate these remarks.

First, we shall give the portrait of an immodest actor, in the sense implied by Jouvet. This actor, Jules Berry, was born on February 9, 1883, at 9 P.M. in Poitiers, after the culmination of Jupiter. Pierre Laroche describes him as follows: "This actor has a very distinctive style—a mixture of impudence, questionable elegance, intellectual ease, and a lack of self-consciousness. He speaks with his hands, wears inimitable cuffs, lights his cigarette in a highly distinctive way, knots his silk cravat with perfect casualness, and always appears as though he is improvising his text, which, in fact, he often does. He goes beyond his roles. All his characters become Jules Berry, but they are Jules Berrys who are more real than the real Jules Berry. He lives his characters with a feverish intensity. He is always giving an 'outstanding performance'." To complete this portrait, we shall quote some remarks taken from an article by Max Favalelli, written on the death of Jules Berry: "It was always in part his own character which he transposed onto the stage, for he brought into his creations the same imagination he put into his existence, and this brilliant witty man seemed to improvise his roles every evening. His effect on the public was remarkable. . . . He was married three times and at the time of his third marriage, he was fifty-one and his wife seventeen. A legend grew up around him which he embellished with countless amusing anecdotes, thus becoming one of the most colorful actors in the French theater. He was an inveterate gambler and money just slipped through his fingers. He squandered a fortune at the gambling tables, and at the Longchamp racetrack, where he had his own racing stable in competition."

In contrast to Berry, we shall describe a modest actor, the great Italian actor Ruggero Ruggeri, who was born on November 14, 1871, at 7 A.M. in Fano at a time when Jupiter was neither rising nor at its culmination. The writer of the article, Silvio d'Amico, portrays very skillfully what differentiates Ruggeri from the immodest actor as defined by Louis Jouvet.

"Ruggeri was not a precocious actor who, at the age of twenty, was promised a glittering future before an admiring public; in short, he was not the 'Great Actor'. He became known slowly and painstakingly through his patient work. The 'Great Actor' is expected to be a massive, domineering figure, muscular, solid, and hot-blooded. Ruggeri does not fit this description. He is pale, controlled in his gestures, and usually has a fixed expression on his face. The 'Great Actor' is noisy, wheras Ruggeri speaks in a measured, melodious tone. The 'Great Actor' is exuberant, while Ruggeri is meditative. Ruggeri's nature is only gradually revealed. He is a refined, restrained person with a remarkable feeling for slight differences in meaning, and he knows his limits. He acts from within, with a controlled intensity."

One of the most famous actresses of all time, Eleonora Duse, was a "modest" actress—an extremely modest actress. She was born on October 3, 1858, at 2 A.M. in Vigevano near Pavia, when Saturn, not Jupiter, had just risen. "Eleonora Duse loathed all ham-acting and lived a simple life uncomplicated by love affairs, completely injecting her entire self, body and soul, into her acting whenever she was before an audience. Off stage, she fiercely safeguarded her privacy." (Henry Lapauze) "Eleonora Duse was admired for her intelligence, her fine breeding, and her depth of character. She was quite unlike most famous actresses. Her art did not consist of fabricating an artificial and exciting reality, but of representing specifically feminine feelings in their truest, most complete, but also starkest form. Someone justly wrote that 'the exercise of her art was a calling for her.' Her life was mysterious and secluded." "Happiness, said Miss Duse, would be to close one's door and, sitting alone at a table in a small room, create life in the isolation of life."[6]

It is obvious that an exceptional talent is necessary to achieve fame with this kind of attitude toward life, especially with such a shy nature, It is also obvious that the portrait of the "typical" actor who is usually at ease, self-confident, and extroverted does not suit this great actress. But some "modest" actors, as Miss Duse proves, have nevertheless acquired fame, although they are certainly not as numerous as the others.

The next celebrity is Charlie Chaplin. Although he is not as "modest" as Miss Duse, Chaplin, as his biographies show, was tormented by the same problems of conscience as those often besetting "modest" actors: "I was born on April 16, 1889, at eight o'clock at night, in East Lane, Walworth," declares Chaplin in his autobiography. At this time Saturn, not Jupiter, had just passed the horizon and the meridian. And in fact, Chaplin is often described as a "doubter," a person who sets problems for himself. In his book *Heroes I Have Known*, Max Eastman writes:

"And that hyperprudence, a kind of timorous canny clinging to what he's got, is the reason Charlie does not even enjoy his creative art to the full, or exploit his unparalleled chance to enjoy it. His studio is as still as a cemetery more than half the time. It is not because he lacks energy or invention or the funds to fill it with a riot of experimental miracles. He lacks free-hearted abandon."

He also has an extremely sensitive professional conscience. It is said that when the film *The Idle Class* was being made, he repeated the same gag nine times running before the cameras and because he was still not satisfied, he made another nine takes the following day. This perfectionism explains why Chaplin's gags have such an impact on the viewer. They are the result of assiduous work and a perfect technique.

Marcia Moore and Mark Douglas recounted another of Max Eastman's stories:

"On one occasion, Chaplin and Max Eastman took a personality test administered by a mutual friend, Dr. Reitell. Chaplin's score on 'introversion' was a figure so high that the doctor exclaimed with surprise, 'You are not so far from being a recluse! Seclusion from the world seems to be your idea of heaven.' At that time, Chaplin's private home was a walled-in hill enclosed with trees. 'If I had a moat and drawbridge,' he said to Eastman, 'I could live here the year round all alone and be happy. I might let you in once in a while for a game of tennis, but only because I need exercise.' In Chaplin's later life, he did indeed become a virtual recluse, shutting himself away with his wife and family in Switzerland."

On self-confidence, Chaplin's score was uncommonly low.

"You are very self-conscious and harbor definite feelings of inferiority," the doctor decreed. "Any bold indications of aggressiveness or strong assertions of power are but a defense, a thin veneer, a cloaking of a timid, worried and perturbed soul."

One day Eastman dropped in to see Chaplin and found him in a state of abject misery. The reason for this dejection was that Chaplin had just turned down $877,-000, which had been offered to him for a series of twenty-five fifteen-minute radio broadcasts.

"Why can't you do it?" Eastman asked. "You can make a speech." "It isn't that," Chaplin replied. "You know I love speech making. I can't come that close to the public. I have to remain remote and mysterious. They have romanticized me. I would lose more than that at the box office if I made myself real and familiar over the radio."[7]

Naturally, in spite of this exaggerated sense of privacy, Chaplin was very fond of the public; but he wanted to capture it in his own way and he succeeded in this. Chaplin, like all complex characters, is full of contradictions. But it is interesting to note that this "little man" who has made the entire world laugh has a character so fundamentally different from the relaxed free and easy personalities characterizing "exhibitionist" actors like Jules Berry and many others.

But let us come back to our specific problem. Using our biographical card file, we decided it would be interesting to divide the actors into two groups in order to determine whether statistically their character differences also correspond to planetary differences at the time of their births.

We researched our actors' file for all the character traits which seem to belong specifically to the typical actor, or, in other words, the "immodest" actor, as defined by Louis Jouvet. This list is not definitive and subsequent studies will no doubt modify it to some extent:

The Typical "Immodest" Actor

"Business sense, airs his opinions loudly, loved by the public, at ease, stylish, lofty, ambitious, expansive, self-assured, bold, authoritarian, adventurous, talkative, needs to assert himself, acts with vitality, ham-acts, capricious, biting, famous, zealous in his acting, quick-tempered, sense of the comical, communicative, extroverted, debonair, critical, not esthetic, sharp, spendthrift, despotic, Don Juanesque, eloquent, enthusiastic, lively, roguish, witty, stunning, given to exaggeration, eccentric, fiery, proud, passionate, promoting theatrical enterprises, spirited, gay, gesticulating often, unruly gestures, mocking, haughty, brazen, lordly, good-humored, a public idol, impatient for success, pitiless, stately, sensational, cutting, independent, undisciplined, disobedient, unbearable, jealous, happy, spiteful, scornful, worldly, a caustic wit, cunning, hostile opinions, original, open, flashy personality, too personal, sparkling, cutting, colorful, attracted by politics, popular, amazing, prodigal, provocative, violent-tempered, bantering, knows how to become rich, harsh, frank, unembarrassed, scandalous, humorous, successful, arrogant, likable, vulgar, noisy, unruly, vain, animated, glib."

As it stands, this description of actors is a good portrayal of the Jupiter temperament. In fact, the actors possessing characteristics mentioned in this list are born more frequently than other actors in general after Jupiter has crossed the horizon or the meridian (see Figure 9). The statistics were derived from 2110 cases. With such a large number, chance cannot be considered responsible for the high frequency. Thus the typical actor seems to have a Jupiterian temperament. But we should note in passing that although the above list is a good evaluation of the Jupiter temperament, it does not comprise the complete Jupiter temperament because this description was drawn only from actors' biographies and is probably incomplete. The study of other professional personalities such as politicians and soldiers should further enlarge the list. But now let us examine actors who have different qualities.

The "Modest" Actor's Temperament

From our file, we extracted all the traits attributed to actors which contradict the traits in the previous list. In this list are the assets and shortcomings of the "modest" actor. These qualities reflect: seriousness, reserve, honesty, sincerity, lack of spontaneity, sociability, and contagious cheerfulness. Here is the list:

"Not very gracious, surly, bitter, few friends, unsuccessful, unlucky, chaste, collector, formal, serious comportment, wrapped up in himself, conscientious, correct, fearful, decent, discouraged, unable to defend himself, disinterested, dignified, discreet, enjoys serious diversions, whining, gentle, honest, inhibited, faithful, has faith, cold, lacks gaiety, limited gestures, serious, grumpy, undecided, honorable, trustworthy, does not assert himself, intellectual, intelligent, not very scheming, loyal, dismal, a second-rate actor, methodical, meticulous, modest, naïve, observant, stubborn, orderly, organizing, organized, quiet, not talkative, lacks enthusiasm, patient, poor pedagogue, perservering, makes sly remarks, punctual, not popular, sedate, precise, upright, has depth, inflexible, likes realism, reflective, gives up easily, reserved, retires prematurely, lives withdrawn, wise, unsociable, erudite, scientific, scrupulous, stern, simple, sincere, careful, melancholy temperament, not very dashing, silent, finicky, timid, cantankerous, plays tragic roles, industrious, sad, virtuous, zealous."

We noted the corresponding positions of Jupiter with all the actors possessing one of the traits on this "modest" list. Then we compared the distribution of Jupiter with the distribution obtained from all the actors whose biographies we studied. The results are shown in Figure 9. "Modest" actors (represented by the dotted line) are not born as frequently as other actors when Jupiter has just passed the horizon or the meridian. This is the exact opposite of the results obtained for "immodest" actors (represented by the unbroken line).

So actors with contrasting temperaments are born under opposite positions of Jupiter. We subsequently furthered our analysis by examining the position of Jupiter at the births of the most characteristic actors of each of the two groups, namely those actors who were depicted as having several traits belonging to either the first or the second list. The more an actor conforms to the "immod-

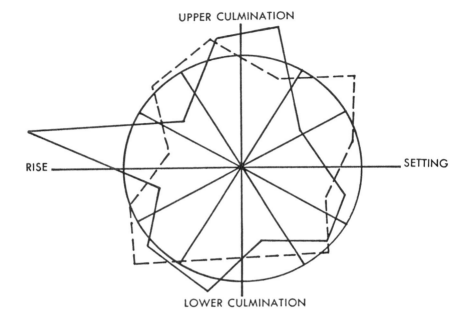

UPPER CULMINATION

RISE

SETTING

LOWER CULMINATION

Figure 9. Jupiter and "immodest" actors versus "modest" actors

The circle represents the average number of actors born with Jupiter in the various sectors of its diurnal motion.

Unbroken line represents "immodest" actors are born more often that their "modest" colleagues when Jupiter has just crossed the horizon or the meridian.

Dotted line represents "modest" actors are less frequently born than their "immodest" colleagues under these same positions of Jupiter.

From M. and F. Gauquelin, *Planètes et psychologie de l'acteur.*

est" depiction, the more likely he is to have been born under Jupiter. This is a general rule, with very few exceptions. Thus, in Lyonnet's *Dictionnaire des comédiens français,* there are seventeen actors with more than five traits from the "immodest" list. These are: P. Achard, Beauvallet, Berthelier, Bocage, Bressant, S. Brohan, J. Brohan, Dantigny, Daubray, Dumaine, Fargueil, Guillot-Gorju, Lemaitre, Ligier, Marais, Mélingue, Thérésa. Nine of these actors were born when Jupiter was at its rise or its culmination (instead of the average number of three). On the other hand, twelve actors have more than five traits from the "modest" list. They are: Agar, Bouffé, Delaunay, Dupont-Vernon, Dupuis, Geoffroy, Got, Jean Paul, Lafont, Maubant, Numa, J. Provost. Not one of these nine was born when Jupiter was rising or culminating.[8]

Vocation and Temperament

The previous examples show to what extent this mysterious tendency called a vocation can go against temperament. An extroverted individual who has a theatrical vocation has more chance of succeeding than an introverted person with the same passion for the theater. And even if he is successful, the introverted or "modest" actor always encounters problems in the course of his career. This is normal. He is exercising the profession of an actor with the temperament of a scientist. As André Villiers wrote: "The artistic and intellectual actor may be condemned to mediocrity by his lack of specific instincts. He will be outshadowed by the 'have you seen me' actor, whose nature is better suited to his career, and may be forced to play subordinate roles."[9] This is exemplified by the case of a relatively unknown actress of the last century, Zélie Hadamard, who was not born "under Jupiter," but when Saturn was rising.[10] "Even in her first roles, she exhibited great experience, an excellent talent for composition, good judgment, perfect diction, and to cap this she was sensitive and highly intelligent. But unfortunately, these are negative attributes in the theatrical world. She was an artist who reasoned as much or more than she felt and for her, like for many other actors, these solid attributes can be a handicap when competing with more outgoing personalities. This kind of artist has to make a greater effort to be assertive . . . and Zélie Hadamard carefully and scrupulously developed her roles. We now know how she developed her characters and why they were always so accurately depicted. But this also explains why they sometimes seemed to lack freedom and spontaneity. Quite recently Mr. Got questioned whether additional coaching was useful to actors and whether the development of critical awareness might not be harmful to an actor's creative talents. Miss Hadamard justifies this opinion, because she is a reasoning rather than an instinctive artist." (Felix Larcher) Miss Hadamard even gave her own views on why she had not acquired great fame: "I am not the kind to have triumphant successes," she said, "yet I hope to make a name for myself by my hard work and convictions." "This is surprising wisdom for an actress," commented Felix Larcher. But to us, this is an admission of inadequacy and modesty.

It is interesting at this point to recall La Bruyère's descriptions of a rich man and a poor man in his work *Caractères.*

"Giton has a fresh complexion, a full face, heavy cheeks, a fixed and confident gaze, broad shoulders, a large stomach, and a firm and measured gait. He speaks with confidence. He is lively, jovial, impatient, presumptuous, irascible, free-thinking, shrewd, and mysterious about current events. He thinks he is talented and witty. He is rich."

"Phédon, on the other hand, is hollow-eyed, has a

ruddy complexion, a lean body, and a thin face. He is absorbed and dreaming and appears stupid. He forgets to say what he knows or to talk about events which are familiar to him. He is superstitious, scrupulous, and timid. He walks gently and lightly as though he is afraid to tread down on the earth. He walks with his eyes lowered and does not dare to raise them and look at whoever is passing. He is poor."[11]

If Giton and Phédon both wanted to be actors, one could wager that Giton would achieve greater fame, because, from this portrait, Giton has the Jupiterian temperament.

CHAPTER NINE

The Saturn Temperament and Scientists

IN THE LAST CHAPTER Giton and Phédon were analyzed as actors. If, however, Giton and Phédon were to pursue scientific careers, Phédon's chances of success would increase considerably. Traditionally, as indicated by our study, scientists are described as tenacious, scrupulous, reserved, shy, unfashionable, dreaming, modest, quiet, studious, discreet, unpretentious, meticulous, precise, gentle, cautious, stubborn, methodical, austere. On the other hand, they are not well-dressed, immodest, exuberant, changeable, impulsive, pompous, relaxed, quarrelsome, self-assured, snobbish, pretentious, domineering, authoritative, pleased with themselves, boastful, talkative, theatrical, opportunistic, self-satisfied.[1]

In short, the "classical" scientist is just the opposite of the actor. And likewise, the planetary configurations of the two groups are opposed. Jupiter is the significant planet for actors and Saturn is the meaningful planet for scientists. So we have chosen scientists as the group to describe as accurately as possible the Saturn temperament.[2]

We followed the same method as for champions and actors, consulting a large number of biographies of famous scientists and doctors. From these biographies, we drew up a list of characteristics forming a general portrait of the typical scientist or, in order words, the introverted scientist.

We are not reproducing the entire list here. As a matter of fact, the characteristics representative of the modest actor are also valid in this instance. One can refer back to this list and add the following supplementary qualities: "Diligent, attentive, handy, composed, not confident, steadfast, model team member, unsociable, infrequent gestures, calm, impersonal, self-controlled, thorough, takes notes, stays in the shade, obstinate, fearful, level-headed, valuable collaborator, cautious, looks worried, uncommunicative, paralyzed by responsibilities, strict, deliberate, secretive, serious, sober, solitary, tactician, tenacious."

Saturn had just passed the horizon or the meridian at the births of scientists possessing traits from this list much more frequently than for all the scientists we investigated. Statistically, there can be no doubt. (See Figure 10.) So we must conclude that the "classical" scientific personality is a representative portrayal of the Saturnine temperament. But this representation is statistical. And just as there are different types of actors, so there are different kinds of scientists. Saturn is significant for those scientists whose character conforms to the above description and these men comprise a large group. But Saturn has no significant role at the births of extroverted scientists. It is possible to have a scientific calling without having the traditional scientific temperament. It is possible to be successful in science even if one is endowed with a completely different temperament: for example, a sociable temperament. This, however, is more difficult because spontaneity and a relaxed manner are not conducive to the painstaking research performed in the quietness of the laboratory which demands patience, reflection, solitude, and modesty.

We could speak of "true" and "false" scientists, but only in a characterological sense, of course, for a man's abilities should not be prejudged by his character. It is actually possible for a man to be a very good actor even though he may have the temperament of a scientist, just as it is possible for a man to be an outstanding scientist with a sociable and cheerful personality. The extroverted scientist approaches his work and research, announces his discoveries, and reacts to criticism in a completely different manner from the introverted scientist. Edison defined scientific genius as 99 percent perspiration, 1 percent inspiration. Scientists of the Saturnine type are more numerous. This is readily understandable because this temperament is more in harmony with the demands of the profession. In the sense implied by Edison, the "perspiration" is a Saturnine characteristic.

Using the classical distinction established by Blaise Pascal between the "geometric mind" and the "intuitive mind," we could say that there are "geometric" scientists and "inspired" scientists. "Geometric" scientists can be found in every branch of learning. The "geometric" scientist measures, compares, and weighs the pros and cons of his observations. This is the Saturnine temperament. The "inspired" scientist is on a completely different wavelength. He works, of course, but he pursues ideas even if they are unrelated to facts. The "geometric" scientist is an experimentalist, whereas the "inspired" scientist is more of a theorist and generally does not have a Saturnine temperament.

Portrait of the "Classical" Scientist

We shall illustrate the Saturnine temperament in the descriptions of these two scientists of the "classical" type.

The biologist Louis Brocq was born on February 1, 1856, at 10 P.M. in a little village called Laroque-Timbaut, just after the culmination of Saturn. Edouard Rist, a member of the Academy of Medicine, has described Louis Brocq's personality as follows:[3]

"He had a tormented, meditative face, with a fine, noble-looking forehead, bushy eyebrows, and deep-set black eyes. . . . This head, which was so intelligent and expressive of a full and concentrated life, rested on a lean and weak-looking body. His black jacket, which was always properly buttoned, gave him an austere air which was further emphasized by his aloofness, his gracious simplicity, and his rather sad air of natural dignity. No one could have tried less to impress, been more removed from the hub of everyday life, or been so undemonstrative in his gestures than this man from the south of France. He always spoke with the same discreet, musical, charming accent that had characterized his early speech patterns. His voice, which he never raised, was serious and he spoke in a rich and warm tone which caught the attention of his listeners. In the course of his career, he never sought any honors. He did not apply for university teaching positions and, in spite of encouragement from his friends, he never sought membership in the Academy. He always said that when it became time for him to retire in 1921, he would abandon medicine completely and go to his country house in Agen, where he would live surrounded by his memories and the beautiful works of art which he had enjoyed collecting throughout his career. His scientific work as a dermatologist was extensive. He was a thorough and keen analyst but he never let himself become too preoccupied by nonessential details. . . . In his extremely active professional life, this great doctor was the very conscience of his profession. He worked without affectation and pedantry. He was an honest and simple man. . . . Not only was he a good man, he was also fair and upright. He really disliked intrigue, hypocrisy, and nastiness and was often very hurt by such behavior in others. This solitary, unsociable, despondent man lived surrounded by many true and faithful friends."

Jean Martin Charcot was one of the greatest French neurologists. He was the first person to establish a relationship between hypnosis and hysteria. Sigmund Freud, as a young man, attended his lessons at the Salpétrière hospital in Paris, learning basic concepts which he subsequently molded into his psychoanalytic theories. Charcot was born in Paris on November 29, 1825, as Saturn was just rising.

The following is a short description of Charcot by Dr. S. Jonas: "His head seemed like the head of some venerable cardinal. His face bore no expression. It was like an expressionless deathmask set in icy stiffness. Charcot had a cold taciturn nature. He sought solitude in order to meditate. As a young man, he formed few friendships. Later in life, his personal relationships were just as limited. He was a stern man who observed keenly and meditated thereon."

Another account of Charcot, by P. Legendre:

"His back was arched as if it bore the weight of his enormous head, overburdened with thought. His features seemed set in marble, like an Olympian mask. He had a hollow voice, spoke in few words, but sometimes hesitatingly like a shy man who did not want to appear so. He did not do well in official examinations. He barely passed the Agregation at his second attempt in 1860. There is a story often told about him. At a certain examination, he was disturbed by an unexpected question and was about to walk out of the examination before his examining time was over. However, a commanding gesture from Rayer, his teacher and examiner, stopped him and he subsequently passed this examination. This inaptitude for improvised, oral examinations put him at an obvious disadvantage beside the other free-talking, well-spoken candidates. He was diligent and methodical and devoutly interested in research and the thorough, patient observation for details."[4]

Brocq and Charcot are two examples of untalkative, meticulous, shy, rather sad "geometric" scientists, and thus they become two good examples of Saturnine scientists.

Now let us turn to another group of scientists who do not have the Saturnine temperament and study the characteristics of three of these men.

Portraits of the "Original" Scientists

To give honor where it is due, our first example will be that of the greatest scientist of the twentieth century, Albert Einstein. He was born in Ulm, Germany, on March 14, 1897, at 11:30 in the morning, according to the municipal records. Saturn, at this time, was still far from its highest point in the sky, while Jupiter had just reached its culmination a few minutes earlier. And, as Ronald Clark wrote in a recently published biography entitled *Einstein, The Life and Times:* "Behind the great man there lurked a perpetual glint in the eye, a fundamental irreverence for authority and an unexpected sense of the ridiculous that could unlatch a deep belly laugh that shook the windows." Perhaps readers are familiar with the photo of Einstein poking out his tongue which was reprinted around the world, or his accounts of current events where the great man appears almost like a clown wearing the mortarboard usually worn by those receiving an honorary doctoral degree. And the following is an incident related by the astronomer Harlow Shapley:

"On this day, the National Academy of Sciences in Washington was honoring several eminent scientists. None of these gentlemen was a brilliant speaker and the formal speeches went on and on monotonously. I felt very uncomfortable. Suddendy Einstein smiled and turned and whispered something to his neighbor, a Dutchman, who scarcely had time to lower his head and repress a guffaw. Later this Dutchman repeated the comment which had provoked his mirth: 'I think', confided the great man, 'I have just got a new theory of eternity.' "

In addition, this story is related by Ronald Clark in his book:

"In 1920, a racist German group decided to refute the theory of relativity, which they considered a manifestation of a 'Jewish plot to contaminate the world.' The group proceeded to hire the Berlin Philharmonic Hall to organize a demonstration against Einstein. This scientist did not hesitate to attend the meeting. There he was, sitting in a box, obviously enjoying himself. At the more absurd statements about relativity, Einstein could be seen bursting into laughter and clapping his hands in mock applause."[5]

The sculptor Epstein had given the following description: "Einstein always enjoyed a joke and had many a jibe at the Nazi professors, one hundred of whom in a book had condemned his theory. Were I wrong, he said, one professor would have been quite enough."

With his sense of humor, cheerfulness, and disregard for convention, Einstein actually seems more of an extrovert than an introvert by nature. We need hardly add that this in no way detracts from his genius, because genius seems to be no more related to the paths of the planets than is intelligence level.

But let us pass to our second example, who differs noticeably from the first. Jacques Gilles Maisonneuve was a famous surgeon at the principal hospital in Paris. In spite of his fine reputation, he was never elected to the Academy of Medicine. This was not because he was too modest, like Brocq. The problem was quite the opposite.

This is Alfred Rouxeau's vivid description of Maisonneuve. He was born in Nantes on November 10, 1809, at 5:15 P.M. At this time, it was not Saturn but Jupiter which had just risen over the horizon at Nantes, and Mars had just reached its culmination in the sky.

"Maisonneuve placed little trust in the teachings of his professors and would only believe what he had seen for himself. He was extraordinarily self-confident and had almost boundless optimism. . . . He almost had to be physically removed from his position to make way for his successor. Although he was excessively self-confident, he was very stern and rigid with his colleagues. As a surgeon, he was extremely bold, although he could easily rationalize this boldness. He performed many "firsts" in surgery. When strongly criticized, he defended himself fiercely and in so doing he created strong enemies. These enemies rejected his application to the Academy of Medicine. . . . They called him 'the riverside butcher' (the main municipal hospital of Paris is situated near the Seine), because he often seemed quite brutal in his surgical operations."[6]

There is no doubt that Maisonneuve cannot be classified as a "classical" scientist. But not all extroverted scientists are so formidable.

The second portrait is that of a botanist and member of the Academy of Sciences. His name is René Maire and he was born on May 29, 1878, at 5:15 P.M. in eastern France when Jupiter had just passed the lower meridian at his native town Lons-le-Saunier. At this time, Saturn was as far away as possible from the horizon or meridian. "In scientific matters, he was animated by a self-centeredness that left people amazed. Such a quality was not indicative of a mediocre mind. Maire related everything to his work with disarming candor. . . . In reality, Maire remained a child in his everyday life, with no trace of meanness. He enjoyed good stories and delighted in puns. He even named his colleagues following the rules of bionomial nomenclature and labeled himself *Macrosatanas rufus.* His table was always surrounded by countless guests whom he offered many culinary surprises. Once dinner was over, he invariably suggested a game of dominoes. . . . In 1932, the French Mycological Society made an excursion to his home. The trip was a great success and he was delighted to show the rarest specimens to his guests His memory for names and shapes defied imagination. . . . His self-centeredness did not stop him from being a very good, very simple, very indulgent, and very kindly man. He was always ready to help his colleagues, who were always welcome to use his abundant library, of which he was extremely proud."[7]

The Theater ad Mushrooms

There are certain important differences between Einstein, Maisonneuve, and Maire, but they tended to be extroverted and self-confident as opposed to the basically withdrawn characters of Brocq and Charcot. Naturally the characteristics common to Brocq and Charcot are found more often among successful scientists. From a temperamental point of view, Einstein, Maisonneuve, and Maire are characterological outcasts and eccentrics. These portraits concur with the statistical results. "Introverted" scientists tend to be born under Saturn and are more numerous than "extroverted" scientists, which makes Saturn the significant planet for this entire group. On the other hand, Jupiter is quite often dominant among "extroverted" scientists. Figure 10 presents these results

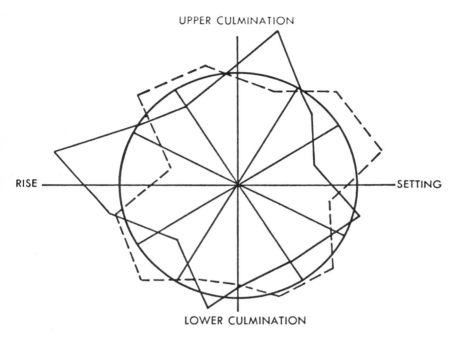

UPPER CULMINATION

RISE

SETTING

LOWER CULMINATION

Figure 10. Saturn and introverted scientists versus extroverted scientists

The circle represents the average number of scientists born with Saturn in the sectors of diurnal movement.

Unbroken line represents introverted scientists are born more often than all of their colleagues when Saturn has just crossed the horizon or the meridian.

Dotted line represents extroverted scientists are born less frequently than all of their colleagues under these same positions of Saturn.

From M. and F. Gauquelin, *Planétes et psychologie du savant.*

in graph form. It depicts the inverse relationship seen for Saturn between "classical introverted" scientists and "eccentric extroverted" men of science.

In short, the extroverted scientist has something of the temperament of the immodest actor, just as the modest actors have some temperamental characteristics of scientists. Once again, this is a question of temperament, not vocation. René Maire, who was not Saturnine, was profoundly interested in mushrooms. He spent his life classifying them, describing them, and naming them. He was happy, egocentric, and he enjoyed socializing with people and joking. Yet, he did not choose a theatrical career. Instead he made the study of mushrooms his theater and audience. A calling is always enigmatic when it so strongly opposes temperament. Yet the modesty, dignity, and reserve of Saturnine actors like Jean Vilar and Eleonora Duse did not stop them from performing on a theatrical stage. And they had absolutely no interest in spending their lives classifying mushrooms.

A Saturnine Football Player

It is possible to succeed in any profession with any temperament, but the difficulty in achieving success and the method in which it is acquired may differ. Attaining theatrical fame with a Saturnine, scientific temperament is difficult but nevertheless possible. An interesting example is that of André Lerond, who was captain of the French football team and an international player on twenty occasions. André Lerond was born just after the culmination of Saturn over his home town of Le Havre in Normandy on December 6, 1930, at 3 P.M. He was really like a "geometric" ballplayer.[8]

"Lerond is doubtless one of the most shining examples of a French football player. He is serious, intelligent, and conscientious. But unfortunately, he is too reserved and even too discreet. These are undeniable features of his personality. Max Urbini and J. P. Rethacker succeeded in obtaining a frank personal interview with André Lerond and were able to break down the wall he had built around himself. Here is part of what Lerond told them in a tape-recorded interview:

"I am looking forward to the blessed day of retirement and returning to calmness—that magnificent day when Jeannette and I will go to live permanently in Lyon where my wife's family resides.... I lost my parents when I was very young, and my grandfather taught me what a professional conscience means. In football, this means courage, enthusiasm, perseverence in training, and attention to minute detail and method.... I swear, I am not a great player, but if I have earned a small place in the game, it is because I wanted it. I would never class myself among the stars of professional football and I do not desire to become one. I want to remain a good club player who does his work as simply as possible. In choosing a profession.... one must also be reasonable. You must try to have luck with you, and in order to do this, you must pay attention to details. So when I return home after training, I overlook nothing. I am very particular about eating the right food, and getting sufficient rest. Perhaps I even go too far, for I have made two files on the players of the first and second divisions. Each player has a card. I feel that it is good to know your opponents as regards their strengths, their weaknesses, and their physical and technical characteristics. Getting back to my professional conscience, it has allowed me to achieve an unhoped-for career.... I read a great deal in my spare time and I am interested in everything concerning physical fitness.... My wife has always supported and encouraged me in my darker moments. My favorite hobbies are reading and doing odd jobs. I am hypersensitive, reserved, and often secretive."

This account is very characteristic of the temperament of an individual born after the culmination of Saturn. The desire to retire, modesty, secrecy, and attention to detail are all typical traits of the Saturnine temperament. A champion sportsman who has an index file on all of his opponents is indicative of a true scientific spirit. Here is another quotation from *Football Magazine:* "With his serious nature, his composure and unquestionable authority, Lerond has become the ideal captain of the French team. He is the most reliable and loyal player and he never plays unfairly. . . . But as he always said he would, Lerond is leaving football at a time when his national and international career is far from completed. And Lerond departed from football as he had played the game: discreetly, quietly, and intelligently. This model football player has left us." This model football player, this veritable chemist of the game, has a Saturnine temperament. His premature but voluntary retirement from sport has enabled him to join a profession more suited to his character. He has become an accountant.

The small psychological world of Saturnine individuals of which Vilar the actor, Brocq the scientist, and Lerond the champion are a part affords a quiet and meaningful life amid the mass of all humanity.

CHAPTER TEN

The Lunar Temperament and Writers

MEN OF LETTERS are most often born when the moon is at its rise or at its culmination. So, by using the biographies of writers, we shall try to describe the lunar temperament.[1]

We shall outline this lunar type through brief descriptions of several people. A good model of this personality is the *chansonnier* Gustave Nadaud, whose portrait we have already depicted. Another is the well-known poet Guillaume Apollinaire. He was born in Rome on August 26, 1880, at 5 A.M., just when the moon had reached its culmination over the Eternal City. He has been described as follows:

"The most original, the most diverse, and also the greatest of the poets who tried to restructure poetry in France at the beginning of this century. He was carefree and unconcerned. Diversity and richness were some of the many facets of his poetic genius . . . not to mention exceptional originality. He was a rather mystifying magician to those who knew him. He was a good storyteller and an avid reader. He was intrigued by everything and was endowed with a great appetite for life and a certain salaciousness which was often sarcastic and provocative, yet he could be tender and romantic too. Apollinaire was an inventor of forms and ideas . . . an ardent, creative, energetic man following in the French lyrical tradition. . . . Like a gypsy, or a secondhand-merchandise dealer, Appollinaire filled his work with odds and ends which were incorporated with fiery virtuosity into his poems, making them learned compositions under the guise of gracious improvisations."[2]

Now, a short description of another poet, not quite so famous, who was popular during the last century. His name is Joseph Albert Glatigny and he was born at Lillebonne in the heart of France on May 21, 1839, at 2 P.M., just after the moon had risen.

"He was a typical bohemian poet, talented and passionately devoted to poetry. . . . Tormented by the poetic demon, he wrote a play and joined a strolling troupe at the age of seventeen. He was an eternal nomad. His specialty was the improvisation of verses, and he had the ability to make rhymes from whatever he heard around him. . . . This colorful dreamer, this paradoxical wanderer, was a remarkable rhymer."[3]

Now I will briefly portray André Berry, a contemporary poet, born at Bordeaux after the moon had reached its culmination on August 1, 1902, at noon:

"Like a troubador, this merry carefree poet essentially likes classical forms and has revived the lay form. His ballads often reflect an exuberant lyricism in which childhood and love are the basic themes. He is imaginative, bohemian in spirit, and a prolific writer. He is well educated, has inexhaustible good spirits and a great creative talent. He is a charming poet who often yielded to the temptation to travel. So he periodically broke away from the university and traveled through several European,

African, and Asian countries, occasionally even on foot, working at odd jobs."[4]

Also in this group of writers with a lunar temperament are the novelist André Gide and the poet Paul Jean Toulet. Gide had a "fluctuating and diverse character." He was born after the moon had reached its culmination. Paul Jean Toulet, who has been described as "very lazy, living like a dandy," and not concerned about collecting his poems, was born when the moon was rising.

A Chameleon Satellite

"Fluctuating and diverse character." In the deliberate vagueness of this expression used to depict André Gide, there is something essential. The lunar temperament is difficult to define, for it is not as distinct or as "monolithic" as the three preceding temperaments. Our everyday vocabulary has difficulty in capturing it, although this may be inherent to the type itself, or perhaps our method lacks the necessary refinement. When a writer describes a fellow writer, the generosity of the terms, which may even be contradictory, make the description difficult to analyze. So it is often hard to establish statistical categories in this jungle of words. But the main difficulty rests with the lunar temperament itself because it has a rather elusive, pliable quality. On a psychological level, the moon is a chameleon satellite.

Once again we used the biographical method of recording character traits to obtain a psychological silhouette of this temperament. However, the traits we are listing should be treated circumspectly and viewed in general, not specific, terms. Only a general outline of the lunar temperamental type seems to have been correctly defined.

Here are some character traits common among writers born just after the rise or the culmination of the moon:

Affable, amiable, has many friends, talkative, bohemian, simple, kindly, decent, charming, good-hearted, gossiping, good company, accommodating, contemplative, debonair, disorderly, devoted, absent-minded, complaining, gentle, good-natured, idle, generous, nice, mannerly, changeable moods, lacks foresight, indulgent, easily influenced, ingenuous, unstable, fashionable, moderate, worldly, dawdling, naïve, careless, nomadic, nonchalant, lazy, poetic, juvenile, widely known, dreaming, obliging, snobbish, superficial, temperate, lacks tenacity, shy, tolerant.

We classified all of our authors according to their chosen literary genre and found that the above characteristics often applied to novelists and poets. They applied less often to essayists, literary critics, historians, and philosophers. The latter, it seems, are situated halfway between the scientist who analyzes and the writer who creates. It is not uncommon for this latter group of writers to be born under Mars and Saturn. Playwrights, on the other hand, are often born when Jupiter is at its rise or at its culmination. Thus they share with actors the characteristics relating to this planet.[5]

Countless Moons

The lunar temperament, which has greater characterological flexibility than the Mars, Jupiter, and Saturn temperaments, can readily be found in every profession, even those least suited to this personality, such as in sports, war, and science. However, the moon is not frequently observed crossing the horizon or the meridian at the births of individuals who enter these professions. This is logical, for the typical lunar personality displays nonchalance, good-naturedness, varying and easily swayed moods, dreaming and indiscriminate social behavior, and these characteristics do not really fit the mentality of a sports champion or a scientific researcher. But the lunar type is so adaptable that there are still a large number of athletes and scientists born under this satellite.

Georges Carpentier was perhaps the most famous French boxer. His match in Jersey City in 1921 against Jack Dempsey for the world heavyweight title is still considered by many as the match of the century. Carpentier was born in the north of France at Liévin on January 12, 1894 at 6 P.M. The moon had just reached its culmination. An article in the *Dictionnaire des Sports* states, "He left behind the reputation of a great boxer, a perfect gentleman, and one of the most popular French champions."

An article by R. Peyronnet de Torrès in *Le Miroir des Sports* is more eloquent: "Dressed extremely elegantly and with impeccable taste, he has young and regular features. His manner is simple and friendly and he is intelligent and bright. His victories, his good company, and his distinction have brought a 'chic public' to boxing matches." Here is another portrait of him which appeared in the magazine *But-Club:* "A handsome lad, he was like a 'prince charming', with his friendly smile, graceful gestures, and a natural dignity which made him well loved. Carpentier was an artist in every sense of the word. Once he became rich, he was more interested in making money on his name than in pursuing serious training. He accepted invitations to many occasions, served as master of ceremonies at many celebrations and attended numerous artistic galas. In the U.S.A., he received considerable publicity throughout the country, and with his polite, genteel manner he quickly became very popular. But this popularity waned just as quickly, because of an unfortunate 'saucepan' affair in which Carpentier's kindness was victimized. Out of consideration, he had allowed his name to be used for a brand of household utensils."[6]

The next example concerns two champion Belgian cyclists. One was born when the moon was rising and the other when the moon was just after its culmination. The former is Jan Adrianssens, born on June 6, 1932, at 7 A.M. in Willebroeck, near Antwerp. "There are no stories available about this quiet racing cyclist. For those who know nothing about his sporting career, Adrianssens can pass unrecognized. He has a round head which is oddly planted on his solid body. He is as reticent with his fellow cyclists as he is with those who watch him pass by anonymously in the mass of cyclists. He respects the orders given him by his superiors. Some people feel that he has been unjustly ignored, but he does not complain about it."[7] The other is Karel Kaers, a world road cycling champion born on June 3, 1914, at 9 P.M. in Vosselaar, also near Antwerp. "His height is impressive . . . he has a broad youthful smile which is frank and trusting. It is the smile of a twenty-year-old boy for whom life has not been cruel. . . . From his lofty six-foot frame, he smiles broadly in order to lose some of his shyness. What is striking about him is his constant good spirits, his continual optimism, which goes hand in hand with a certain carefreeness."[8]

Would sport become a gentlemanly encounter and not a harsh battle if all champions were born when the moon was at its rise or at its culmination? This is impossible. The Mars temperament, which is the typical temperament of a champion sportsman, is very different from the lunar temperament. The variability of the lunar temperament can be a handicap for champions. Carpentier, who gave up training before a world championship match, was knocked out by his opponent Battling Siki in 1924, and this was the end of his career. Adrianssens never really became a first-rate cyclist, and Kaers, after his surprise victory in the world championships, did practically nothing more in spite of his obvious ability. But the best example we have given of the lunar temperament is the description we gave of the typical weak-willed champion Armand Blanchonnet, so talented, yet so lazy. He also was born just after the moon had risen. His temperament is very different from the ambitious temperament of Eddy Merckx, the indefatigable superchampion. However, at Merckx's birth, Mars was just after its culmination.

Scientists also are not often born when the moon is at its rise or zenith. But this is understandable because the Saturnine temperament forms a poor combination with the lunar temperament. There are lunar scientists, but they tend to be theorists rather than researchers. Research demands perseverance at the task which the individual with a lunar temperament finds difficult to sustain. His strong point is inspiration, surprising discoveries, and ideas arising from a prolific imagination, and he prefers to let the Saturnine scientist prove or disprove his theories by patient research.

The following portrait is of an "inspired" scientist, Henri Lebesgue, a famous mathematician and member of the Academy of Sciences. Henri Lebesgue was born on June 28, 1875, at 7 A.M. in Beauvais in the north of France when the moon was at its culmination.

"He was a good husband and excellent father, sociable and a good companion. . . . Lebesgue had the ability to find humor in everything he said. . . . Lebesgue's irony was not sharp or biting. He avoided personal allusions and his humor lay in the caricature of general popular opinions so no one was hurt by it, not did it offend people's personal pride. Lebesgue published very little in spite of the tremendous impact of his ideas on mathematics. He savored the pleasure of imagining and planning new theories. But he had no interest in performing the painstaking, laborious, confirmatory work. . . . He had a very personal and individual way of reading reports written by others. . . . He would glance rapidly over the article and, proceeding from the salient points, he would attempt to rewrite the author's work, while commenting on the possible mistakes which the author had avoided making.[9]

It was through his mathematical talents and his outstanding intellectual ability that Lebesgue became a famous scientist, not through his perseverance or meticulous nature.

The Moon and Saturn: A Poor Combination

The lunar and Saturnine temperaments form a poor combination, as was proved statistically in our biographical study of champions. We noted the positions of both Saturn and the moon at the time of birth of every champion possessing a characteristic recorded in the Saturn list (p. 000). For example, André Lerond was described as follows: "He is serious, he is conscientious, he is unfortunately very reserved and even too discreet." These traits are tabulated in the list for the Saturnine temperament. So we recorded the sectors in which Saturn and the moon were situated when Lerond was born.

After this had been done for every champion, the results were grouped in two statistical curves, the first corresponding to Saturn, and the second to the moon. We then superimposed these curves (see Figure 11). The contrast between the curves is striking because the distributions proved to be exactly reversed. We had expected that Saturn would be found most frequently just after the horizon or the meridian at the birth of champions described previously in Saturnine terms by sports writers. But we were more surprised to find that it is very rare for the moon to be in these positions at the birth of champions. The two temperaments do not form a good combination.

On the other hand, there are certain common tendencies between the lunar and Jupiterian temperaments.

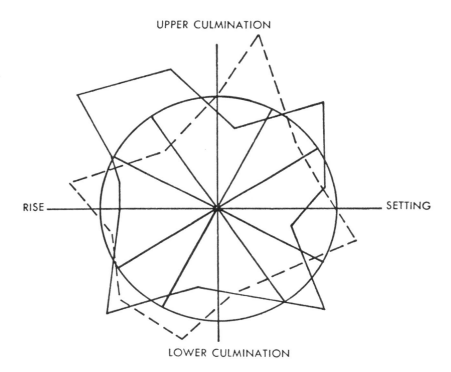

Figure 11. The moon and Saturn form a poor combination for champions

The circle represents the average number of champions born either with Saturn or with the moon in various sectors of their diurnal motion.

Dotted line represents champions possessing traits from the list for the "Saturn temperament" tend to be born after Saturn is at the horizon or the meridian.

Unbroken line represents, on the other hand, these same champions "avoid" being born when the moon is in these same areas of the sky.

From M. and F. Gauquelin, *Planètes et psychologie des champions.*

This was evident in the study of professional groups because the moon and Jupiter yielded the same results for politicians and journalists. The moon also appears quite frequently at the birth of comedians. In fact, some of the descriptions of lunar types, such as the boxer Carpentier or the mathematician Lebesgue, show evidence of the kind of extroverted joviality characteristic of Jupiterians. But the lunar individual is more amiable, more carefree, and also more tolerant. He does not act crassly or authoritatively toward others, nor does he have such an assertive personality. The Jupiterian is a persuasive extrovert, but the lunar individual is an extrovert who can be led. This, at least, is the impression we obtained from our present research.

CHAPTER ELEVEN

The Diagnosis of Temperament

Four Psychological Continents

PEOPLE LIVE TOGETHER, associate with each other, converse with each other, exchange ideas, and either like or dislike each other. But they live in psychological worlds which are sometimes situated many light-years from each other. There are at least four of these worlds, namely, Mars, Jupiter, Saturn, and the moon. Characterologically, these worlds coexist but are not interdependent. People may practice the same profession and succeed brilliantly at it, yet their attitudes, behavior, life-styles, and way of thinking may differ. They may be able to appreciate each other, but never really understand one another because their intimate experiences, through which they have learned life, are not transmittable. Jean-Louis Barrault, Jean Vilar, Marcel Achard, and Gustave Nadaud were chosen as examples because they represent the four psychological worlds, even though their lives were restricted to the theater. Barrault represents Mars, Vilar Saturn, Achard Jupiter, and Nadaud the moon.

Planetary Typology

Thus, a planetary typology has been outlined, but it has not yet been completely defined. Our study has included champions, actors, scientists, and writers. But there are other groups, such as politicians, soldiers, and artists, whom we have now begun to investigate. As of now, we can publish a provisional list of key words for each of the Mars, Jupiter, Saturn, and moon temperaments. This list is applicable when the planet is situated just after the horizon or the meridian at the moment of birth.

Key Words

MARS	JUPITER	SATURN	MOON
active	at ease	formal	amiable
eager	ambitious	reserved	many friends
quarrelsome	opportunistic	conscientious	simple
reckless	authoritarian	cold	good company
combative	talkative	methodical	good-hearted
courageous	likes to assert	meticulous	accommodating
dynamic	himself	modest	disorderly
energetic	sense of the	observant	absent-minded
fiery	comical	organized	generous
untiring	communicative	not talkative	imaginative
fighting	debonair	precise	easily
aggressive	spendthrift	reflective	influenced
afraid of	gay	retiring	fashionable
nothing	gesticulating	reserved	worldly
straightforward	often	wise	nonchalant
strong	good-humored	melancholy	poetic
daring	independent	timid	dreaming
valiant	happy	industrious	obliging
full of vitality	worldly	silent	rather snobbish
lively	prodigal	sad	superficial
self-willed	bantering		tolerant
	likable		
	vain		

A Language Problem

Our everyday language is not specific, so we occasionally encounter semantic difficulties.[1] The same word may have very different characterological meanings according to the context in which it is used. Take, for example, the word *tenacity*. The tenacity of a champion who conquers fatigue to be first is not necessarily the same as the tenacity of an actor who wants to "succeed" at any cost, or the tenacity of a scientist who works tirelessly on the same experiment.

This semantic difficulty can also be found at the level of planetary relationships. Saturnine *shyness* is quite different from lunar *shyness*. The former is deep and lasting, while the latter is only ephemeral and disappears after initial contacts have been made. Another example is the *organizational ability* often attributed to both Jupiterian and Saturnine personalities. But the Jupiterian type is an *organizer* whose efforts are to direct others, like Louis XIV, whereas the Saturnine type organizes himself, like the football player Lerond, mentioned in the previous chapter.

This explains why the present boundaries between the four planetary continents are still not distinctly demarcated. For example, champions possessing a trait from the "Mars temperament" list (see p. 000) *also* tend to be born, more often than other men, after Jupiter has risen or reached its culmination. This tendency is less pronounced than the "normal" tendency of these champions to be born under Mars, but it is nevertheless significant. The explanation for this could be that our language contains adjectives which can be used to designate quite different characterological attitudes. Words like *eager*, *bold*, and *adventurous* can refer to the Mars type and the Jupiter type. But the motivations behind this eagerness, boldness, or this spirit of adventure would not be the same

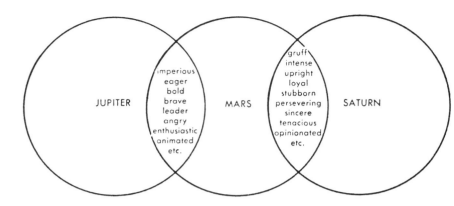

Figure 12. Temperamental traits common to Mars, Jupiter, and Saturn

Among champion sportsmen, there is a degree of overlapping between the Mars and Jupiter traits on the one hand, and between the Mars and Saturn traits on the other. This is due to the inadequacy of our language to describe minute variations in these psychological tendencies. This "annexation" of Mars by Jupiter and by Saturn, in this diagram, is representative of the group of champions. The list of common traits would differ if we were considering actors and scientists. (This figure simply indicates the first few common traits shared by the planets from our lists.)

even though the same word is used to designate them.[2]

There are also common traits shared by the Martian and Saturnine temperaments among champions. Listed in alphabetical order, they are: composed, grumpy, having faith, industrious, intense, loyal, opinionated, perservering, rugged, self-controlled, sincere, stubborn, surly, tenacious, and upright. The champions with these traits show a marked tendency to be born either with Mars or Saturn at the rise or culmination

Figure 12 indicates, for champions, some of the traits common to the planetary continents of Mars, Jupiter, and Saturn. In order to better define the boundaries between these types and to reduce this no-man's land between them, we must conduct many more comprehensive studies. This research has already begun.

CHAPTER TWELVE

The Planet with a Thousand Faces

EVERY MAN IS A unique individual. His personality is never completely identical with that of another individual. Similarly there are not two identical stones or identical planets in nature. Yet the mineralogist classifies stones and the botanist classifies plants according to certain similarities. This classification enables us to better understand the subtle relationships between them. Psychologists strive to do likewise with man, classifying us, defining us, categorizing us in order to be able to predict our behavior. This is the specific aim of planetary typology.

A planetary type is one of the many factors on which a personality is built. It is an important factor, but not the only one. For a planetary type is a large family and each member is different. We shall use Jupiter as an example (we could just as well take Mars, Saturn, or the moon). People with a Jupiterian temperament have a "family tie." But their personalities may differ in many respects. Jupiter has a thousand faces, pleasant and unpleasant, famous and anonymous. Here are a few quick portraits which will allow the reader to comprehend the Jupiterian bonds linking the many personalities.

Jupiter and Entertainers

Tristan Bernard, born on September 7, 1866, at 10 P.M. in Besançon, one and a half hours after Jupiter had reached its culmination, was one of the most famous French humorists in the first half of this century. We have reported some of the comments made in the newspapers after his death in 1947.[1]

"Novelist, journalist, comedy writer, or dramatic critic, Tristan Bernard managed to put animation and subtlety into everything he wrote, which made him one of the most popular French writers. . . . He had, it seems, a sense of humor right to the tips of his fingers." (*France-Soir*, December 9, 1947)

"He had deep-set, mischievous, large black eyes under a pair of bushy eyebrows. His nose was aquiline and his beard had more or less become legendary. He was a great gambler at Deauville, Cannes, and even at Paris, playing poker and baccarat, etc. One evening, he was complaining of having lost too much. 'How much?' 'Oh,' he said, 'at least a hundred performances.' " (*L'Ordre*, December 9, 1947)

"He was one of those legendary personalities of whom people are no longer sure if they are still alive or even if they ever lived. His beard alone was 'a historical monument' and the source of many stories, fables, comments, and anecdotes, even though most of these were never told by him. His real name was Paul Bernard. Tristan was the name of a horse that had brought him luck. All his life he adhered to a bantering and sometimes gently cynical philosophy. But this smiling charm concealed a sensitive humorist and a genuine moralist. Tristan Bernard's fame was universal and his work was prodigious." (*Combat*, December 9, 1947)

A year before his death, he celebrated his eightieth birthday. "Eighty years old? Tristan Bernard, the wittiest man in the world! This has to be one of Tristan's jokes!

One of those sparkling pirouettes which always dazzle us! An octogenarian? This bright storyteller whose name is synonymous with joviality, subtlety, and imagination! He is eighty years old! The man whose name signifies 'smile'?" (Maud Jacobson, *L'Ordre*, September 7, 1946)

Similar to Tristan Bernard is Armand Fallières, "Father Fallières," President during the Third French Republic. He was born when Jupiter was at its culmination on November 6, 1841, at 2 A.M. at Mézin in the south of France.[3]

"His stocky silhouette, his goatee beard, his tufted hair, and his spotted lavaliere made Fallières a caricaturist's dream. Nevertheless, he acquired real popularity. Many French people saw themselves in this bourgeois man from Gascony with his distinctive accent and his steadfast optimism tinged with nonchalance." (Jean-François Genest, *La France de la Troisième République*, 1971, p. 203)

Here is another historian's account which confirms the first: "Barely known at first, the President very quickly became popular. His debonair manner, his tufted hair, and his liking for spotted lavalieres and his goatee beard certainly helped. Although he was far from naïve, the President did not mind if people believed he was. Many of his sayings were widely reported. At a Rodin exhibition, he commented on a piece of sculpture: 'Another road accident!' At another exhibition of avant-garde paintings, he exclaimed to his guide, the painter Sisley, 'I am following you with my eyes closed.' He earned the reputation of being not only a courteous and benevolent man, but also an extremely shrewd and intelligent president. Paul Boncour evaluates him as follows: 'Of all the presidents, he said, he was the most effective.' Father Fallières no doubt could have run for office again, but he did not choose to. With his typical bright wit, he declared,

'The position is not a bad one, but there is no advancement in it.' " (Joseph Bonnafos, *Historia*, special edition, no. 19, pp. 149–51)

There are many similarities between this President of the Republic and the dramatic writer Tristan Bernard. Both were noted for their unusual appearance, their sense of humor and their witty turn of phrase. Another man, the dramatist Marcel Achard, also resembles them in many ways (see the detailed portrait of him above). He was also an entertainer with an industrious, opportunistic nature concealed by an air of nonchalance.

Jokes, practical jokes, and hoaxes are characteristic of the Jupiterian temperament. "Every Friday Alibert, a music-hall star and traveling comedian, would gather his friends to indulge in a garlic-flavored mayonnaise and relate jokes. His favorite hoax was to disguise a friend as a waiter and get him to spill the mayonnaise down the low-cut dresses of the ladies." (*France-Soir*, April 24, 1970) Alibert, who went on the stage wearing a white suit, white shirt and white tie, shining shoes, and an immaculate straw hat gently pulled down over his eyes, was born on December 3, 1889, at 11 A.M. in Carpentras, not far from Marseille. Jupiter had just risen.[4] His jokes were without malice or nastiness . . . but often Jupiterian types are more aggressive and their immoderate side becomes apparent.

The Immoderate

Alfred Jarry is famous for a play he wrote called *Ubu Roi*, a farce parodying political autocracy. Born when Jupiter was rising on September 8, 1873, at 5 A.M. at Laval in the Mayenne department, Jarry was not an absolutely reliable person. This is what Louis Perche has written about him:[5]

"Jarry's mother admired the boy because he demonstrated a character that she would like to have seen in her husband. He was dogmatic and did not give in easily. He spoke forcefully in a loud voice and seemed sure of himself, asserting his personality. As a schoolboy, he had no problems making friends. He was quite confident, knowing how to push himself forward without asserting himself too much, and his heavy body seemed to bear down on his bowed legs, emphasizing his short stature. He did not give the appearance of being stocky, but rather sturdy with a massive build, and his face was like a Kalmuck mask with penetrating eyes, according to the description of one of his friends. He was always loudly proclaiming truths in a decisive tone. He settled disputes shamelessly and had a distinctive vocabulary full of cutting remarks. He was jealous of his independence, curious and eager for life. Stubborn, shy, wild and sarcastic, cruelly mocking, he loved to be involved in scandals, being one of those boys who are always jumping into the water just to prove his freedom. When he left the Rennes High School, his friends remembered him as being predominantly lazy, but brilliant when he wanted to be and undisciplined when he chose to be, yet always ready to display his crude vocabulary filled with sexual allusions. His vanity and pride were expressed in the only way open to an adolescent—through words."

Jarry's nature as a child did not alter as he grew older. "An eccentric individual, he stubbornly believed that his personality differed from that of everyone else whom he met. He was proud of his faults, which he refused to consider as faults. He chose to ignore social convention and was proud of his habits and pleasures." Alas, one of his habits and pleasures was a consuming passion for alcohol. Drunk on absinthe, he died at the age of thirty-three, on May 28, 1906.

The Jupiterian temperament is often associated with immoderation of all kinds: wine, food, gambling, and women. The great actor Lucien Guitry, born when Jupiter was rising, was a gourmet, although "glutton" might be a more accurate description. During the year before his death, Guitry would bring dozens of oranges daily to his friends and eat almost all of them, *after stuffing them with pieces of sugar* (he happened to be a diabetic). In spite of several serious sick episodes, Lucien always refused to follow a diet. On May 9, at a single meal, he devoured one hundred snails. The next day, he became critically ill. On June 1, he felt better. Around four o'clock, feeling very hungry, he ate a whole bowl of potatoes! Soon after, he suffered another heart attack, which was to be his last. At 6:15 P.M. Lucien Guitry died.[6]

This uncontrollable gluttony, which is so destructive to the individual afflicted by it, seems to be a definite characteristic of a certain Jupiterian temperament, as is evidenced by these statistics obtained from an examination of 1116 chronic alcoholics who were institutionalized at the Sainte-Anne hospital in Paris for alcoholic psychosis, delirium tremens, etc. A study of the position of Jupiter at the time of their births indicated a tendency for alcoholics to be born after Jupiter had risen or culminated.[7] Although it only reflects a tendency, this figure is significant, because the chances are only one in a hundred in this instance. Among these Jupiterian individuals, the urge to enjoy life can take an opposite and sinister route toward a psychiatric institution, for the Jupiterian individual is often given to immoderation. But people can be immoderate in a thousand various ways, such as a desire for glory, adventure, conquests, with dignity or dishonor, each according to his own personality.

The Conquerors

The pioneer aviators were often Jupiterian types, as statistics[8] and biographical studies have confirmed. The psychology of the pioneer aviators is based on bravery, independence, vainglory, and courage. These are traits which often reflect a combination of the Mars and Jupiter types. We shall try to define the Jupiterian aspect of this type through the personalities of two famous pilots.

Hubert Latham, an early aviation enthusiast, was one of the unfortunate heroes of an attempt to fly across the English Channel. The first to accomplish the crossing was Bleriot, but Latham was the first to attempt it. He was born in Paris into a rich family on January 10, 1883, at 3 P.M., at which time Jupiter was rising in the east.

"He attempted the first flight across the English Channel, but failed and came down in the sea. When the sailors who were acting as his convoy arrived to pick him up, they found Latham sitting in the seat of his floating aircraft, smoking a cigarette and whistling a hunting tune."

"A public idol, his father had given him a liking for travel and a passion for adventure. From his grandfather, he inherited a certain boldness of character and an ungainly build. But with his small mouth and high cheekbones, he became the idol of French crowds, especially the women. Debonair and distinguished, his composure, his free and easy manner, and his playboy charm captured all hearts. But people loved him not only for his fine features and dandyish manner; they also loved him for the risks he took and the skill he displayed. Even though he was eclectic and lacked perseverance, people willingly pardoned him for these whims of a spoiled, carefree child who flew for his own pleasure and the thrill of the risk. In the air, he was an amiable virtuoso, relying more on his talent than on his experience. All those who associated with him were charmed by him and loved to repeat his impertinent remarks. For example, when the President of the Republic, Armand Fallières, asked him, "Well, my boy, what do you do besides fly?" he replied, "I'm a society man, Mr. President!"

"This impetuous young aviator once said, 'You must know how to strike the imagination of crowds. That is what we are here for. For as aviators, a great deal of our success is publicity.' "

For his landing in England, "Latham chose the highest hillside in the area. He was told that this was madness but he did not listen, preferring to follow through with his childish whim. Latham argued convincingly and ostentatiously. 'I wager I shall have crossed the Channel before August 1.' He had his gloves in his hand, a smile on his lips, and a carnation in his buttonhole, as though he were discussing something of no great magnitude. Latham, unconcerned and full of boyish enthusiasm, thanked the bystanders with little hand gestures—aristocratic gestures—for Hubert Latham was not an unknown. He detested the *nouveau riche*, and loved to please the crowds."[9]

Looking for easier successes, Latham gave up aviation. He led a safari in Africa and was killed by a buffalo which suddenly sprang in front of him while he was in the jungle (Latham did not retreat and tried to fight it). He was afraid of nothing. Was he simply bold or reckless also? Dead at the age of twenty-nine, Latham's life was not crowned by the halo of universal glory which he had vainly sought during the last five years of his life. Idleness was repulsive to this fiery nature which loved confronting danger and surmounting obstacles. He loved this saying of Marcus Aurelius: "Exert yourself for the things you despair of accomplishing."[10]

This motto could very well apply to one of the greatest French aviators, Hélène Boucher. Hélène Boucher was born in Paris on May 23, 1908, at 11 A.M. when Jupiter was rising. We shall make her relive for a few moments through this extract from her biography by Jacques Mortane:[11]

"Hélène Boucher, as a young girl, did not amuse herself by making toy airplanes. On the contrary, certain aspects of her character proved her spirit of independence at an age when children generally had to be obedient. But she could never obey. As a young girl, she would refuse to offer her hand when crossing streets. Each time, there would be an argument and Hélène would emerge victorious. . . . With her iron will, she would stand up to her father, who was just as firm. The resulting scenes were a terrible torment to her poor mother. . . . As a child, she already knew how to bargain. 'Oh,' she would say to her mother, in a mocking tone, 'how dare you ask that, you'll see!' and she bargained over prices so persuasively that she always obtained the reduction she wanted. At that time, she was only ten years old, yet people seemed compelled to submit to her. It was quite obvious that she would not yield and would wait until she had obtained some degree of satisfaction. But this did not stop all the shopkeepers from adoring this little woman who knew how to get her way with them, but proved very nice— after her victory! Her entire life's behavior was modeled on this motto: 'To be useful and daring.' 'I do not want to live in mediocrity. I want total success or nothing.' What could be expected from such an independent, active temperament? She also declared: 'What a horror to have to live knowing that the whole future depends on marriage; to have to ask oneself every morning before getting up, will I meet my future husband today? Marry and have a mediocre life, never! I intend to show that I can succeed by myself and that my lord and master, my prince charming, will not be my protector!' However, there were plenty of suitors for the hand of this girl, with her appealing body, her fresh, open face, gray almond-shaped eyes, mocking mouth, sparkling teeth, and firm chin. She was popular and adulated. But she knew how to get rid of the unwelcome suitors with great irony!"

When Hélène Boucher discovered aviation, she decided she would excel as a flier. Making a strong effort and using persuasion and boldness, she succeeded in obtaining a license and then began to break records. Thus she realized her dream of living intensely and achieving fame. "Happy and lively, she was very harsh and severe toward unwelcome suitors, and she had the facility to maintain long-standing grudges. Although she saw her friends crash, her courage never wavered. She said: "I know I shall end as they have all ended. There are no two ways about it. I shall die on the land. It is the most beautiful death."

After breaking the female world record for speed flying at 445 kilometers an hour, Hélène Boucher died on November 30, 1934, while at the controls of a Caudron Rafale.

The Tyrants

Not all conquerors have the purity and nobility of the pioneers in aviation. There are other challenges which men desire to conquer besides the sky for the fruit of their victories, power and glory. If other men get in their way, they remove them or trample them. Conquerors are often to be feared, as the Nazis certainly proved.

Let us look for a moment at the results of a statistical study grouping the positions of Jupiter at the births of 508 men who occupied important positions in Adolf Hitler's Third Reich.

These subjects included 259 top dignitaries of the Nazi Party, 130 chiefs of the S.S., and 119 generals of the German High Command from 1939 to 1945.

The planet Jupiter, which is already significant for German soldiers and politicians in general, takes on an added importance here. In the sectors just following the rise or the culmination of Jupiter, 118 Nazis (instead of 83, which would be the normal number of births for these sectors among the general population) were born when Jupiter was in these areas. The possibility that this could be due to chance is less than one in 50,000.[12]

A large number of Nazi leaders were therefore Jupiterians, and formidable Jupiterians at that. Here are some brief portraits of the best known among these leaders:

Heinrich Himmler, head of the S.S., was born at the very moment when Jupiter was reaching its culmination on October 7, 1900, at 3:30 P.M. in Munich, Bavaria. "Those who lived with him," wrote André Brissaud, "have all declared that he was a very deceiving, hypocritical person, filled with a wild desire to dominate. This desire was moderated only in the presence of Adolf Hitler. Furthermore, he was madly egotistic and profoundly indifferent from an emotional point of view. Capable of accomplishing large amounts of work in a routine, automatic way, he often suffered from extreme inner agitation which was manifested by red blemishes on his cheeks and forehead. His outwardly cool fanaticism was profound, tumultuous, and phantasmagorical, yet it burned with sincerity."[13]

Reinhard Heydrich was born on March 7, 1904, at 3 P.M. in Halle, Saxony, when Jupiter was at its culmination (and also Mars, because the two planets were in conjunction). As the head of security, he was "debonair, sporting, as pretentious as a film star and an ardent pursuer of females. This earned him the sobriquet "king of the nightclubs of politics." He was not given to lengthy utterances, was as sharp as a razor, and systematic. His personality was extraordinarily powerful and his ambitions were boundless. Nothing and no one could oppose him. All his life, Heydrich was an 'iron-hearted' man, a technical expert in crime, and inspired by his love of power."[14]

The following men were also Nazi leaders born just after Jupiter had crossed the horizon or the meridian: Goebbels, the minister of propaganda, infamous for his vicious onslaughts and deceitful words; Eichmann, exterminator of the Jews; Lammerding, a general of the S.S. and commander of the Reich division which committed many atrocities in France at Tulle and at Oradour sur Glane; Franz Witt, the S.S. Brigade leader, who at thirty-five was the first commander of the Hitler Jugend S.S. division; Martin Bormann, Hitler's second in command at the end of the war, and many other politicians and soldiers, including Adolf Hitler himself, who was born on April 20, 1889, at 6:30 P.M. at Braunau am Inn near the Austrian border, when Jupiter was just after its lower culmination. We will not describe Hitler in detail, because more than enough has been spoken and written about him.

Nazism was characterized not only by a Nietzschean desire for power. It also had a theatrical aspect to it. These two features were complementary to each other. The Soviet writer Chakhotin had noted this: "And so the mass parades, the thousands of portraits of the Führer, the thousands of swastika banners were destined to arouse the enthusiasm of the crowds, who were ready to blindly follow this force displayed before them. But on the other hand, those who resisted this force could not defend themselves adequately from it because they were paralyzed by fear." For them, according to Chakotin, "the swastika became a threatening symbol" forcing them into Nazism, like hares blinded and paralyzed by car lights unable to escape. . . ." For example, Chakotin has written of the effectiveness of the revolutionary gymnastics which were aimed at reinforcing the frenzy through psychological contagion by means of the large Nuremberg parades.

The salutes, the cheers, the goose-step marching, and the silent episodes were part of the same procedure as were the fanfares, songs, and hymns."[15]

This was like being at the theater, for Jupiterians are always rather theatrical. But in this instance, the theatrical event was a particularly disturbing one. How could people resist it? Perhaps the only way is to be a Jupiterian oneself, refusing to be dominated by a stronger power. The Friends of the Liberation and the great French Resistance fighters were, in fact, born more frequently under Jupiter than ordinary men. But of course, there are many other characterological ways of defeating Jupiterian tyranny.

When Two Jupiters Meet

When one Jupiterian temperament crosses another and their wills conflict, compromise is difficult, and usually the stronger breaks the weaker. This is illustrated in an episode concerning Louis XIV and his finance minister, Nicolas Fouquet.[16] When Louis XIV came to the throne, Fouquet, an unscrupulous but brilliant and refined man, was the richest man in the kingdom. He invited the king to an absolutely luxurious feast in his castle at Vaux-le-Vicomte. The dishes at the banquet were of gold and the food was the finest and most exquisite. The feast ended with a sumptuous fountain display in the ornamental garden lakes. To provide water for the fountains, Fouquet had diverted an entire river. He treated the king with the utmost honor. But the king was young and relatively poor and he could not stand this blow to his pride and vanity. As he was driving home to the Palais du Louvre in his carriage in the early hours of the morning, he shook his fist and cried: "I should have had him arrested on the spot." This he eventually did several months later, and Fouquet was condemned for having become rich dishonestly. He spent the rest of his days in an impregnable fortress. The king's grudge did not soften. Louis XIV took not only his wealth, but also his architects, his decorators, and all his artists, and made them build the famed Versailles chateau.

We have now concluded our review of several Jupiterian temperaments. They naturally include various personalities but all have the common bond of belonging to the Jupiter family. As in any large family, there are worthy members like Tristan Bernard, heroines like Hélène Boucher, perpetrators of evil like Heydrich, and failures like the chronic alcoholics. Jupiter has a thousand faces, but all have the same silhouette.

CHAPTER THIRTEEN

Planetary Types and Modern Psychology

SINCE THE TURN of this century, a great many character classifications have been proposed. It would be interesting to compare our planetary typology with other typologies.[1] A complete study is not possible in this book, so we shall only compare our planetary typology with the two most famous classifications of temperament, the types listed by the Swiss psychiatrist Carl Jung and the physical types established by the American psychologist W. H. Sheldon. Some interesting convergence points will emerge.

Introversion and Extroversion

Although Plato had already hinted at this dichotomy of personalities, the classification of characters as extroverted and introverted was first proposed by Jung.

This is how Jung describes the extroverted type: "If a man thinks, feels, acts, and actually lives in a way that is directly correlated with objective conditions and their demands, he is extroverted. . . . His whole consciousness looks outward because the essential and decisive determination always comes from outside. . . . Not only people but things seize and rivet his attention. Accordingly, they also determine his actions. . . ."[2]

And now, his portrait of the introverted type. "The introvert interposes a subjective view between the perception of the object and his own action which prevents the action from assuming a character that fits the objective situation. The normal reaction of the introvert is to stop, criticize, and withdraw."

Let us compare our planetary types with Jung's types. On a value scale going from introverted to extroverted, the first type is the Saturnine one. Jung's declaration, "The normal reaction of the introvert is to stop, criticize, and withdraw," can be directly applied to the Saturnine type. "If someone suggests an important professional venture to me," stated Jean Vilar, born when Saturn had completed its culmination, "I regard the person making the offer, especially if it is a large one, as my greatest enemy. At first I recoil and even refuse. . . ." Another example: Recognizing the tremendous talent of Eleonora Duse, who was born after Saturn had risen and who was then acting in an unknown Italian troupe, a very famous impresario proposed to launch her on a famous career. For several years, Miss Duse refused this proposition. She finally accepted but only in the hope of improving her art and not for her own financial reward. These reserved, inscrutable, rather shy people are generally Saturn types.

Continuing up the scale, we have the Mars type, who is a rather ambivalent individual. His dynamism and determination is directed outwardly, but with a good deal of selectivity. The Mars type is not always very sociable. On the other hand, the Jupiter and Moon types both show traits of extroversion. They have open natures and are readily influenced by people and events.

The Jupiterian temperament likes to assert himself over others. His tranquility, caustic judgments, his gaiety, and his desire to please and succeed are extroverted traits. For example, the Jupiterian Marcel Achard makes confirmed enemies with his malevolent wit. Not everyone appreciates his humor.

Of the two, the lunar type is the most extroverted. The lunar temperament admires the latest tenor because everybody else does, which is something a Jupiterian would not do. The lunar temperament is susceptible to influence. He has many friends and does not favor any of them. The lunar Nadaud "seeks to please in the salons: always amiable, always cheerful . . . Very well known, very sought after, he rarely ate at home. A place was set for him in every house. . . . He had friends everywhere and no enemies. His gracious popularity combined pleasantly with his fame in no way detracting from anyone else's self-esteem."

Introversion and extroversion are unevenly distributed among the four planetary types, as can be seen in Figure 13.

Body Build and Cosmic Types

Does a person have a certain temperament because of the shape of his face or his physique? Since very ancient times, writers have affirmed this, believing that there is a cause and effect relationship between body build and character. The most convincing study in support of this theory was published thirty years ago by W. H. Sheldon, a professor at Harvard University.[3]

Through very detailed observation, Sheldon demonstrated that the tremendous diversity of human physical builds could be grouped into three main morphological categories; that the great variety of human personalities could also be grouped into three temperamental categories; and that there was a close statistical relationship between these morphological and temperamental categories.

Table IV, describing the three morphological and psychological types, summarizes Sheldon's ideas.[4]

Where do our planetary types fit in Sheldon's classification? First, it must be noted that Sheldon describes only three temperamental types, whereas we have four planetary types. So there can be no direct correlation, for our types do not fit squarely into Sheldon's categories.

By studying this table and comparing it to the one on p. 000 which contains the important key words describing the planetary types, we see that:

Sheldon's somatotonic temperament is situated between the Mars and Jupiter types. Like the Mars type, "he is energetically active and has physical courage, competitive aggressiveness, and a need for action." Like the Jupiter type, "he is vigorously self-assertive, loves power, domination, and risks, but lacks sympathy and tact."

Sheldon's viscerotonic temperament is situated between the moon and Jupiter types. Like the Jupiterian, "he enjoys comfort, companionship, joviality, is always ready to eat, and enjoys the company of his fellow man." Like the moon type, he is "generally relaxed, tolerant, and amiable. He needs affection and the approval of others."

Sheldon's cerebrotonic temperament is very close to the Saturn type. They both "tend to be inhibited, like privacy, and enjoy solitude."

Although Sheldon described a relationship between physique and temperament, our studies are not sufficiently advanced for us to be able to establish a link between the human physique and planetary type. Initial results seem to indicate that this relationship is much more nebulous in our case than it was for Sheldon—that

TABLE IV
Physique and Personality According to Sheldon

PHYSIQUE	PERSONALITY TRAITS
ENDOMORPHY	**VISCEROTONIA**
Predominance of the rounded and soft forms in the various areas of the body. The viscera are often very developed.	Generally relaxed attitude. Enjoys comfort. Sociability, joviality, tolerance, amiability. Loves good food and the companionship of other people, their affection, their approval. Even-tempered. In times of stress, needs others.
MESOMORPHY	**SOMATOTONIA**
The somatic structures (bones, muscles, connective tissue) tend to dominate. The blood vessels are developed. Hard, firm, straight, relatively strong and sturdy.	Vigorous self-assertion. Energetically active and physically courageous. Loves domination, power, and risks. Direct, forthright manner. Competitive aggressiveness. Psychological insensitivity. Lack of sympathy and tact. In times of stress, needs action.
ECTOMORPHY	**CEREBROTONIA**
Weak muscular and visceral development. Large surface area in proportion to mass. Greatest sensory exposure to the outside world. Delicate, flat-chested. Whole body is of fragile structure. Long and lean extremities.	Tends to be inhibited and reserved. Likes privacy (intimacy and solitude). Unpredictable attitudes and feelings. Very attentive. Extremely rapid reactions. In times of stress, needs solitude.

is, if there is any relationship at all. Moreover, other writers have criticized Sheldon, claiming that the measurable aspects of the body are not representative of the temperament. It is possible for a man to be physically very strong, yet be a "gentle giant" by nature. Or he might be physically underdeveloped yet possess enormous psychic energy. The "double decimeter" aspect of temperament seems a rather naïve concept. Nevertheless there may be some secondary relationship between physique and character, as they do both seem to depend on one and the same cause, which is to be found in the individual's biochemistry. The "physical" relationship between character and morphology therefore seems to be primarily one of a biochemical nature and not purely structural.

The Biochemistry of Behavior: An Explanation?

Biochemistry is still a developing science. Some of the most recent biochemical revelations have a direct bearing on our observations. For it has been proven that there is a relationship between the uric acid level of the human body and social success. Individuals with a high uric acid level are more energetic and enterprising than other individuals. Dr. Escoffier-Lambiotte, who reported these studies, writes: "A team of American scientists showed that the uric acid level is related not exactly to intelligence but to social success and that, genetically, it determines a specific kind of behavior which is characteristically ambitious, energetic, proud, and authoritative, thus facilitating this success."[5] There was considerable criticism raised against this initial study. It was argued that if the uric acid level is higher among people who eat a great deal, this is only because those who are successful tend to eat more and therefore have a higher uric acid level, not the reverse.

To settle the dispute, some very important research was undertaken by several teams of scientists throughout the world. The Institute of Social Research at the University of Michigan conducted a study on thirty-six professors there. Again, "it indicated that the level of uric acid in the blood is related, not to intellectual ability, but very significantly to certain behavioral traits which are very meaningful for *success*: namely, enjoyment of authority, energy, dynamism, eagerness, and perfectionism— regardless of the social backgrounds in which these subjects were raised." The Institute then followed a group of Pittsburgh college students for four years, examining their social backgrounds, their intelligence, and their performances. Once again, uricacidemia seemed closely related to ambition, eagerness, or "desire for success." Finally, another experiment, the results of which were published in August 1970 by the Yale Department of Public Health, was conducted on 340 students attending three secondary schools for boys in Michigan. This study fully confirmed the above results, indicating that the uric acid level in the blood does influence the results of performance tests which were used to measure determination, speed, and desire for success, but not intelligence. The uric acid level also influences professional ambition. Young people who were questioned about the careers they hoped to pursue showed a tendency to choose more difficult and competitive professions when they had an elevated uric acid level. Similarly, the students with higher uric acid levels showed a much greater interest in extracurricular activities, and they attached less importance than the other students to human relations and emotional ties. Finally, the psychological tests showed that they are not as anxious as the other students and that their latent anxiety seemed inversely proportional to the uric acid levels."

As further evidence, the University of Edinburgh

showed that a group of business leaders had distinctly higher uric acid levels than a test group of bank employees when both groups were eating identical diets. This leaves no doubt of the fact that uric acid is related to certain behavioral traits, foremost among which are energy and ambition.[6]

But to return to the planetary types and the behavior associated with them, it would be interesting to test the following theory: Can the various planetary types be distinguished by their different uric acid levels? The Mars type is energetic, active, and dynamic; the Jupiter type, ambitious, opportunistic, and authoritarian. In this case, the amount of uric acid in the blood of a person born when Mars or Jupiter was rising or culminating should be higher than that of a person born when neither Mars nor Jupiter was in the sectors associated with their rise or culmination. As we have already noted, important industrial managers are born more frequently than other men after Mars has risen or reached its culmination, and experiments have demonstrated that business executives have a distinctly higher uric acid level in their blood.

Body and Facial Language

There is another "physical" domain where there is a possible correlation with the planetary types. This consists of the subject's general facial expressions, gestures, and manner of speaking—but in particular his expression, which is called a mirror of his soul. Referring to our biographical file, we have discovered that sharp, keen, nervous, steely expressions usually belong to the individuals born with Mars at the horizon or at the meridian:

Sad, serious, meditative, cold expressions are frequent among individuals born with Saturn in these areas of the sky;

Planetary Types and Modern Psychology

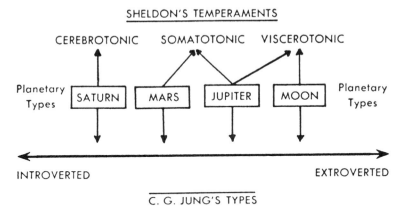

Figure 13. Sheldon's temperaments and C. G. Jung's types

This diagram indicates where the planetary types seem to fit in relation to Sheldon's and Jung's classifications.

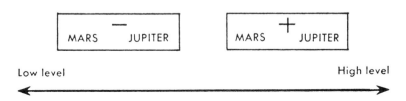

Figure 14. Uric acid level of the blood

This diagram outlines the theory of a possible relationship between uric acid level in the blood and the Mars and Jupiter types.

Happy, expressive, sparkling, malicious, merry, domineering, authoritarian expressions generally belong to persons born with Jupiter at the horizon or at the meridian;

Dreaming, gentle expressions usually belong to those persons born with the moon in these parts of the sky.

Similarly, jerky, staccato voices are indicative of the Mars type. The Jupiter type gesticulates frequently when he talks, and he talks a great deal. The Saturn type has few gestures and does not talk very much, etc.

These observations are often difficult to correlate, but their incidence is too high for them to be attributable to chance. The reader should reread the many character portraits described in this book, paying particular attention to the descriptions of facial expressions, and he will see what a close relationship there is between types of expression and the planetary types. There is, in an individual's expression, something of his soul, or, to be more prosaic, something of his biochemical makeup which partially determines his behavior.[7]

"Like Father, Like Son"

BY THE LAWS OF heredity, our parents pass on to us not only some aspects of their physical appearance, but also their intellectual gifts and character traits.[1] Naturally there is nothing fixed about this. It is a statistical resemblance, like every other genetic phenomenon, but it is a fact. The hereditary tie is formed at the level of the baby's genetic structure. As Joseph Nuttin, professor at the University of Louvain (Belgium), wrote, "It is highly likely that hereditary factors are the base of certain endocrine systems which influence both the physique and the temperament of a personality."[2] In popular speech, this is expressed in simpler terms by the proverb "Like father, like son." A good illustration of this proverb can be found in two great French men of the theater, Lucien Guitry and his son Sacha. We shall examine these two men through accounts written by those who knew them well.

Lucien Guitry was born in Paris on December 13, 1860, at 10 P.M. He also died in Paris.[3] He was one of the greatest French actors, but pride and vanity were among his worst faults. "He was too egotistical to be true. His personality was too excessive, even physically, for him to subordinate himself to the wishes of an author. . . . Actors, in order to make characters live, should not have too overwhelming an ego, or at least they should know how to control it. Lucien Guitry found his own ego so interesting and so superior to his contemporaries that he displayed it somewhat too much. Yet he was a great actor and there are, in truth, very few really great actors. Most actors resort to tricks of the trade and they have a repertoire of studied mannerisms. But this was not the case with Lucien Guitry, for he really worked. But he observed himself more than he observed others and he was too enamored of himself to have the courage to be self-critical. This is why outside criticism annoyed him. This great actor would have reached higher pinnacles of success if he had been more modest and more humble."[3]

The season before his death, he had been acting in Monte Carlo and he used to walk along the pier, majestic and imposing in his flowing coat. Beside him, frail, fresh, and blonde was the lovely little Miss Pierry. All his life, Lucien Guitry loved women and fine food. We have already related how he devoured one hundred snails several days before his death, when he should have been following a very strict diet.

Another example, related by Jacques Lorcey: "He had many mistresses. 'Who is this?' asked his friend Jules Renard, about the latest. 'I don't know,' answered Lucien Guitry, cynically."

Not well educated, bohemian, eccentric, and an actor even in his early youth, with a powerful, impulsive, materialistic, and sensual nature, Lucien matured with marriage and fatherhood. He very quickly learned to frequent the fashionable salons, adopting the measured speech, elegance, and refined politeness he heard and observed there. He also had the foresight to surround himself with witty, cultured men who taught him the advantages of irony and self-control."[5]

"He was exceptionally witty," wrote Louis Schneider, "and like all witty men, he occasionally was unkind in his humor."

Claude Berton wrote: "Lucien Guitry, an excellent mimic and imitator, is a perfect narrator. There is no doubt that he has a ready flow of language. He speaks fluently and has a gift for relating stories."

Obviously, by his character, Lucien Guitry belongs in the category of "immodest actors" as defined by Louis Jouvet. And, in fact, at the time of his birth, Jupiter had just risen.

Sacha Guitry, Lucien's son, was born on February 21, 1885, at St. Petersburg while his father was performing in Russia. We do not know the time of his birth. Even as a young boy, Sacha was undisciplined and given to pranks. His only ambition was to work in the theater and to write plays. He was expelled from several schools because he was not studious. Sacha sketched caricatures, which he sold, and wrote farces in which he himself acted. Originally, his father did not want him to go into the theater: "As long as I am there," declared Lucien Guitry, "you will not act. I will not have you spoiling the name I have made for myself." "Very well," retorted Sacha," I'll wait." Sacha Guitry very quickly became a Parisian personality. His *mots* were notorious, as were his numerous lawsuits. He was married five times and each time with considerable publicity. He said to his last wife, Lana Marconi: "You will be my widow." At one of his marriages, he made the mayor believe that he was on his deathbed. The mayor came to his house very apprehensive. Sacha's face was made up and he was lying in bed, deathly pale as though he were about to expire. As soon as the couple had been pronounced man and wife, he jumped up laughing, to the bewilderment of the mayor and his assistant. He then invited them to drink his health with champagne. He loved this kind of practical joke. He was completely ego-centric, considering only himself, and his vanity easily equaled that of his father. He had a habit of saying "I" (moi) so emphatically at the beginning of a sentence that his enemies nicknamed him "Moa." Then he retaliated by writing a play called *Toa* (You). It was a charming, brilliant play, but the humor was difficult to understand. During one of his many lawsuits, involving one of his ex-wives, the wife's lawyer said of Sacha Guitry that the author-actor had an egocentric cerebrum and the whole city knew about everything he did because he took such a delight in publicizing himself. "What are your faults?" he was asked one day. "I think I have them all. I smoke three packs of cigarettes a day. I have been playing roulette since the age of four . . . I pay too much attention to what I drink and too little to what I say. I have the terrible habit of making puns." But at his death, Marcel Archard said of him: "You were the greatest comic poet of our time, the best artist of all the comedy writers and actors. You had every gift, and the most precious gift of all, imagination."

Sacha Guitry had a brother, two years older, who died prematurely in an automobile accident. "Jean was even more dreadful than Sacha. He was asked to remove himself wherever he went." "He is unspeakably impertinent and lazy," said his teachers. Often he would disappear for several days. When things had calmed down, he would return home to his mother in the middle of the night. He captured the heart of a fourteen-year-old American girl, with whom he had a love affair.

"I loved Jean Guitry," said the dramatist Francis de Croisset. "He had a generous heart and a sense of humor which delighted me." One day when Sacha was making his debut in the theater in a small role, "Jean installed himself in the front row of the balcony with a whole group of boisterous friends. Sacha's entrance was greeted with an extraordinary ovation. Every step he took, every gesture he made brought tremendous applause. His friends' enthusiasm was boundless and their shouts, cries, and enthusiastic outbursts scandalized the other spectators and shocked the stars of the show.[4]

Obviously, Lucien, the father, bequeathed through heredity his charm, his ease, his wit, his pride, his ambition, his desire for women, his ostentation, his liking for practical jokes, and his complex character to his two sons. Naturally the sons were not exact replicas of their father, far from it. Some traits very likely stemmed from their mother or even from more distant ancestors. The personality of every human being is unique. However, there is a basic resemblance between Jean and Sacha Guitry's temperaments and their father's.

CHAPTER FOURTEEN

Cosmic Genetics

The Wolves and the Lambs

HAS A WOLF ever given birth to a young lamb or a ewe given birth to a wolf cub? As far as the human race is concerned, if a child is born from a whole line of amiable, calm parents with no marked spirit of adventure or aggressiveness, it is quite probable that the child will be neither violent nor combative. He will belong to the "lamb family" like his ancestors. But if, by chance, this child is born when Mars has just risen, what will happen? Will the baby grow up to be a tough aggressive adult because of this Martian influence? Born of docile parents and predisposed to be of a similar nature himself, will this lamb become a young wolf because at the exact moment of his birth, Mars, the god of war, was appearing in the east? How could this influence override the amiable and calm predisposition granted him by heredity? When the child is born, it is after nine months of gestation during which his body has developed. Once the "chromosomal lottery," which occurs at conception, is drawn, the hereditary future of the child seems decided. There is no present justification for believing that the planet's action at birth can modify the child's chromosomal structure. In any case, the "lamb" will not turn into a young wolf.

This presents a real problem in that, while there is a relationship between the planets and the individual's character traits, the temperamental predisposition of a person nevertheless seems determined by his heredity. There is no valid reason for supposing that there are two types of character determination, one entirely independent of the other, that of the planets on the one hand and that of heredity on the other. So, to resolve this dilemma, and to explain the nature of the relationship between the planetary position and temperament, it seems logical to believe that planetary temperament is part of the individual's genetic predisposition. In this way, the contradiction is eliminated. Just as wolves give birth to wolf cubs and sheep to lambs, parents give birth to children who tend to be born under Mars if the parents themselves have a Mars temperament. Thus, being born under Mars would be a hereditary predisposition and the position of the planet is simply evidence of the child's temperament.

Hereditary Sensitivity to the Cosmos

Once again, we must understand the various possibilities and to do this we shall cite the works of several scientists.

Every organism reacts differently, according to its temperament, to outside aggression, to disease. One individual will catch many colds while another has much more resistance. There are many cases of allergies of a temperamental origin to food, medicine, and to pollen from flowers. Furthermore, one single tablet of a given drug will be sufficient to relieve Peter of his insomnia and allow him to fall asleep, but Paul will require twice that dosage. With John, the medicine may not act or may even make him sick. As Professor Maurice Lamy, a member of the Academy of Medicine, wrote: "The knowledge of these facts is of vital importance. It has given rise to a new science, *pharmacogenetics*, which studies the sensitivity or resistance to the action of drugs, which is influenced by the individual's *biochemical constitution* and obeys the dictates of his heredity." In short, an external factor, such as a drug, when given in strictly equal doses, can exercise a different action according to the subject's constitutional makeup. Similarly, Professor Lamy insists on "the existence of a specific sensitivity of a special type which allows the action of the medicine."[1]

This modern concept of "specific hereditary sensitivity" should be used in the interpretation of our results to provide an accurate understanding of the relationship between cosmic factors and temperament. Thus it establishes the basis for cosmic genetics.

Cosmic Genetics

Cosmic genetics implies that the level of cosmic sensitivity varies from one subject to another and that it is linked to our genetic constitution. The following is a rather common example of two different reactions to the same cosmic phenomenon: namely, the action of the sun's rays on fat and lean people. If a fat and a lean person are exposed to the same degree of solar radiation, the lean person will tolerate it better. The difference in the reaction will be even greater if the lean person should have an olive complexion and the fat person is fairskinned. Everyone seems agreed on the explanation for this. Because of his hereditary constitution, the fat fair-skinned person does not tolerate solar rays as well as the dark-skinned subject. However, he does have greater resistance to the cold.

But is not this "fat person" the viscerotonic type, described by Sheldon as easygoing, relaxed, and sociable? And isn't the "thin person" Sheldon's cerebrotonic type who is hypersensitive and solitary? From this very simple example, we can form an equation: different hereditary constitutions = different reactions to the sun = different characterological temperaments.

An American living in Germany, Manfred Curry, has carried the equation even further: "Tell me how you react to the weather and I will tell you what sort of person you are." In 1946 he developed a theory dividing people into two groups according to how they react to the weather. There are Type K and Type W. Type K individuals are very uncomfortable when there is a sudden drop in temperature. Physically they are thin, they have lean faces and a reflective air. They have introverted personalities. Type W individuals have extroverted personalities. Thier bodies are solid and their figures are rather rotund. Type W individuals are uncomfortable with sudden elevations of temperature.[2]

This reactive typology is nothing more than meteoropsychology because it is based on weather changes and not cosmic ones. But the cosmic influences are only one step away, for our reactions to the cosmic clocks are also influenced by our inherited psychological characteristics.

Professor G. Piccardi, director of the Physical Chemistry Laboratory at the University of Florence, has clearly stated this in the preface of one of our books: "Two individuals belonging to the same species but with different hereditary backgrounds will not react in the same way to cosmic phenomena. However, those with the same hereditary background will react similarly."[3]

In other words, "tell me how, on the day you were born, your body reacted to the planetary movements and

I will tell you what sort of person you are." Hence the theory which we formulated ten years ago: namely, that children tend to be born at certain times of the day, when parturition is activated by planetary influences. But the sensitivity of children varies and depends on their genetic constitution. Movements of planet A may activate the birth of child A, but will have no effect on child B.[4]

If you were born when Mars was rising, this did not happen fortuitously. You will have an active, courageous, dynamic temperament. When the time came for you to be born, your body reacted in preference to the effects produced by this planet rather than to the effects of the other planets. You inherited this tendency to be born after Mars had crossed the horizon or the meridian, just as blue eyes or fair hair, height, and intelligence are inherited. Your parents showed the same tendency to be born when Mars was passing the horizon or the meridian. Or perhaps it was only one of your parents who possessed the tendency that gave you your active, courageous, and dynamic temperament. Thus, there is a planetary effect in heredity.

Births of 25,000 Parents and Children

It still has to be proved that there are more planetary similarities between parents and children than among persons with no blood relationship. We examined this theory during the period from 1959 to 1964. The birth registers from many city halls once again provided the material on which our study was based. We examined twenty-five thousand dates and times of birth of parents and their children. These births extended over almost a century from 1850 to 1945 and all the documents used were recently published by our Laboratory.[5]

For every birth, we calculated the position of the

planets of the solar system in their diurnal motion covering the thirty-six sectors previously defined. For every planet, we compared the sector in which the planet was located at the time of birth of both the parents and the child. This involved 16,037 comparisons per celestial body, considering a total of ten such celestial bodies. Thus there were more than 160,000 planetary comparisons which we analyzed statistically.

The Planetary Effect in Heredity[6]

The total picture drawn from the data examined indicated a correlation between the cosmic conditions of the birth of parents with that of their children. This genetic effect was noticed with the moon, Venus, Mars, Jupiter, and Saturn. Or, in other words, children tend to be born after the rise or culmination of one of these celestial bodies if the same circumstances held for the birth of one of the parents. This tendency is obvious, for the probability of the results is very small: only 1 in 500,000.

Figures 15 and 16 give a general indication of how this planetary effect is manifested in heredity.

The effect seems related both to the distance of the planet from the earth and to its mass.[7] For example, the moon, Venus, and Mars are closer to the earth than Jupiter and Saturn and the effect seems more pronounced with the first three planets than with the latter two. Furthermore, no statistical tendency has been found for Mercury, the smallest planet, or for Uranus, Neptune, and Pluto, which are invisible to the naked eye and revolve far away from us in the confines of the solar system. It is impossible to detect a hereditary effect with these stars which can only be observed with a telescope (see Figure 17).

The astronomical roulette wheel "deviates" for the

The planetary clock often
shows the same hour for parents and children.

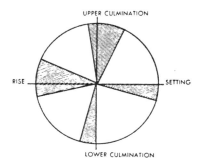

Figure 15. Planet at the birth of the parent

The father or the mother was born after the planet had
passed the horizon or the meridian and in particular after
the planet had risen or reached its culmination (shaded
areas).

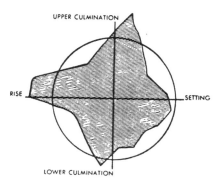

Figure 16. Planet at the birth of the child

The child tends to be born when the same planet has just
crossed the horizon or the meridian and in particular
after the planet has risen or reached its culmination. This
hereditary effect was observed with the moon, Venus,
Mars, Jupiter, and Saturn. This figure combines the 35,-
907 observations made of these five heavenly bodies.

From M Gauquelin, *L'Hérédité planètaire.*

moon, Mars, Jupiter, and Saturn, as it does at the births of famous people. But in this instance, it also "deviates" for Venus. So Venus must also be able to influence parturition.

Finally, thanks to our archives, we have been able to extend our observations of the planetary effect to children of the same families (6691 birth comparisons). Planetary similarities at the horizon and meridian are more frequent between siblings than between unrelated children.[8]

Concurrence with Genetic Laws

Nothing could be more shocking to a geneticist than this cosmic interference in hereditary matters. Yet the planetary effect is in perfect harmony with the classical laws of genetics. One of these laws states: "If both parents of a child have the same hereditary factor, the chances of the child's inheriting it are doubled."[9] This is also true in cosmic genetics. If *both* the mother and father were born when planet A was crossing the horizon or the meridian, there will be a tendency for the child to be born under the same position. This tendency is twice as great as when only one of the parents was born under this configuration. On the other hand, if *neither* parent was born under planet A, it is quite unlikely that the child will be born under this particular configuration. All of this is in accordance with genetic laws. In the first case, the child is twice as likely to inherit temperament A since both parents have this temperament. In the second case, it would be unusual for the child to inherit temperament A unless this temperament could be traced back to a previous generation.

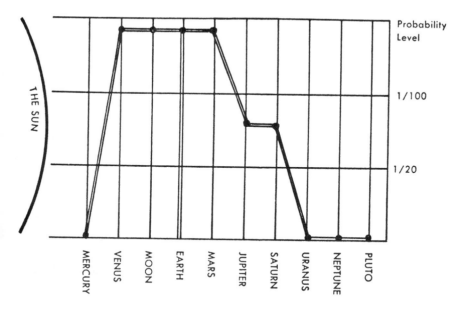

Figure 17. The planetary effect is partially related to the distance of the planet from earth

On the x axis, the planets are aligned in order of their distance from earth.

On the y axis, the probability level exceeded by the values of the statistical test of chi square.

This graph shows that only the five planets situated closest to earth have yielded significant results.

From M. Gauquelin, *L'Hérédité planétaire.*

The Father's Strange Role

Another strange and rather perplexing aspect of cosmic genetics is that the role of the father and mother are equivalent. Thus the planetary effect is independent of the parents' sex. This, however, does not contradict hereditary laws, and this time it is not the geneticist who is shocked but the obstetrician. His objection is as follows: How can the paternal and maternal heredities have an equal influence on parturition when all evidence indicates that the father cannot play a role in the onset and length of labor? His role was significant nine months ago, whereas the mother's role is the crucial one at the time of delivery.

However, at the time of conception the chromosomes of the father and mother combine, and genetically the fetus is the result of both its parents. In the next chapter we shall discuss a recent medical discovery indicating that at the time of birth the mother's is not the sole role. The fetus has some ability to guide the speed of delivery and to be born at the appropriate cosmic hour suitable for it. This answers the obstetrician's objection. The father's heredity plays a role during the delivery through an intermediary and this intermediary is the fetus. There is nothing strange about the fact that the planetary relationship should be as strong between the father and his offspring as between the mother and her child. It would indeed be strange if this were not so.

CHAPTER FIFTEEN

The Baby's Role in Timing Birth

THE CHILD WHO IS about to enter the world carries on an obscure dialogue with the planetary gods. Obscure, because "within the maternal womb, the infant is rather like the astronaut in his spacecraft, a little cramped but wonderfully protected from all outside influences that could affect him." By resolving the mystery of his birth, we can discover how this dialogue is possible. But first, it must be proved that the child plays a role during labor and delivery, that he in some way directs the physiological processes which cause him to be born at a certain hour.

What is the opinion of specialists today? They have compared the parturition process to the driving of a car. So who starts the motor and controls the wheel? Why, on a certain day, *approximately* nine months after conception, does the mother's body expel her infant? The exact moment of birth is unpredictable, but in the past ten years or so, numerous studies have succeeded in explaining the exasperating mystery of what controls the time of birth.

Although every foreign body tends to be rapidly rejected by the body, the mother keeps the fetus in her womb for nine months. There is therefore a physiological *brake* which permits this, just as a car will not roll down a hill if the brake has been properly applied. Why, on a certain day, at a certain time, does labor start? How is this brake released within the mother's body? Every vehicle must have an engine. The engine allowing the child to be expelled from the maternal womb is the mother's uterus. The uterus is a powerful muscle, and its contractions, which gradually become more frequent and often more painful, are the engine for delivery. But what causes these uterine contractions and accelerates them? Or, in other words, who is at the wheel for the delivery? Could it be the fetus?

The Brake

We must now consider the placenta, which develops along with the fetus. Until the third month of pregnancy, its primitive role as an undeveloped organ is primarily to facilitate metabolic exchanges between the mother and the fetus. But during the last six months of pregnancy the placenta plays an essential endocrine role. At least this role is played by the fetal part of the placenta, which is the most important part, as it has developed from the same fertilized cell as the fetus and possesses the same genetic structure as the fetus.[1]

The placenta secretes two hormones through its villi: estrogen and progesterone. Progesterone has the property of diminishing the contractile capacity of the uterus, while estrogen has the opposite effect. It stimulates the muscle. So it seems that the "brake" which keeps the child in the maternal womb is progesterone. It inhibits the uterus from contracting unwittingly (early contractions are commonly called "false labor" or "premature labor" and may occur at between six and eight and a half months) as this would result in the premature expulsion of the fetus.

Professor A. Csapo of the Medical School at Washington University, St. Louis, has been the advocate of this idea. "The progesterone produced by the human placenta is responsible for sustaining pregnancy . . . the termination of this significant role for progesterone allows gestation to end."[2]

This mechanism is called "the progesterone block." Dr. Csapo has proved the existence of this mechanism in a whole series of very detailed experiments on animals. But it is necessary to prove the existence of a specific kind of progesterone induced block in the human species.

A Hormone "Out of Circulation"

Dr. Csapo's idea is as follows: the progesterone acts *locally* on the uterus. The hormone, instead of being transmitted through the blood circulation, as usually happens with hormones, acts directly on the uterus and is gradually absorbed by the muscle. Thus, to continue the metaphor, it acts as a sort of physiological "hand brake." Dr. Csapo formulated this idea in 1959, after managing a very exceptional clinical case. Two twins were each developing in separate uterine compartments. They were therefore fraternal twins, developing from different eggs, and they were born two months apart. During this whole time, the progesterone level in the mother's blood had remained constant. Yet the "brake" formed by the progesterone ceased to act earlier in the first born of the two children. As each of the twins had its own placenta, Dr. Csapo felt that the progesterone secreted by the placenta was in direct communication with the closest part of the uterus and therefore did not have to pass through the blood circulation. He believed that the same part of the placenta of the second twin had more resistance than in the first twin because the local effect of the progesterone continued to maintain its function as a "brake" for a longer time.

In short, these pseudo twins were not born on the same day at the same time because they were not genetically identical. The progesterone formed in the placenta of the second twin was secreted longer, and this delayed the child's birth. This was an exceptional case, but a very informative one regarding the role of the fetal placenta. And Dr. Csapo added: "The local effect of the placental progesterone does not disappear once labor has begun."[3] In other words, through the intervention of the placental progesterone, the fetus maintains a control over the delivery process which can be retarded at any given moment.

The Fetus Gives the Signal

Most scientists acknowledge the validity of this local progesteronic block. But this does not explain why one day its action ceases. In other words, how is the brake released? Several explanations have been proposed, but the most interesting is that the fetus itself determines when it will be born. Actually, it was the oldest explanation for the onset of parturition. Twenty-five hundred years ago, Hippocrates declared: "When the time comes, the baby stirs and breaks the membranes containing it and emerges from its mother's abdomen." But an objection was raised against this role of the fetus. This was an empirical objection, stating that if the child dies *in utero* (i.e., still in the womb), the expulsion nevertheless still takes place. But it was undoubtedly a mistake to generalize from this rare pathological case on what actually occurs in physiologically normal instances.

This concept is now in vogue again thanks to the work

performed by Dr. G. C. Liggins of the National Women's Hospital, University of Auckland, New Zealand, in particular,[4] but it is a modified version of the Hippocratic theory, of course. We no longer believe that the fetus has only a simple mechanical role, for science has demonstrated that it also has a subtle hormonal role. First there is this obvious fact: *anencephalic* babies who are born with only the base of their cranium and no brain are not born at term but a long time afterward. Yet they are born alive. An anencephalic child has no pituitary, and consequently no adrenal function. Using this empirical observation as a starting point, Dr. Liggins tried to verify experimentally if the fetal adrenal glands could influence the onset of parturition. During gestation, he removed the pituitary from the brain of fetuses of several animal species (cows, sheep) and then resutured the uteri. The fetuses, although still alive, remained unborn. But was this because they no longer had a pituitary? This seems quite probable. If the pituitary hormone ACTH (adrenocorticotrophic hormone), which activates the adrenal glands, is given parenterally, the fetuses in which the pituitary glands were removed were born at the expected time.

"Consumption" by the fetus

Therefore the fetal adrenal glands and in particular the adrenalin and corticoadrenal hormones which they secrete are able to release the brake and initiate parturition. Why? This is simply because the fetal adrenal glands "consume" the progesterone for their own use. The fetus grows larger, its "appetite" increases, the progesterone level decreases, and thus the "brake" is released.

Liggins' works were discussed at a 1969 meeting of specialists. The chairman of this convention, Dr. G. S. Dawes from Oxford University, declared in his opening address: ". . .There is evidence to suggest that the fetus itself normally initiates the process of parturition, liberating itself from the intrauterine environment which has protected it from cold and light."[5]

The role of fetal adrenalin in initiating parturition has been established in several animal species. It has yet to be definitely proved in man, and undoubtedly this will establish some experimental problems.

The Accelerator

Once the brake has been released, the vehicle starts to move. But what is the accelerator that causes the uterine contractions to occur regularly and with increasing frequency until the child is born? A large number of substances can play this role of accelerator which, in technical terms, has an oxytocic role.

However, the list has been narrowed to one substance which is secreted by the posterior lobe of the pituitary. Its stimulating properties on the uterine muscle are well known to all obstetricians—hence its name, oxytocin. If synthetic oxytocin is injected into the mother, labor can be induced. Furthermore, higher levels of this substance can be found in the uterus at the end of parturition. The specialists refer to this level as high, but in this very subtle domain everything is relative. The amount of oxytocin necessary to initiate uterine contractions is so small that it is almost impossible to detect. With these virtual homeopathic levels (four milli-units of oxytocin per minute perfused into the blood are sufficient to cause a reaction), the oxytocin cannot be detected in the blood in spite of the very precise, newer detection techniques.

Other substances also have a well established accelerating role. These are the estrogens secreted by the placenta and the fetus; adrenalin, secreted by the maternal adrenal glands and the fetal pituitary itself; and probably other substances which have been demonstrated in the amniotic fluid in which the fetus is enclosed and develops until birth.

A Schedule for Births

Until now, it was always believed that the mother-placenta-fetus system existed in a closed-circuit relationship. Yet, when it is time, parturition can be initiated by an outside source and even sometimes accidentally. If, for example, during the ninth month of pregnancy, the mother suffers a fright or shock, the associated emotional discharge may initiate uterine contractions.

Another even more interesting fact is that the start of labor pains does not occur randomly at any time, but follows a very definite daily rhythm. Concordant statistics have shown that parturition begins more often around midnight, when the mother is asleep, than around midday, when she is busy with her household chores. A factor linked to the waking-sleeping cycle facilitates the commencement of parturition at night and partially inhibits it during the day.

What is the explanation for this? Biologists have noticed that our bodily reactions are constantly changing in the course of the twenty-four-hour day. Many physiological substances show marked daily variations in concentration. (In medicine, this is called a diurnal variation.) This is also the case for premandiol and estrol, which are the metabolites of progesterone and estrogen. Doctors who wish to know the levels of these two metabolites in the blood of a pregnant woman must calculate the average level over a twenty-four-hour period, for the level at a single given hour is not very significant. Modifications also occur in the nervous system. In a waking state, the uterus may be more tonic. But it becomes relaxed when the expectant mother falls asleep. Thus the "surveillance" exercised over the uterus is also lifted and permits the uterine contractions to start. The state of imbalance of the maternal-fetal system around the time of parturition is in fact very great, and slight daily variations are often enough to initiate parturition.

Naturally, if labor begins around midnight, it often ends in the early hours of the morning. Even at birth, we are already part of the daily rhythm. Obstetricians are well aware of this procedure, which happens nightly at about the same time. Moreover, as Dr. J. Malek of Prague has shown in a study of more than five hundred thousand cases, it is easier for a woman to give birth at night than during the day. The delivery is faster, easier, and less painful.[6]

Parturition During Office Hours

Giving birth at night was almost a standard practice until a few decades ago. Then, thirty years ago, the statisticians realized that their demographic studies did not concur with the "classical" law which states that most births occur toward the end of night. A Swiss scientist, Fasler, comparing times of birth in Basel, found there was a greater number of births in the afternoon, contrary to the findings of his colleague Goehlert, who, fifty years earlier, had obtained the "classical" curve with most births occurring at night in his study of a hundred thousand births in Switzerland.

What is the explanation for this? In 1959, Françoise Gauquelin offered the first explanation for these facts.[7] The techniques of parturition have evolved. Until some twenty or thirty years ago, nature was allowed to follow its course and the daily "physiological" rhythm of giving birth was respected. Now, much more frequently, the obstetrician uses medicaments which can accelerate the woman's labor. Occasionally labor is induced. Naturally for the sake of convenience, these interventions tend to take place during the day rather than at night. So the birth rhythm has been reversed. The "natural" rhythm has been supplanted by a "medical" rhythm, which is characterized by a greater number of births during the day.

In modern maternity hospitals where induced labor is the rule, the graph of births shows that for some hours no births are registered—namely, during the early hours of the morning. Then the frequency curve increases, and the two hours before lunch are the busiest time. The curve drops again at lunchtime, but then follows another busy period between 4 and 8 P.M. So one could say that babies are now born during office hours. Françoise Gauquelin has since extended her investigation to other countries besides France with similar findings.

But do we now know enough to initiate births artificially "by appointment"? Some practitioners believe so and are directing deliveries in this way. This is not a new concept. There were doctors pioneering this idea before the last World War. Dr. de Forest of New York was one of them, and he has described his procedure. At the term of her pregnancy, the patient would be given an early-morning appointment in the doctor's office. Around 9 A.M. the labor was artificially induced and, wrote Dr. Forest, "ordinarily around the middle of the afternoon, the labor was advanced to the expulsion stage and the infant would be born before dinner . . . this routine practice has been so successful that I have adopted it as my 'standard' procedure."[8]

A French specialist, Dr. Claude Sureau, is more conservative: "The effectiveness of the various methods (the fact that there are so many of them proves their unreliability) is not evidently related to their nature but to variations of internal receptiveness, i.e., to the persistence or disappearance of the uterine block. This is the real problem . . . this is the reason why no method of inducing labor can be considered totally physiological and harmless."

Before depressing the accelerator pedal (infusing artificial oxytocin), it is best to ascertain that the figurative hand brake has been released (i.e., the progesterone block). Otherwise the attempts at acceleration will act on the mother's uterus in the same way as trying to accelerate in a car with the brake on. The uterus does not open properly and the fetus suffers as a result. There is also the risk of having to intervene surgically and perform a Caesarean section. This is why, unless there are very definite indications for it, the time has not yet come to induce all births at set times. But this time is getting closer. "We would not hesitate to say," concluded Dr. Sureau, "that research into the best method of inducing labor as the pregnancy approaches its term in order to have 'a fixed date of parturition' is a worthwhile goal. . . . The progress achieved to date . . . leads us to hope that we will have mastered this procedure in the relatively near future."[9]

Certainly by the year 2000, births will take place by appointment!

A China Shop

But we must return to 1973, for there is a definite philosophy behind all these observations. There are multitudes of forces to make a child enter this world. The mother, the placenta, the fetus, external events, and the doctor all play their distinctive roles. There are some extremely subtle relationships between the various hormones. Their actions and reactions control the inaction or acceleration of the uterus. One fact has been clearly established today: the fetus can directly, or by secretions from the placenta, be the brake, starter, and accelerator of the parturition processes, which would in turn explain certain intensifications of uterine contractions followed by unexpected suspensions of the same during labor. In a sense, the child is able to choose the time at which he will be born. But is the fetus really free? There are some mysterious influences affecting it. Is it possible that throughout the entire labor procedure, it has some invisible contact with the planetary signals? For if the fetus gives orders to the maternal uterus, this is because it is in turn receiving orders. Are there some subtle directives coming from above whose orders modern medicine, with its drugs, is disturbing like an elephant entering a china shop? Do we have the right to cast aside the role of the cosmos in this way and deprive ourselves of natural data on the temperament of the newborn? If the child is born at a time set by the physician, it will no longer keep its appointment with Mars or Jupiter. By the year 2000, births will take place by appointment—unless between now and then scientists become interested in our studies.

CHAPTER SIXTEEN

Planetary Effect and Parturition by Appointment

A YOUNG CHICK breaks its shell and comes into the world when the right moment comes—unless this shell should, for some reason, be broken earlier. Likewise, if an infant is prevented from being born at his chosen time, the planetary evidence of his temperament will not be available. If labor is induced by the physician, the planetary configuration specific to the birth of this fetus can no longer be assessed. This has been demonstrated in our studies.

Planetary Effect and Caesarean Births

Let us consider the most dramatic cases from the medical files we consulted: births which necessitated surgical intervention such as a Caesarean section or the use of forceps to facilitate the baby's birth. The distribution of these difficult births over the twenty-four hours of a day is entirely different from the normal physiological rhythm observed by demographers. This is a typical example of the "medical" curve, as defined by Françoise Gauquelin. Births following medical intervention tend to occur in the late morning or early afternoon, which are times when, under normal conditions, very few babies are born.

We have examined 1440 hereditary comparisons in which infants were born by Caesarean section or with the aid of forceps and have noted that the hereditary effect disappears in babies born under these circumstances. For example, if the father was born when the moon was rising but if his child is born following surgical intervention, the moon may be in any position. This is also true of the other planets.[1]

The Action of Medicaments

Nowadays, there are cases which are less dramatic but much more common. The natural process of a large number of births has been modified by the use of drugs capable of accelerating labor or reducing the mother's pain.

The graphs representing birth times are very informative on the parturition procedures practiced at a given time and in a given place. They are a valuable source of information. In fact, when our statistical data show a predominantly physiological rhythm over the twenty-four hours of the day, we know that the deliveries are for the most part natural, and we can expect visible hereditary effects. On the other hand, if the physiological rhythm is not evident, we can be sure that a large number of deliveries were "controlled" with medications, and in these cases the hereditary effect is somewhat attenuated.

By controlling parturition, physicians are eliminating planetary information. This rule has been confirmed in all the birth groups examined (see Figure 18). The following is a typical example: The births which we examined in the Parisian area since 1937 took place for the most part in the obstetrics department of a large hospital which was built around this time in Créteil, a small city situated on the outskirts of Paris. Immediately we noted a very dis-

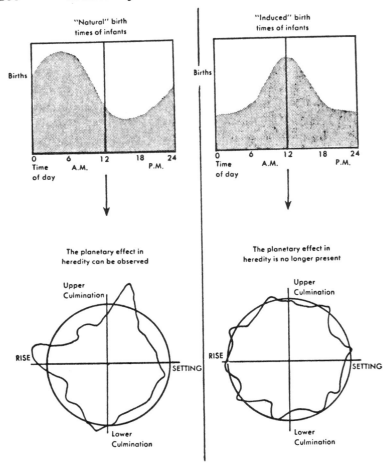

Figure 18. The planetary clock is no longer hereditary if the baby's birth is not a natural one

Diagrams 1 and 2 show the position of the planets (moon, Venus, Mars, Jupiter, and Saturn) for children of parents born with one of these stars rising or culminating. But in Diagram 1, the birth times are those of natural births and in Diagram 2 they are the times of induced births.

From M. Gauquelin, *L'Hérédité planétaire*.

tinct variation in obstetric events based on the distribution of births over the twenty-four-hour period. The "natural" rhythm, which was quite evident until 1937, had almost completely disappeared during the period extending from 1938 to 1945. As a result, the planetary effect is not as apparent during this latter period.

When the Planet is Fast

But we were very surprised to note that the planetary effect after 1938 precedes the schedule it was following prior to 1938. The births that occurred after 1938 correspond with planetary positions whose greatest frequencies near the horizon and meridian no longer coincide exactly with those of their parents. Instead, they precede their parents' planetary position by about an hour. Here, for instance, is an illustration of what happened with respect to the births at this hospital. If the parent was born after Mars had reached its culmination, the child would have shown a preference to be born under the same Martian schedule prior to 1938. But after 1938, we noticed that the child's birth was advanced on the hereditary calendar. The child showed the greatest tendency not to enter the outside world when Mars had just passed its culmination, but, significantly, one hour earlier. Thus the child's planetary timetable was no longer exactly the same as its parents. However, this discrepancy is not surprising. Modern obstetrical techniques have shortened the parturition process, thus advancing the time of birth. We did some research in the obstetrics department of the hospital where the children of the post-1938 group were born. This enabled us to establish an important fact. A medicine called spasmalgin was given almost routinely during this period as soon as the woman arrived at the hospital to ease her labor pains, which had already begun.

"This product is used extensively at the present time

in the practice of obstetrics," wrote Professor H. Vignes, "and it is correct to say that it has favorably assisted in delivery in a large number of cases. Its effect on contractions results in a more rapid dilatation of the cervix. It reduces the interval between contractions and it eliminates irregular contractions."[2]

The use of spasmalgin therefore decreased parturition time. Moreover, we confirmed that from 1938 to 1945, the average delivery time had decreased by about an hour. One hour! This also corresponded with our planetary statistics.

An Accumulation of False Evidence

With or without faster births, the planetary influence in heredity is becoming increasingly befogged with time. The administration of various drugs alters the normal mother-child relationship during parturition. By assisting the mother, doctors and midwives are disturbing or obliterating the child's role. Moreover, we know that it is through the child that the planetary effect in heredity operates. So, as the "natural" diurnal rhythm of delivery is disappearing, so too is the planetary effect in heredity. Modern medical practices are replacing the cosmic environment and masking its role.

Our hereditary observations stop in 1945. But today there are many more new obstetrical techniques. The very onset of labor is often induced artificially for reasons of convenience. A study on the planetary effect in heredity made on births today would necessitate a concerted effort to separate physiological births from births induced by medical means. There are still some natural births and there always will be.

We have shown the diagnostic value of planetary evidence in determining an individual's temperament. But now doctors are confusing the orderly relationship between man and the planets. A child who should have been born when Jupiter had just risen or culminated, because both his parents were born under that configuration, now has his time of birth determined by a physician. In contrast, the child may be born as Saturn is rising![3] If we were to apply the rules formulated in the preceding chapter, we would diagnose this infant as a future introverted type, yet his psychological destiny is such that he will become an extrovert. For the mysterious physical knowledge the fetus has of cosmic conditions when it comes time for his birth is only a reaction phenomenon. The child reacts to the passing of the planet which is simply evidence of his temperament—simply evidence. It in no way modifies the child's future personality at birth and does not give him anything not already in his genetic constitution. Even when this evidence has been obliterated, the infant remains true to his own nature. If a doctor decides to deliver a baby who has inherited a Jupiterian temperament from his parents under Saturn, he will suppress the Jupiterian evidence in favor of false Saturnine evidence, but this will not make the child a future Saturnine. This amazing and astonishing means of knowing a child's temperament from the moment he is born is now in danger of disappearing just at a time when we have come to understand it scientifically—unless our cry of alarm is heard. Naturally, we do not advocate a return to the Middle Ages, where nature alone ruled supreme. We do not want to deny a mother assistance when she needs it, but many deliveries could progress normally without complications and without unnecessary intervention. Mothers, if you are anxious to know the temperament of your offspring, avoid that little injection which brings you relief during labor. Do not deprive yourselves of this valuable source of information concerning your child![4]

CHAPTER SEVENTEEN

The Sun: Heart of Planetary Influences

THE SUN IS A star and plays its stellar role in our solar system. It is the heart that controls the subtle cosmic mechanism of the planets. Without the sun, the planets would be devoid of their master, and we who live on one of these planets could not exist.

It is a strange paradox. The effects of the sun's mass and radiation far exceed other cosmic influences. Planetary influences are infinitely weaker than those of the sun. And yet we have not been able to illustrate any solar effect on birth similar to that observed with the planets. We have searched for possible solar influences in the professional groups, in biographies, and in hereditary comparisons, and we have come up with nothing tangible. The natal distribution of the sun remains in complete conformity with the laws of chance. As far as the sun is concerned, the astronomical roulette wheel reflects only the majestic indifference of this heavenly body which dominates and controls the destiny of our solar system. However, it is possible that the sun plays a *more important role,* a different role. As the heart of the solar system, it is also the guiding unit of our planetary system.

In order to understand this, let us return to the bounds linking solar activity to our globe. We speak of solar activity because the sun is not an immutable golden sphere shining with a uniform brightness. On the contrary, it is the site of intense constant chemical and physical activity. When this activity is more pronounced, we speak of increased sunspot activity. These spots are observed as areas of lesser luminous intensity which develop on the agitated surface of the sun. They do not develop fortuitously over the years, but follow a periodic cycle. In addition, the sun is also subject to sudden feverish outbursts called solar flares, at which time it projects more light and matter than usual into space. It is also the site of many other poorly understood phenomena. Scientists believe that the planets may be responsible for some of these phenomena because everything in the solar system is interrelated.

The Earth's Magnetism

The sun's activity influences the earth's magnetic field. This magnetic field is weak (0.3 to 0.4 oersted) and can be equaled by simple little magnets. However, to scientists, the study of terrestrial magnetism is no child's game. It has been intensely studied for the past hundred years, and scientists have discovered that the earth's magnetic field is not constant, but is in a permanent state of flux. The principal variations are caused by cosmic factors and, in particular, the sun. Thus they felt that by measuring the fluctuations in terrestrial magnetism, they could obtain a good estimate of the intensity of solar flares. In other words, they were trying to establish a sort of thermometer to gauge the solar system.

Another interesting fact is that variations in terres-

trial magnetism can affect living creatures. These variations are extremely weak and for a long time it was believed that they could not be experienced by living organ-
isms. Until recently, scientists had only subjected plants
and animals to very strong magnetic fields, without obtaining any noteworthy or confirmatory results. This is
why they believed that magnetism had no influence on
life. The thought of working with very small magnetic
fields seemed ludicrous—like playing with a toy magnet.
But in fact, living creatures are extremely sensitive to the
magnetic forces in the environment. Over the ages, life
has evolved in the earth's magnetic field. Life has existed
here for millions of years, so it is not surprising that it can
be influenced by minimal magnetic changes. We now
know that living creatures are very receptive and sensitive to them, even if the magnetic fields are extremely
feeble—less than 0.4 oersted, which is the average value
of the terrestrial field. Professor F. A. Brown has been able
to deliberately alter the direction taken by a planarian
worm by rotating a very small magnet beside it. Professor
J. D. Palmer obtained similar results with the volvox, belonging to the Protozoa family. According to H. L. Yeagley, the homing pigeon's ability to return to its nest is due
to its magnetic sense. And in man, the effects of terrestrial
magnetic disturbance have been demonstrated by H.
Friedman, R. O. Becker, and C. Bachman on mental patients and by W. Cyran on the onset of labor. As Professor
F. A. Brown has written, living creatures have, in addition
to the "biological clock" which regulates their activity in
relation to time, a "biological compass" which serves to
orient them in space. Space and time are two factors in
the same unit field. Thus man, without being aware of it,
can be affected by slight variations in terrestrial magnetism. Not only man, but also the fetus that is about to
abandon its maternal shelter and whose extreme biological sensitivity has been proven.[1]

Planetary Heredity and Terrestrial Magnetism

Obtaining a relationship between the planetary effect at birth and magnetic disturbance would be sufficient evidence to prove that the planetary effect is controlled by the sun. For geomagnetic fluctuations are more or less a thermometer of solar activity. When the sun's heart beats faster, the magnetic thermometer will faithfully reflect this disturbance on earth. When the solar heartbeats return to their normal rhythm, the magnetic thermometer records the relative calm.

Since 1884, geophysicists have been measuring the daily magnetic variations. Their thermometer is called the International Magnetic Character Figure (Ci). It is graduated from 0.0 to 2.0. A reading of 0.0 indicates quiet days when everything remains undisturbed on earth and in the cosmos. A reading of 2.0 indicates days on which magnetic storms have occurred. Several hours prior to these storms, solar flares erupt from the sun.

We have classified in chronological order the sixteen thousand births examined previously in our study of heredity and correlated the sixteen thousand birth dates with sixteen thousand records of geomagnetic disturbance. The results indicate a definite solar influence. Terrestrial magnetic disturbance therefore influences the planetary effect in heredity. The planetary effect increases when the magnetic fluctuations increase (Figure 19). We have divided our data into two groups:

Children born on disturbed days (Ci from 1.0 to 2.0);
Children born on quiet days (Ci from 0.0 to 0.9).

The number of hereditary similarities between the child and the parent is *two and a half times greater* if the child has entered the world on a magnetically disturbed day than if the child is born on a calm day. The exact statistics emphasize the importance of this phenomenon. They refer to the planetary observations in the sector

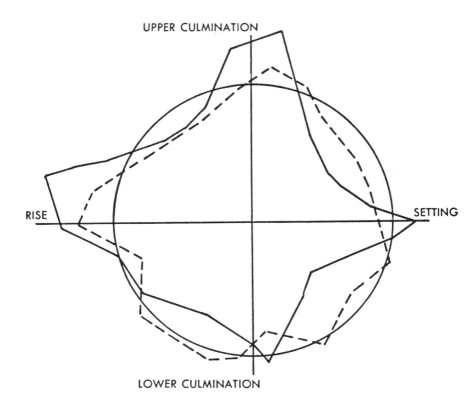

UPPER CULMINATION

RISE

SETTING

LOWER CULMINATION

Figure 19. The intensity of the planetary effect in heredity is related to terrestrial magnetic disturbance

A child born of a parent who was born when the planet had just passed the horizon or the meridian is twice as likely to be born under similar planetary configuration if he is born on a magnetically disturbed day (unbroken line) than if he is born on a quiet day (dotted line). The results from the five planets have been combined.

immediately following the rise or the culmination. If the figure 100 is taken to indicate the absence of a planetary effect in heredity (as is the case with people having no family relationship), we find that the planetary effect increases to 105 among children born on quiet days and to 113 for children born on disturbed days. Because of the large number of cases examined, the difference is so great that it could only be attributed to chance once every million times. This planet–magnetism relationship is valid for Mars, Jupiter, Saturn, and, above all, Venus (Figure 19).

What do these results mean? The planetary sensitivity of a child is more readily manifested in a disturbed magnetic atmosphere. The discovery of this trend is already an important step in the understanding of the problem. How then does the planetary effect work? Today we view the solar system as a great organism, composed of many forces which interact on many levels. The most plausible theory is that the sun is the motor and the solar field is the medium. The moon and the closest and largest planets to the sun cause agitation in this field. The stronger this agitation, the greater the effect on the child at its birth. This theory takes into consideration the fact that the influences of very distant planets such as Uranus, Neptune, Pluto, or Mercury, the smallest planet in the solar system, cannot be recorded. It may be considered that these planets are too small and too distant for their agitation in the solar field to have any significant influence on the fetus.

Rocks in a Stream

To understand why the planetary effect increases during solar activity, we shall use the analogy of rocks in a stream. If the stream flows gently, the rocks will have no great influence on the current. But, if after a large storm, the stream swells so that the rate of flow is greatly increased, then it will be violently altered by the presence of the rocks in the riverbed. Anyone swimming in the river on that day could be carried along by the current. Naturally, if some of the rocks are large, the swimmer will feel the violent effects of the current as he gets closer to the rocks.

The cosmos in which we live is comparable to this rocky stream. The stream represents the "solar field" or "wind" which blows over us and beyond Pluto to disappear into the frozen infinity of space. The rocks are the planets, varying in size and in distance from our terrestrial globe. The intensity of the solar wind varies in relation to the sun's activity. When this stream of particles and waves suddenly increases, it strikes violently against any obstruction, which in this instance is the planets. The new currents created by this encounter leave a wake behind them called magnetic tails. And the greater the impact, the longer the tails. These impacts cause the earth's magnetic field to be disrupted, and everything living on earth experiences their effects to a greater or lesser degree. Under these conditions, the planetary sensitivity of a child about to be born is increased. There are two possible reasons for this: the magnetism facilitates a biological alteration, or the planetary signals to which the infant reacts arrive more intensely on these days. Thus the hereditary evidence becomes more apparent. But on days when the sun is calm, and the solar stream is weak, the planetary and magnetic signals are similarly feeble. The planetary sensitivy of the child will not be manifested so readily and the hereditary evidence will not be so apparent.

Thus all the factors are interrelated. But without the sun, there would be no planetary effect on humans. The sun is the "energy power station," the planets are "transformers," and the full-term fetus is the "resonator" on an earth whose magnetic agitation functions rather effectively as a "facilitator." (Figures 20 and 21 present the above theory in diagrammatic form).

However, we must add that these symbols by no means answer all the questions, and in particular these two: What is the exact nature of the energy involved? and How does the fetal planetary sensitivity work during parturition? The full-term fetus must be a fantastic discriminator to be able to choose from the thousands of strong or weak influences surrounding it, the weakest of those forces originating from a distant planet and the only one suited to its temperament. We must openly admit that, for the moment, we are unable to explain this. We do not have enough information. But we may be able to find some clues from the scientific research being performed in this same field of cosmic influences. We outlined some of the discoveries of these scientists in our previous works. So, to avoid repetition, we shall only describe two new experiments which further attest to the validity of the planetary sensitivity of a full-term infant.

The Chick Embryo's "Intuition"

The first experiment could be termed "How a chick embryo within the eggshell knows what is happening on the outside." This experiment is a sequel to the ones conducted on rats by Professor F. A. Brown in the nineteen-sixties. Although they were placed in a completely controlled environmental situation, the rats' activities followed the rhythm of a lunar day. These animals, which could not possibly see the moon, became more active when the moon was below the horizon and quieted down as the moon rose. In the subsequent experiment which we are describing, one of F. A. Brown's colleagues, Dr. Leland Johnson, currently at Augustana College, South

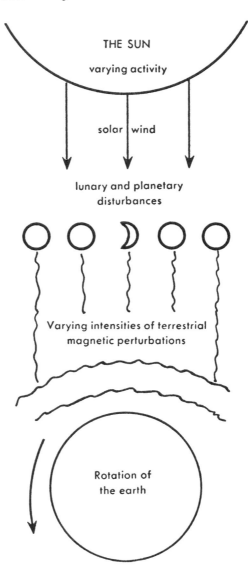

Figure 20. Hypothetical diagram of the planetary action

During its diurnal motion, the planet undergoes cyclic influences as it passes the horizon and the meridian.

The planetary effect

↓

Selective action on the fetus—a function
of its hereditary temperament.

The magnitude of this action
is controlled by the intensity
of the terrestrial magnetic agitation.

↓

Fetal reaction
(probably hormonal)

↓

Action on the mother's body
during parturition

↓

Contraction of the uterus

↓

Delivery

Figure 21. Hypothetical diagram of the biological mechanism of the planetary effect during diurnal movement

Carolina, chose the chick embryo for his experiments.[2] He measured the respiratory rates of chick embryos during the early stage of their development, long before they hatched. So during the entire experiment, the chick embryo remained in its shell. Up to the fourth day, "the chicks exhibited a daily metabolic pattern which resembled in a striking manner that reported for potatoes. Peaks in metabolic rate occurred about 7 A.M., noon, and 5 P.M. . . . By day 7, however, the daily pattern in oxygen consumption of the developing chick increased, remained high all the day, and then dropped as the sun set. The same pattern recurred on day 8. It is important to remember that these chicks had never seen a sunrise nor a sunset, nor equivalent light change, nor had they felt the additional warmth of the daytime, and yet, at this time, their metabolic pattern came essentially to match that of normal adult chickens." Like potatoes until the fourth day, the chick embryos in their shells then behaved like living chickens in a barnyard following the solar rhythm. Why? The embryologist Professor Victor Hamburger, with his associate Dr. M. Balaban, was discovering at the time of Johnson's work that at four and five days of incubation, chicks have no functional eyes, functional muscles, or functional nerves. In other words, they are essentially living vegetables. Then everything changes. "By day 7 of incubation, the chick, which is an animal highly adapted for daytime activity, is able to set its activity pattern adaptively to the light-dark cycle of the particular time zone without ever experiencing a single day-night in nature."[3] There is only one possible explanation, concluded Professor Brown: The chick must receive some kind of information from the geophysical environment enabling it to "know" almost exactly what part of the day it is.

By the seventh day, the chick embryo has acquired sufficient intimate knowledge to recognize different parts of the day. So we must now ask ourselves if, when it is ready to be born, it does not break its shell at a certain hour under the influence of external forces. It can also be speculated that if a chick embryo imprisoned in its shell acts this way, then perhaps the full-term fetus does likewise in its dark fluid environment in the amniotic sac. There is definite food for reflection here, although the comparison should not be interpreted beyond reason.

The Brain, a Cosmic Control Center?

Another discovery that bears consideration is why man's cosmic control center is located in the brain. But to understand this, we must review some discoveries of other scientists. Professor G. Piccardi has worked for twenty years on chemical reactions and has proved that the speed of these reactions can be easily influenced by cosmic forces.[4] In his attempt to comprehend this fact, he formulated the theory that the cosmic forces act at a very low energy level. Chemically speaking, water, the liquid of life, is structurally very unstable. And it is so easy for water to be involved in major reactions that these reactions have been termed the "trigger effect." But what could be responsible for these reactions, since they are not spontaneous? According to Piccardi, the cause is extremely long electromagnetic waves extending several thousand kilometers. These are "extremely low frequency" waves (ELF), with a weak energy level, and neither Faraday cages nor the walls of houses and laboratories nor perhaps the barrier of the human body seems able to stop their path. In 1960, Dr. H. L. König of Munich noticed that these very low frequency waves are more abundant at sunrise. They act on the germination of corn, the growth of bacteria, and on the hatching of insects. They also act on man by slowing the speed of his reflexes.[5] H. L. König also made this significant remark: "The rhythm of the brain's alpha waves is of the same frequency as the extremely low frequency waves from outer space." And this leads us to another interesting example, taken from a memorandum by Dr. J. R. Hamer published by Northrop Space Laboratories: "The purpose of this memorandum is to discuss theoretical and experimental work which has been directed towards understanding the biological 'head' clock of man. In particular, the thesis to be discussed is that the prominent 'alpha' rhythms of the human brain may be entrained by electromagnetic fields close in frequency to the individual alpha rhythms found in man."[4] The conclusion of J. R. Hamer's paper is positive: since the electromagnetic fields are part of the earth's natural environment, they could, by synchronizing with the brain's alpha waves, transform the brain into the "biological head clock of man" with the ability to accelerate or retard this clock as circumstances warrant.

Could the very weak electromagnetic fields modify man's biological clock and in particular the twenty-four-hour cycle which is such an integral part of the human organism? R. Wever of the Max Planck Institute in Erling-Andechs, Bavaria, has proved this in his laboratory.[5] Wever confined two groups of men in an underground bunker containing two living rooms. The two rooms were not connected with each other. The subjects in each room were allowed to live at their own daily rhythm. One room was unmodified. But in the other room, unknown to the subjects, Wever liberated an artificial very low frequency electric current. "This field, simulating one of the natural fields in the earth's atmosphere, could not be perceived." The results: "In ten experiments for three or four weeks, the artificial field was introduced for at least a week. In all cases, the presence of the weak field resulted in a shortening of the diurnal periods (for an average of 1.27 hours)." Therefore, when subjected to a very weak electromagnetic field, the human clock starts to lose 1.27 hours per day! The artificial electromagnetic field is identical to the fields coming from outer space, or the cosmos. The author therefore generalizes logically from this experiment that these natural fields "must have similar effects on the daily rhythms of humans."

Dr. Wever's human guinea pigs, isolated from the world in their underground bunker, were influenced by very weak electromagnetic forces from an invisible electrical field. According to Dr. J. R. Hamer, the receptor for these waves is probably situated in the brain.

Within its mother's womb, the infant is also isolated from the world. Perhaps his brain is already a control center capable of receiving signals from outer space and relaying the orders throughout his entire body. Obviously, the procedure underlying parturition is not a simple one. But the infant is not deaf to the messages coming from the cosmos and he reacts to them. Nature has decided that at his birth man is to be entwined in the invisible network of forces which link the earth and sky.[6]

The Woman in the Moone, an *Astrological Comedy*

THE SERIES OF EXPERIMENTS described in the previous chapter diverted us slightly from our original goal of deciding if the universe demonstrates astrological features. Originally we found some inexplicable planetary effects for the births of famous people. But it is not chance that is inscribed in the stars, it is temperament. Do the planets influence a child at birth by according him a specific character? No. The planetary effect simply triggers the birth for a given time as a result of the genetic sensitivity which the child has inherited from his parents. Do the planets therefore act directly on the child? This appears unlikely. The planets, it seems, act solely as disrupters of the primary action of the sun. The relationship between the planetary effect and variations in terrestrial magnetic activity which results from solar activity seems to be a rather convincing proof of this.

Indeed, these recent discoveries contradict the idea of an astrological universe. And yet, the undeniable fact still exists: that associating the time of birth with the planets is an astrological concept. And to extend this basic point, we shall prolong this study of planetary influences on human destiny by referring to an Elizabethan comedy based on astrology. This will be our final interlude.

This reference was taken from Dr. Johnstone Parr's well-documented work *Tamburlaine's Malady and Other Essays on Astrology in Elizabethan Drama.* [1]

The comedy is entitled *The Woman in the Moone* by John Lyly. "In Lyly's play," wrote Dr. Parr, "the shepherds of Utopia petition Nature to create for them a woman comrade, and Nature endows her creation, Pandora, with all the excellencies of the gods and goddesses in heaven. The seven planets, however, are envious because they have not been consulted in Pandora's creation, and accordingly determine to work her ruin. Each planet in turn attempts to bring about Pandora's actions and the relation with the shepherds, caused by these planetary influences, form the simple plot of Lyly's play." This amusing scenario takes an exciting turn for us because Dr. Parr decided to compare "the character" of each planet as described by Lyly with the opinions of the most renowned astrologers. Thus Dr. Parr concludes: "With one minor exception, the qualities which Lyly assigned rather carefully and painstakingly to each of the seven planets and the effects which they produce on Pandora, are in general those which would have been admitted by a competent astrologer." Thanks to Dr. Parr's erudition, *The Woman in the Moone* is an excellent test of the symbolism of the planets. Furthermore, this test is quite objective because "Lyly was not interested chiefly in astrology" and Dr. Parr did not believe in it! So these are ideal circumstances in which to examine the astrological symbolism of planetary temperaments.

In Lyly's comedy, each planet in turn "ascends" to "signorize awhile over Pandora" in the following order: Saturn, Jupiter, Mars, the sun, Venus, Mercury, the moon.

When Saturn "ascends" to "signorize awhile" over Pandora, he says:

> I shall instill such melancholy moode;
> As by corrupting of her purest blood,
> Shall first with sullen sorrowes clowde her braine,
> And then surround her heart with froward care:
> She shall be sick with passions of the heart,
> Selfwild, and tougtide, but full fraught with teares.
>
> (I.i. 144–49)

Then, as Dr. Parr notes, Pandora finds that she is "unfit for company" and that a "fretful sorrow captivates her tongue." One of the admiring shepherds kisses her hand and this displeases her. She scowls but says nothing and finally runs away when the shepherds try to soothe her melancholy mood with music.

Dr. Parr remarks: "Saturn's power for causing melancholy, sullen sorrows, froward cares, and for making one solitary, tongue-tied, silent, self-willed, and weepy is well authenticated by the astrologers. In fact, Claudius Ptolemy wrote:

" 'Saturn . . . will make me ill-disposed . . . fond of solitude . . . void of natural affection.' "[2] Alchabitius has remarked: "Saturn is evil . . . produces and fosters . . . men of melancholic complexion. He signifies . . . profound silence . . . mistrust and suspicion, moving men to complaints and mutterings."

Augier Ferrier has described Saturn's influence as follows: "Sad, solitarie, fearful, melancholie, faint-hearted . . .; rejecting the counsell of others: fearing that the world doth deceive him; uncivil . . . fleeing the compagny of men unless it is to deceive them."

And finally, Henry Cornelius Agrippa wrote: "The gestures and motions of . . . Saturn . . . are . . . beating of the breast or striking of the head; . . . bowing of the knee, and a fixed look downwards as of one praying; also weeping, and such like."

Lyly's play continues with the arrival of the next planet, Jupiter:

> Now Jupiter shall rule Pandora's thoughts,
> And fill her with Ambition and Disdaine;
> I will inforse my influence to the worst,
> Least other Planets blame my regiment.
>
> (II.i. 2–5)

And immediately Pandora comments:

> Though rancor now be rooted from my heart,
> I feel it burdened in an other sort:
> By day I Think of nothing but the rule,
> By night my dreames are all of Empery.
> Mine eares delight to heare of Soveraintie,
> My tongue desires to speak of princely sway,
> My eye would every object were a crowne.
>
> (II.i. 6–12)

Dr. Parr then describes the Pandora-Jupiter behavior as follows: "Thereupon Pandora becomes haughty, insolent, and filled with proud disdain." She demands exaggerated demonstrations of respect from the shepherds, making them "kneele and crowche," watch her "stately looks," and "yield applause to every word" she speaks. In the manner of a haughty potentate she commands them forth to slay a "savage Boare" and perform other exploits to please "Her Majestie."

This Jupiter-Pandora, a real Louis XIV, is in the astrological tradition, although it is represented in a negative aspect. Jupiter is, in fact, usually considered more favorably. John Indagine, who is quoted by Dr. Parr, states that Jupiter bestows "Beauty, richesse, honor, . . . wysedome, knowledge, eloquence and magnanimitie." Albohazen is in complete agreement with his colleagues when he writes:

"Jupiter . . . makes one . . . honorable, virtuous, and pure, of fine reputation, just, morally upright and religious, frank and free, gentle of disposition, quiet, unruffled, eschewing vain things. . . . He is truthful in speech, honest in deed, and fortunate in all his activities and influences, loving councils of wise men, just ordonances, and discriminating judgements."

But Jupiter can be "poorly positioned," and "poorly situated in the sky." In this case, according to Auger Ferrier, "it will give sometimes foolishness, . . . pryde, . . . prodigality; . . . yeeld hym an hypocrite, and in place of honestie, it will make hym dreame of tyranny."

Finally, the great authority Ptolemy says, "Jupiter . . . posited ingloriously . . . will endow the mind with . . . profusion . . . bigotry . . . arrogance . . . folly . . . carelessness and indifference."

Thus concludes Dr. Parr, "Lyly is justified in maintaining that even the benefic Jupiter's influence could be deterimental, causing Pandora to become haughty, overly ambitious and commanding."

Next Pandora comes under the influence of Mars and everything changes.

> Now bloody Mars begins to play his part
> Ile worke such warre within Pandora's breast,
> That after all her churlishness and pride
> She shall become a vixen Martialist.
> (II.i. 177–180)

Pandora in the guise of Mars becomes quarrelsome, violent, and seeks trouble:

> Mars hath inforst Pandora 'gainst her kinde,
> To manage armes and quarrel with her friends:
> And thus I leave her, all incenst with yre:
> (II.i. 236–38)

This malevolent Mars is in keeping with the traditional picture of Mars. Ptolemy declares: "Mars . . . makes men . . . warlike, daring . . ., bold, . . . contemptuous, tyrannical; . . . cruel, sanguinary, . . . boisterous, ruffianlike, rapacious, pitiless, . . . hostile."

According to Albohazen Haly, Mars "is a planet . . .

fiery and violent; he is a destroyer and a conqueror, delighting in slaughter and death, in quarrels, brawls, disputes, contests; . . . he is . . . quickly moved to vehement and devastating anger. . . ."

The sun, which is next in turn, communicates its state of mind to Pandora. So relinquishing all "rancor" (Saturn), "pride" (Jupiter) and "anger" (Mars), Pandora now becomes "gentle, kinde, liberall and chaste, discrete and patient."

This description also corresponds to the traditional image of the sun. In fact, Firmicus Maternus described the solar type as follows: "completely trustworthy, . . . proud, but wise, and governs all with moderation and humanity; . . . husbandry, efficiency, judiciousness."

Then Venus replaces the sun in Pandora's soul. Suddenly Pandora can think of nothing but love, dancing, and music. Pandora sings and invites the shepherds to a banquet. She says she is so in love with love, even more so than Helen of Troy, that she "made her husband twenty-times a cuckhold."

Venus has always been considered as the goddess of the arts and love. As Ferrier wrote, "Venus . . . in good disposition, makes the man pleasant, merry, dancing, laughing, content, amiable, gracious and of good conversation."

Firmicus agrees: "Venus makes a person . . . joyous and cheerful, . . . passionate and voluptuous by nature but religious and righteous, . . . rejoice in the practice of music and the arts, achieve many amatory affairs."

Pandora loses her lasciviousness when Mercury arrives saying:

> Now is Pandora in my regiment
> And I will make her false and full of slights,
> Theevish, lying, subtle, eloquent;
> For these alone belong to Mercury.
> (IV.i. 8–11)

Here too, Lyly is in complete conformity with the traditional symbolism of Mercury, God of orators, merchants, and, by association, of thieves. Thus Ferrier writes: "Mercury . . . makes one . . . full of wit; . . . a poet, an orator. . . . If evilly disposed, it makes him . . . inconstant, a lyer, a mocker, a deceiver." And Ptolemy affirms that Mercury "renders the mind clever . . . inventive . . . skilful in argument, . . . but void of truth . . . inconstant, avaricious, unjust."

Finally, the moon, the last of the seven heavenly bodies, intervenes to control Pandora's mood. And the moon exclaims:

> Now other planets influence is done,
> To Cynthia, lowest of the erring starres,
> Is beauteous Pandora given in charge.
> And as I am, so shall Pandora be,
> New Fangled, fyckle, slothfull, foolish, mad.
> (V.i. 1–6)

Pandora then becomes a "lunatic" and nature permits her to choose a planet where she may retire. Pandora chooses the moon, declaring:

> Cynthia made me idle, mutable;
> Forgetful, foolish, fickle, franticke, madde;
> These be the humours that content me best,
> And therefore will I stay with Cynthia.
> (V.i. 307–10)

In reference to the lunar influence, the astrologer Ferrier comments that the moon gives one "inconstancie, lightness of spirite" and Ptolemy says that Luna makes one "susceptible of change, obtuse, variable of purpose." Abraham ibn Ezra says the "human traits" which Luna bestows are "excessive introspection, meditation in a mind lacking knowledge." And William Lilly writes that the the moon makes one "inclined to flit and shift his habitation, unsteadfast . . . a vagabond, idle person; . . .

delighting to live beggarly and carelessly."

So we will leave Pandora with the moon. This interlude with its amusing and somewhat sacrilegious aspect compels us to ask ourselves some pointed questions on the relationship between our work and astrology. The gloomy, melancholy mood which engulfed Pandora when Saturn took over her soul; the ambition and pride which Jupiter bestowed; the quarrelsome aggressiveness which accompanied the arrival of Mars—all these traits confirm our observations, as is evidenced by comparing Pandora's different mental states with the list of planetary characterological traits published on page 000. It is quite evident that the similarities with the corresponding astrological "mentalities" are "surprising." On the other hand, the influences of an authoritative, noble sun, an amorous, artistic Venus, and an inventive, literary Mercury contradict our observations. Artists do not enter the world under Venus, nor writers under Mercury.

However, the question has now been raised and we must try to resolve it.

CHAPTER EIGHTEEN

Neo-Astrology?

"The name Mars has been given to a pebble; then it is considered of war, and it gives a "martial" nature to its subjects: but had the stone been labeled Jupiter, would it have a 'jovial' nature?"

—PAUL COUDERC,
astronomer at the Paris Observatory

LYLY'S PLAY TELLS US that in astrology every planet has a distinct influence on the character of individuals. To what extent do our planetary types resemble those of astrology? We are trying to answer this question statistically in our laboratory. But this is a lengthy task and we are compelled to consult hundreds of books from many countries and extending over many years. Until we have the results of this investigation, we can draw no conclusions, so we shall simply review the three thousand years of astrological symbolism. We shall discuss three eras in the history of man—the dawn of this symbolism in Chaldea, the end of the Middle Ages, and the twentieth century—and compare their beliefs with our own findings.

Planets and Gods

The birth of astrology can be said to be in Chaldean times. The Chaldeans first stressed the importance of planetary symbolism and second the importance attached to the rising and setting of the stars. Each heavenly body controlled a type of plant, an animal species, a precious stone, and a color. Furthermore, they also controlled "certain events, certain functions or professions, and each day and each hour were incorporated into this cycle of a divinity."[1] Each planet was the abode of a god, and it was this god who influenced humans. The Chaldeans believed that the influence and symbolism of each planet was derived from its appearance. Sparkling Venus was the home of Ishtar, goddess of fertility. Glowing Mars was the dwelling place of Nergal, god of war. Jupiter, following its regular, majestic path, was the abode of Marduk, the powerful and terrible king of the gods. And lastly Saturn, yellow and quivering, was the residence of Ninib, who was personifed as a gruff old man.

The Chaldeans were also interested in the rising and setting of the planets, and by the fifth century B.C. they were using this as a means of predicting the king's future. As the residence of Marduk, king of the gods, Jupiter was also the king's planet and the destiny of Babylon was "interpreted" through this planet. The priests believed that the rising of the heavenly bodies was a favorable omen, as is illustrated in this omen translated by A. Sachs: "If a child is born when Jupiter is rising, his life will be orderly and favorable. He will become rich and he will live to an old age." On the other hand, the priests believed that the setting of the planets was unfavorable. Jupiter's setting was considered a bad omen for the king. And "if a boy is born when Venus is rising and Jupiter is setting, his wife will be more powerful than he."[2] Venus, at its rise, represents the female in Chaldean symbolism and in this instance dominates Jupiter, the king, who is disappearing into the mists of the setting sky.

The idea of attaching importance to these specific astronomical moments of rising and setting is somewhat surprising, but let us note that the Chaldeans were not interested in the culmination. However, this theoretically benevolent or malevolent influence of the rising or setting of planets is in no way reflected in our results. Moreover, we know the Chaldean's symbolic explanation for it. As it rises, the planet is reborn for a day; this is why its influence is a good one. The setting star is dying and falling helplessly into the black pit which follows dusk. This is why its influence is a bad one.

Much more interesting is the type of influence attributed to each planet. Nergal-Mars is the god of war and our soldiers and champion sportsmen are often born under Mars. Marduk-Jupiter, the majestic, is the king's planet. Louis XIV, the Sun King, was born as Jupiter was rising and we have seen why this monarch with his supremely regal temperament should have been called the Jupiter King. Finally, according to the Chaldeans, Ninib-Saturn was a gruff old god, which is rather in conformity with the Saturn temperament we have described.

We must admit that we do not have sufficient accurate information at the present time. So to acknowledge a definite resemblance between Chaldean planetary symbolism and the results of our statistics would be premature. For we have not been able to confirm the symbolism of Ishtar-Venus, or that of Mercury, home of the god Nabo, whom the Chaldeans called "the wicked, the incendiary, the leopard," etc.

Yet there is no valid reason to reject a priori the idea that the Chaldean priests could have been correct in some aspects of their doctrine. No doubt their theories were based on animism rather than science, and there is no reason to revert to this animism. Even if the Chaldean "explanations" of man-star relationships are completely removed from modern theories, they may have been justified in trying to establish this strange relationship between birth and the course of the planets. It is even possible that among all the false intuitions based on doubtful analogies, the Chaldean priests could have *observed* certain facts about the mode of influence of the planets. Therefore, we should not automatically reject the *astronomical* observations made by the Chaldeans. Perhaps some aspects of their *astrological* observations, although poorly interpreted, poorly formulated, and "unscientific," should also be retained. But where does science really begin?

These questions will have to remain unanswered until the experts studying the cuneiform texts have revealed all the secrets contained in these clay manuscripts, which lie still untranslated in the cellars of the British Museum.

Stars and Humors

A Greek concept, the Hippocratic theory of temperaments, has also been passed down over the centuries. According to medieval belief, into which this concept was incorporated, every man is a microcosm, a small world unto himself, and he contains within him the four basic elements of the macrocosm, i.e., the universe. These universal elements—air, fire, water, and earth—are found in man as: blood black bile, yellow bile, and lymph. An individual's personality is determined by the balance of his humors, which have properties identical to those of the elements. If a man has an excess of one of these humors —blood, for example—he will have both the character and the predisposition to disease of the sanguine type. Thus individual temperaments are determined by the predominance of one of the humors. This dominance is caused in turn by planetary influences. The planets affect man's behavior because they possess elements corresponding to the humors.

Planet	Humor	Element
Jupiter	Sanguine	Air
Mars	Choleric	Fire
Moon	Phlegmatic	Water
Saturn	Melancholic	Earth

This concept of temperaments was very important during the Middle Ages, and it has become popular again today, but in a different form. The four temperaments were described as follows:

Sanguine: The sanguine type is a sturdy man with a ruddy complexion. He is generous and courageous and he enjoys good food and love.

Choleric: The choleric person is thin, hairy, impulsive, quick to anger, courageous, and ambitious.

Melancholic: Melancholic individuals are of slight build. They have pale faces. They are obstinate. They enjoy tranquillity. They are quiet and constantly tormented by fears and worries.

Phlegmatic: The phlegmatic individual is small and fat, lazy and apathetic.[3]

Naturally, it is too simple and even inaccurate to try to explain characteristic human behavior patterns by an excess or insufficiency of humors in the body. But there is a new science, behavioral biochemistry, which is renewing interest in this concept, and once again there seem to be certain common features between these four humors and our observations concerning the Jupiter, Mars, moon, and Saturn temperaments.

Planets and Professions According to Astrology

The last "official" French astrologer, Morin de Villefranche, was the man who recorded the exact time of birth of the future King Louis XIV. He wrote a book entitled *La Théorie des déterminations astrologiques.* At the end of his book, he gave the principal analogies between planets and professions, and his comments are of interest to us since our results have been derived from a study of professions. Following planets, according Morin to be "in a good celestial state," are significant for these professions:

"*Saturn:* Generally speaking, scientists and men of learning: theologians, philosophers, mathematicians, treasurers, sculptors, architects, mining engineers;

"*Jupiter:* Men in government: statesmen, provincial governors, counsellors, presidents, chancellors, diplomats, politicians, magistrates, administrators, mayors, high church dignitaries, court dignitaries;

"*Mars:* Soldiers, hunters, lawyers, doctors, iron merchants;

"*Sun:* Popes, emperors, kings, princes, governors, magnates, nobles, all those invested with honor and position, ambassadors;

"*Venus:* Artists, musicians, those ordained in religious orders, pharmacists, perfume vendors, cloth merchants, jewelers, etc.;

"*Mercury:* Mathematicians, geometricians, astrologers, astronomers, philosophers, orators, men of letters, poets, artists, scribes, secretaries, merchants, inventors, craftsmen, etc.;

"*Moon:* Queens, princesses, travelers, fishermen, hunters, the common people."[4]

We have not surveyed all the professions mentioned by Morin. But we can compare his judgments with our own observations. We are in agreement with him in the following cases. For Saturn: scientists, men of learning, mathematicians. For Jupiter: men in government. For Mars: soldiers and doctors. However, there are some specific instances where we do not concur with him. In particular, for Saturn: philosophers (in our studies, they are born under the moon), and sculptors, for whose births we have no positive results.[5] For Jupiter: bishops, who do not tend to be born under this planet and, above all, Morin has omitted soldiers and actors from this category. For the moon, we found that travelers tend to be born under Mars and Jupiter; also, Morin did not link the moon with writers and poets, who, in fact, are often born under this heavenly body. Furthermore, Morin wrongly ascribed these latter two professions to Mercury; and geometricians, astronomers, and artists were also wrongly ascribed to the moon. Finally, there is no correlation with our observations for the sun and Venus.

All in all, the number of discrepancies is distinctly greater than the number of similarities, especially if we specify what Morin meant by planets "in a good celestial state." By this Morin does not mean the planet's position at the horizon and meridian, but (to quote him) "the position of the planet in the zodiacal path and the quality of the aspects (i.e., its angular relation to other planets) which it maintains." In the next chapter, we shall examine the so-called influences of the zodiac and the aspects. So it is logical to feel that the likelihood of finding correlations between Morin's work and ours is so slight a priori that the few that do exist are in themselves a significant indication in favor of planetary symbolism. But we shall leave you to draw your own conclusions, because for us these tenuous correlations are simply additional useful pieces of information.

Twentieth-century Symbolism

We have deliberately reviewed these past eras of astrology, returning to its source. Moreover, this symbolism has been handed down to us today almost unaltered, as can be seen in the following extract. The writer, Dal Lee, wisely did not try to be too original. (We shall refer only to the five planets with which we have obtained positive results):

"*Moon:* It is impressionable, changeable, frank and open, refined, kind and modest, motherly. Those strongly under its influence but who do not understand how to make the best of their gifts are usually visionary, lazy, fond of frivolity, procrastinating, and easily influenced by others.

"*Venus:* This planet represents the beautiful, the harmonious, the friendly. It is affectionate, sympathetic, refined, fond of pleasure, social, artistic. It brings softness and smoothness to such matters that happen to fall under its influence. Undeveloped Venus people are generally sensuous, lazy, vain, vulgar, profligate.

"*Mars:* The planet of force and energy, it is good or bad according to the way man uses it. It is constructive, courageous, fond of the out-of-doors, hot-tempered, aggressive, grasping. Undeveloped people who have Mars strong in their horoscopes will be lavish, impatient, sensual, coarse, passionate, cruel, self-centered.

"*Jupiter:* It expands, enlarges, brings good fortune; is noble, sincere, kind-hearted, religious, honorable, faithful. Those people under Jupiter who do not know how to use their attributes properly are usually extravagant, conceited, fond of gambling, self-indulgent, hypocritical, fanatical.

"*Saturn:* Life's great teacher; the planet of experience. He limits, and limiting he bestows wisdom. People strong under Saturn favorable are reflective, careful, fearful, economical, laborious, chaste. If they do not hold themselves well in hand, they tend to become morose, too suspicious, nervous, jealous, timid and even fatalistic."[6]

The correlation is rather good for Mars, Jupiter, and especially Saturn. But it is questionable for the moon and obviously bad for Venus. But Dal Lee, like all modern astrologers, is not content to add only the sun and Mercury to his list; he also describes the symbolism of the more recently discovered planets such as Uranus, Neptune, and Pluto. But we have been completely unable to find any influence coming from these planets.

It is also interesting to note that our everyday language has conserved the astrological meanings of the planets. Consider, for example, these dictionary definitions:[7]

Saturnine: "supposed to be under the influence of the planet Saturn which tends to make people morose; morose, of a gloomy temper; heavy; grave; phlegmatic."

Martial: "from Mars, the god of war. Pertaining to war; suited to war; military; given to war; warlike."

Jovial: "(because the planet Jupiter was believed to make those born under it of a jovial temperament) gay; merry; joyous; jolly."[7]

Likewise, the words *mercurial, moony, lunacy, lunatic,* and *venereal* are part of our everyday vocabulary. Planetary symbolism is firmly anchored in our minds although we may be unaware of it.

Our Observations: Neo-astrology?

The general impression from these comparisons is that our statistical studies could lead to a *partial* restoration of the very old planetary symbolism which has been transmitted from author to author over the centuries. If this symbolism could be freed of some of its archaic concepts, defined and codified, it could perhaps still be used —an idea which is both fascinating and awful, because it challenges the conscience of researchers like ourselves. For if we are forced to admit that the traditional beliefs in the influence of the stars do have basic elements of truth, then are we not automatically forced to acknowledge the astrological doctrine *in its entirety?* Both the adherents and the opponents of astrology sometimes feel this way.

In a well documented and interesting book, two men who are sympathetic toward astrology, while not professionals in it, J. A. West and J. G. Toonder, have written: "Gauquelin's work proves once and for all, and incontestably, that there is *something* to astrology. . . . Gauquelin has given quantitative expression to an ancient qualitative belief: i.e., that the planets are meaningful." And, in their opinion, Gauquelin, in spite of his deep reservations concerning astrology, "seems destined to go down in the history books as *l'astrologue malgré lui.*"[8]

Here is another judgment, written this time by an open-minded, enlightened scientist, Dr. J. Porte, head of research at the National Center of Scientific Research in Paris:

"After examining a large number of beliefs from traditional astrology, Mr. Gauquelin feels that he can affirm, on the basis of empirical information, the reality of certain 'influences of the stars.' Although they have no direct connection with traditional astrology and are distinct from the rather mystic beliefs in which most astrologers indulge, Mr. Gauquelin's conclusions have the same 'absurd' qualities as the concepts of traditional astrology."[9]

Finally, his is the opinion of R. Imbert-Nergal, a member of the Rationalist Union of Paris, a group which is extremely hostile to anything that seems eccentric in science.

"Because he has freed astrology of everything making it most unacceptable (its interpretations of destiny and its divining powers), Mr. Gauquelin believes that he has desacralized it and made it acceptable for our rationalist requirements. We are grateful that he has condemned horoscopes with such conviction and relevance that many dilettantes will be forced to reconsider their beliefs. But these concessions do not eliminate the essential aspects of astrology, namely, that stellar forces characterize a child at the moment of his birth."[10]

We have even been called "neo-astrologists" by another member of the Rationalist Union, the French astronomer Paul Couderc, who is a fanatical enemy of all concepts dealing with stellar influences.

A Question of Degree

The question of terminology is really quite unimportant from a scientific point of view. Facts count more than words. But the terminology is important where the "politics of science" are concerned. For those people who have labeled me as nothing more than a horoscope reader are quite ready to reject my theories without even examining them. They consider them occultism. This is the first reason why my works should not be termed "astrology." Then there is the example of Professor J. B. Rhine, who, without rejecting the basic ideas of traditional *psychics*, has changed the name to *parapsychology* because this term does not immediately conjure up a vision of clairvoyants and fortunetellers. We have come to feel that the term *astrology* should be abandoned in favor of a new designation which better covers the new science of cosmic clocks. We suggest astrobiology or cosmobiology as examples, because these terms have not yet been too abused by nonscientific persons.

But this change of designation would be a poor excuse and a kind of intellectual deception if the validity of horoscopic doctrines were proven in their entirety. This is not the case. For, in my opinion, this is the least debatable reason for abandoning the word *astrology.* I am not necessarily speaking about all the ideas that form the basis of the doctrine. I can only explain it by saying that it is a question of degree. If I say that a man is honest because he acts honestly in five instances out of a hundred, I am wrong, for there are ninety-five remaining instances when this man behaves dishonestly. In my opinion, the comparison is analogous with astrology. It is not only a symbolic concept of the influence of the stars at birth—a concept dating from our most ancient history—because this certainly covers fewer than 5 percent of all the astrological laws. I must insist that the modern, visible form of the ancient art of the stars is the horoscope—the same horoscopes that can be found everywhere, in newspapers, on the radio, or even in computers. These horoscopes also have a long history. They have been used to tell you your character and also to predict your health, your fortunes in love and financial matters. In other words, to predict the events of your life and even those of your death.[13]

So now let us explore the mysteries of the horoscope.

CHAPTER NINETEEN

The Three Astrological
Roulette Wheels

"Scientific observation is always a polemic observation."

—G. BACHELARD

A HOROSCOPE IS A PICTURE of the sky at the time of an
infant's birth from which his future destiny can be predicted.

In general terms, this picture is based on three astrological roulette wheels: the zodiac, the aspects, and the
houses. And within these wheels, there are ten balls moving around, representing the ten planets of the solar system. To an astrologer, the sky is like a busy gambling room
in a casino. But this casino is immense, for it includes the
entire cosmos. The stakes are priceless—a man's destiny.
At birth, each of the ten moving balls becomes lodged in
the mysterious slots of the three astrological wheels,
which are intertwined one with the other. Thus, *"les jeux
sont faits."* As the croupier of the cosmos, the astrologer
records the position of each stellar ball in the sky at that
moment. Then he pronounces his verdict because, although we are unaware of it, our whole lives are preor-
dained at birth. Have we won, or have we lost? The horoscope can tell us.

The laws of astrology are numerous and complicated.

The critics claim that these laws are arbitrary and without foundation, but the advocates of astrology reply that they were elaborated slowly and patiently over the centuries after much careful observation. One day a Chaldean or Greek astrolger realized that people born under the sign of the ram were more dynamic than others. After observing this several times, he formulated the law that the ram is the symbol of courage and a venturesome spirit. Modern astrologers have noticed the same thing. So this long series of observations is like an early accumulation of statistics. In fact, as in all observational sciences, alleged facts are nothing more than the sum total of statistics, even though these statistics may be intuitive and rather unobjective; but they are statistics nevertheless. Was it possible that the astrolgers did not know how to observe and that they confused coincidence with truth? The claims of astrology can be verified only by making numerous objective observations—and these are statistics. The statistical method is not an esoteric procedure, used only by conservative men. It is simply an objective way of observing in order to avoid confusion between coincidences and laws.[1]

First Roulette Wheel: The Zodiac

The zodiac is divided into twelve sections called signs. When crossing any of these signs, the sun, moon, and planets play different roles. The twelve signs are: Aries, Taurus, Gemini, Cancer, Leo, Virgo, Libra, Scorpio, Sagittarius, Capricorn, Aquarius, and Pisces. They exercise different influences at the birth of people. We shall not describe them in detail here but Figure 22 presents the zodiacal wheel with two or three key words illustrating the influence of each sign.

Each sign relates to a type of character or destiny. We

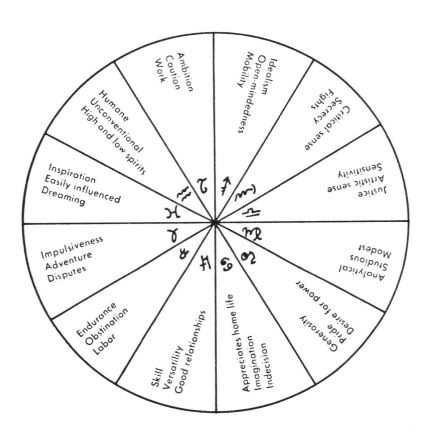

Figure 22. The zodiacal wheel

shall explain how we can prove or disprove the validity of this alleged relationship. For example, the influence of Aries, the first sign of the Zodiac, is defined by astrologers as follows: "Active, dominant. Some favorable attributes are: courageous, strong-willed, independent, pioneering. Some unfavorable: restless, impulsive, hot-tempered. It is ambitious, energetic. Strong on military matters." Now let us examine several thousand births of well-known soldiers, military leaders, or famous heroes. It is almost self-evident that they have proved themselves on the battlefield to be "strong on military matters, courageous, ambitious, energetic," etc. In the horoscopes of great soldiers, Aries should therefore be represented more often than the sign of Cancer, whose influence is described by astrologers as: "silent, dormant, receptive. Some favorable attributes are: self-reliant, kind, deep-thinking. Some unfavorable: feelings too easily hurt . . . not happy in surroundings where emotions might easily be upset"[2]— all characteristics not conducive to a successful military career.

We have drawn up the horoscopes of the 3439 well-known military men whose birth data we had previously collected. Then we calculated the frequency of the sun, moon, and planets in each of the signs of the zodiac. The sign Aries was not represented any more frequently than Cancer. In fact, there were no predominant or inconspicuous signs. We also examined the zodiacal distribution of the "ascendant," which is the degree of the zodiac rising above the eastern horizon at the time of birth, and which is considered by astrologers as a very important factor in the determination of character. The distribution of the ascendant conformed with the calculated astronomical frequencies. We then surveyed all the sixteen thousand births of professional celebrities, comprised of scientists, sports champions, writers, etc., with no significant results. The zodiacal roulette wheel worked by chance for every astrological factor we examined. And yet, our celebrities have their unusual and exceptional personalities and destinies.

Our observations, published in 1955, were criticized by astrologers, who felt that they lacked depth and failed to get to the heart of the problem. They said they would never accept our negative statistical verdict unless we could prove *case by case*, using biographies if necessary, that zodiacal influences did not exist. We now have these biographical proofs and we have been able to refute their objections through our analyses of the character traits published in the biographies which were the basis of our research. Once again, after examining each case individually, we were unable to discover any zodiacal influences.

This example, concerning champions, is very significant in this respect. Using our list of character traits for "iron-willed champions" as a reference, we selected all the champions who were described *several times* as "active, aggressive, courageous, determined," etc.[3] Only ninety-five champions, including Mattler, Merckx, and Nakache, fitted into this category. We prepared a horoscope for each of these ninety-five champions, carefully noting the positions of the planets in the signs of the zodiac at the time of their births. We were interested in discovering whether the "dynamic" signs, such as Aries, would predominate over the "meditative" signs, like Cancer. But there was no evidence of this, even for such important celestial factors in astrology as the sun, the moon, the ascendant, and Mars. In fact, the sun was infrequently situated in Aries, for there were only two births under this configuration (whereas theoretically there should have been an average of eight). Scorpio followed closely behind Aries with only four births. Yet Aries and Scorpio are the two signs "governed" in astrology by the dynamic planet Mars. On the other hand, there were thirteen and twelve births respectively in the signs of

Gemini and Aquarius. These two signs are not traditionally noted for the expenditure of physical energy.

These observations again indicate the uselessness of
the astrological zodiacal wheel. Mattler was born with the
ascendant in Pisces, the sun in Capricorn, and the moon
in Sagittarius. The "superchampion" Merckx was born
with the sun in Gemini, the moon in Virgo, and the ascendant between Leo and Virgo. If we now refer to the
key words of the zodiacal wheel published in Figure 22,
we see that the psychological traits which should apply to
Mattler and Merckx are completely unrelated to their
temperaments, which have already been described.

Second Roulette Wheel: The Aspects

The aspects are the angles formed between the stars
of the solar system as seen from earth and considered two
by two in the zodiac. The stars appear to move at different
speeds along the zodiac, and they can assume every possible angular distance from 0° to 360° in relation to each
other. Astrologers attach particular importance to certain
of these angles. Some are considered beneficent aspects,
like the sextile (an angle of 60° between the stars) and the
trine (an angle of 120° between the stars). Others, like the
quarter (angle of 90° between the stars) and the opposition
(angle of 180° between the stars), are considered harmful
aspects. Conjunction, which occurs when there is no gap
between the planets and they are side by side in the
zodiac, is very important because the influences of the
two planets are thus mingled. This aspect is interpreted
favorably with "good" planets and unfavorably with
"bad" planets. Figure 23 presents the celestial "aspects"
and their interpretations in diagrammatic form.

We have attempted numerous times to prove the validity of the "aspects," but without success. However, we

shall review one of our studies on the planetary aspects at the moment of death. Astrology claims that at the moment of death, the planets, in their path across the sky, reach positions similar to those of the birth horoscope, thus activating the setting in motion predictions already contained in the birth horoscope. The "death transits" which are considered the most dangerous, occur when the "bad" planets Mars, Saturn, and Uranus are passing over vital factors of the horoscope, such as the birth positions of the sun, moon, and the ascendant. This law was proposed by the astrologer Paul Choisnard, and he tried very hard to get it accepted by the scientific world by compiling statistical data to verify it. He wrote: "This is clear proof that men do not die indiscriminately under any pattern of the sky."[3]

We compared the birth horoscopes of more than seven thousand subjects with the patterns of the sky at their deaths. Then we analyzed the angles between each birth factor and each death factor over the 360° of the zodiacal belt. By the end of the study we had gathered more than one hundred thousand specific coordinates, and our statistics are conclusive for both the "good" and the "bad" planets. We found no significant aspects. There is the same chance of dying under each of the aspects. Contrary to traditional astrological belief, the quarters and the opposition are no more harmful than the sextiles and trines are protective. In this research, as in all the research we conducted on the aspects, chance seems to play the only significant role and the aspects appear to be uninfluential.

Third Roulette Wheel: The Houses

Because the earth rotates on its polar axis every twenty-four hours, the stars appear to cross the twelve

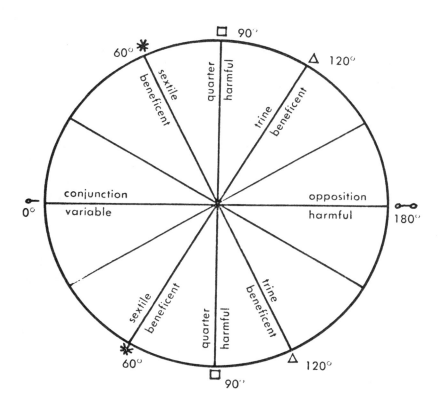

Figure 23. The astrological aspects

astrological houses. These areas of the sky are numbered from I to XII, in Roman numerals. Their meaning and the positions they occupy astronomically in the sky are indicated in Figure 24. We shall try to represent these different areas of the sky astronomically. As the planet rises, it leaves the first house and enters the twelfth house. In the course of twenty-four hours it will progress gradually across the sky passing through the twelve houses, which have been numbered in a reverse direction to the diurnal motion of the planets (see Figure 24). Also in Figure 24, the edges of houses I, IV, VII, and X have been scored more heavily because these are the areas immediately preceding the passage of the planet over the horizon or the meridian. These are the "angular" houses, and they are believed to be more influential than the others, thus conferring greater importance on the planets as they pass through them.

This astrological wheel of the diurnal motion can also be checked by following the notations given in Figure 23. But here we must be very careful. The diurnal motion of the stars, which astrologers have divided into twelve parts, is the same astronomical domain as the one in which we recorded an unexpected relationship between a child's birth and the planets. So we must acknowledge with astrologers that the most important boundary areas are the points where the ecliptic meets the horizon at the *ascendant* and *descendant* and where it meets the meridian at the *midheaven* and the *imun cocli*. Thus these angles have a distinct role and special meaning, as do the planets as they pass through these areas. However, these four "angles" have no actual physical reality because they are merely geometric constructions. Furthermore, our observations certainly cannot be superimposed on the laws of traditional astrology,[4] as can be proved by comparing the "ideal frequency curve" on p.00 with the astrological wheel of the "houses." First, the areas of the

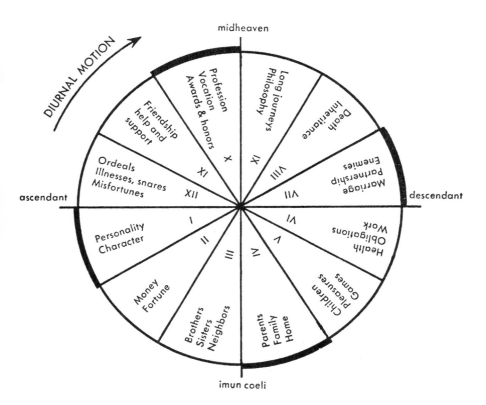

Figure 24. The wheel of the twelve astrological houses

planet's greatest influence are located according to our results past the horizon and meridian. This corresponds roughly with houses XII, IX, VI, and III. In traditional astrology, these areas of the sky are called the *cadent houses,* and the planets are supposed to have only a very weak or even a harmful influence in these houses. Second, the elements of destiny which astrologers attribute to houses III, VI, IX, and XII have absolutely no correlation with our observations. In fact, their symbolism is as follows: *Third house:* The subject's social world, brothers and sisters, short journeys, small animals. *Sixth house:* Obligations and work, health, chores, severe illnesses in particular. *Ninth house:* Long journeys, religion, philosophy, large animals. *Twelfth house:* Called "the hell of the zodiac." Secret enemies, snares and ambushes, illness, and various misfortunes.

The art of astrology is unable to correctly interpret our results. The contradiction between the pessimistic interpretation of the sixth and twelfth houses and the brilliant professional successes of the subjects we examined is quite striking. Moreover, the influences attributed to the third and ninth houses are so incongruous that it is not surprising that they are contradicted by facts. It is hardly necessary to give further examples. The first house, situated before the rise, symbolizes character, so it should be extremely important. But we found that among "iron-willed" champions, the dynamic planet Mars is *less often* in the first house than it is at the births of "weak-willed" champions. Iron-willed champions seem to prefer to enter the world later, after Mars has risen and is located in the maleficent twelfth house, the symbol of snares and ambushes.

The tenth house, situated before the culmination, is the area of the sky symbolizing professional success. Obviously, this is of particular interest to us in view of the fact that most of our studies were conducted on such professional celebrities as famous scientists, renowned artists, etc. But we discovered that the taciturn and scientific planet Saturn is *much less frequent* in the tenth house for scientists than it is for artists. This is in contradiction to traditional astrology. We found that more scientists are born when Saturn is occupying the ninth house, which traditionally symbolizes long journeys, religion, and large animals.

It must also be emphasized that our results after the rise and culmination of the planets correlate only with character traits, excluding all other aspects of human destiny included in the astrological houses, and that only the planets closest to earth seem to play a positive role in the birth of a child. Therefore, we are tempted to deduce that the astrological wheel of houses, like the two preceding wheels, does not reveal any horoscopic truths.

These Roulette Wheels Are Not Hereditary

We decided to continue our investigation of classical horoscopes because we desired to know if, in spite of everything, it was possible to prove the validity of these astrological claims by another means: astral heredity. In other words, do parents and children show a tendency to enter the world under the same signs of the zodiac, with the planets in the same houses or under the same aspects between these planets? We undertook this research as a token of our good faith toward astrology. In fact, the question of astral heredity has been important to astrologers since Kepler wrote: "There is one perfectly clear argument beyond all exception in favor of the authenticity of astrology: this is the common theme between parents and children." (*Harmonia mundi*). Kepler further explained his thoughts in a letter written in 1598 to his master, Malin, the skeptic: "Look at the relationship between births. You were born under a conjunction of the sun and Mercury and so was your son. Mercury was behind the sun at the moment of both your births. You were born at the trine of Saturn with the moon; your son was almost born at the moon-Saturn sextile. There was virtually a Saturn-sun trine at both your births. You were born under Saturn, while your son was born under the sun and Mercury. Venus was in opposition at the time of your birth and at the time of your son's birth."[5]

In the beginning of the twentieth century, Paul Choisnard hoped to prove his law of astral heredity statistically: "The planetary positions in the horoscopes of blood relatives demonstrate a more frequent similarity than the themes of unrelated persons."[6]

Choisnard's principal laws of heredity imply that there is a tendency for children to be born with the moon, the sun, or the ascendant in the same zodiacal position as at the births of their parents. Karl E. Krafft subsequently confirmed Choisnard's statements in his work entitled *A Treatise in Astrobiology.*

For a long time, these works led astrologers to believe that their beliefs in astral heredity had been ratified by various statistical studies. However, in 1955 we conducted a series of more extensive experiments which showed that these astrological laws were illusory.[7] We conducted a second very detailed investigation several years later and published our results in the *Cahiers Astrologiques* of May–June 1962.[8] We compared twenty-five thousand horoscopes of parents and their children in an attempt to verify the astrological doctrine of astral heredity but we obtained no positive results, neither for the zodiac, for the aspects, nor for the houses. So the hereditary possibility of a child's being born with a planet in the same astrological house as that of his parents has not been proved. The theory has been tested unsuccessfully with each of the ten stars of the solar system. In fact, if a parent is born with a planet in one of the powerful angular houses such as the first house (character) or the tenth house (profession), there is no valid reason for his child to be born under a similar configuration. This latter conclusion is important because the houses are an astrological division of the diurnal motion, a domain in which we have demonstrated a close relationship between birth and the planets.

There is no astral heredity in the sense implied by Kepler, Choisnard, Krafft, and many other astrologers. The planetary sensitivity which a child inherits is manifested only within the very limited cosmic framework of our previous observations. Moreover, the astrological concept of astral heredity is radically different from our interpretations of it. To astrologers, this heredity is not explained by a physical relationship between the planet and the child, but by an accord controlled by an occult force between the configuration of the sky and the destiny of the newborn child. We use the word *destiny* in a most general way, but the texts by Kepler, Choisnard, and their successors are clear in this respect: their "astral atávism" is quite comparable to the Hindu karma doctrine. This is why, for these astrologers, there is no contradiction in believing in astral heredity while continuing to predict the good and bad fortunes in a man's life, for they believe they are both cosmically intertwined. These are the mysterious "harmonies of the world" so dear to Kepler. On the other hand, our concept of a child's planetary sensitivity at birth denies any possibility of predicting astrologically the future of his life.

The objection may be raised that all this is very tenuous and that we should at least credit astrology for having conceived the hereditary possibilities of astral factors. And we must agree. But as Henry Ford said: "Ideas by themselves are very valuable but they are never anything but ideas. Anyone may conceive them, but what matters is to be able to apply them positively." And this is certainly not within the grasp of everyone. Facts are the only elements that finally matter, and what we wrote at the conclusion of our article in 1963 still seems to be valid today:

Since some positive hereditary relationships are apparent under certain planetary conditions, why are they not apparent when we examine them under the horoscopic tradition? This seems to exclude any possibility that the zodiac, the aspects, and the houses may influence human lives. But how sure are we? Perhaps a more talented investigator will one day be able to correct this firm and conclusive judgment.

CHAPTER TWENTY

The Scientific Shock

> "I prefer to be wrong with Galen than to accept Harvey's theory of the circulation of the blood."
>
> —*An honorable seventeenth-century practitioner*

> "If statistics are used to prove astrology, then I no longer believe in statistics."
>
> —JEAN ROSTAND, *member of the French Academy*

"AS THOMAS S. KUHN POINTS OUT in his classic study, *The Structure of Scientific Revolution*, it is a myth that science admits all factual evidence and revises its theories to fit," wrote Damon Knight. Knight added: "It is another myth that science grows in a linear and organic fashion, refining its theories step by step. Kuhn shows that any science, at a given time in history, is the prisoner of its basic preconceptions, which he calls 'paradigms.' Paradigms are defined as 'universally' recognized scientific achievements that for a time provide model problems and solutions to a community of practitioners."[1]

The history of scientific advancement has shown that the impact between the accepted science of an era or the so-called normal science and a new concept is always rather violent. A whole generation must often mature before the new idea can triumph over official conservatism. According to the cynical comment by Max Planck, Nobel Prize winner in physics: "Great scientific theories do not usually conquer the world through being accepted by opponents who, gradually convinced of their truth, have finally adopted them. It is always very rare to find a Saul becoming a Paul. What happens is that the opponents of the new idea finally die off and the following generation grows up under its influence. He who holds the allegiance of the young holds the future."

The impact is even more intense when the collision is between "normal" science and our facts, which appear like the reformulation of an old idea abandoned a long time ago.

Our twenty-year battle to awaken interest in our discoveries within the scientific community was bitter, especially at the beginning. Our archives are filled with letters from scientists saying, in essence, "We refuse to examine your work on planetary influences, for planets cannot exert influences."[2]

Fortunately, there were some investigators who, unlike their more conformist colleagues, showed interest in our research. J. Porte of the National Institue of Statistics in Paris, Professors H. Bender at the University of Freiburg, G. Piccardi at the University of Florence, and F. A. Brown, Jr., at Northwestern University, accepted invitations to write prefaces to our books. Sponsorship by these men made it possible for us to present our results regularly at international scientific conventions and to publish our observations in scientific journals.

Other Researchers Confirm Our Observations

Twenty years ago a committee of Belgian scientists, called "Comité Para,"[3] was formed for the purpose of verifying experimental scientific work that has resulted in apparently strange conclusions. The committee comprises thirty scientists of various disciplines, particularly astronomers and statisticians.

After several years, this committee decided to repeat

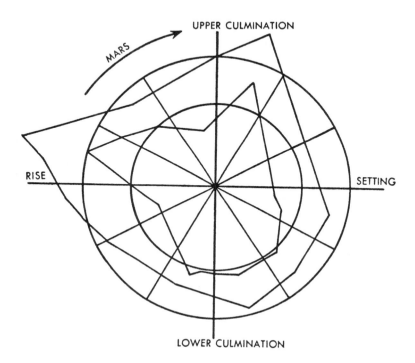

Figure 25. Belgian astronomers have observed the same results as ours for Mars and the sports champions

one of our experiments, using new material. They chose champion sportsmen, at whose birth the planet Mars appeared to be abnormally distributed in its diurnal movement. The Comité Para gathered a new group of 535 French and Belgain champions, and submitted the birth data of these champions to a computer previously programmed with the complex movements of Mars.

The results of this analysis, done in 1968, showed major frequencies of the planet Mars after its rise and culmination at the champions' births, as it had in our groups. Figure 25 shows the remarkable resemblance between the distribution of Mars with the 535 champions gathered by the Comité Para and the distribution of Mars with 1553 other champions gathered by us.

The members of the Comité Para were surprised and uneasy about the results of their own computations. For four years, they studied all possible objections and organized numerous control experiments. This detailed cross-examination at the Royal Observatroy of Belgium demonstrated again a link between the positions of Mars and the birth of champion sportsmen.[4]

Has the planetary effect on heredity been accepted into the "normal" science of which Thomas S. Kuhn speaks? Not yet. Even the members of the Comité Para could not fully accept the results of their own experiments. Other battles still have to be fought, other victories won, in the fields of astrology and science, before this happens.

Allergic to the Planets

The basic proposition of astrology concerning the relationship between the planets and the child at birth has, in our opinion, been proved. The steller symbolism may perhaps conceal some profoundly true intuition, even though every attempt to prove the accuracy of horoscopes has resulted in failure. This is a paradox with which no one is satisfied. It angers the horoscope makers and arouses righteous indignation among conservative scientists. Yet we cannot change the facts to make them suit a prefabricated way of thinking. We must rely on our observations. That a diagnosis can be made on the hereditary temperament of a child if we know which planet was just after the horizon or the meridian at the time of his birth is a very significant proposition. It could modify our entire perception of the world. In any case, it should be verified, expanded, explained, or refuted by all those who are not satisfied with acceptable illusions but are ready to make certain sacrifices to unfold another of nature's secrets.

We would like to conclude this work with a statement made by Mrs. C. Capel Boute, head of research at the University of Brussels. This declaration, made at the fifteenth Health Congress held in Ferrara, Italy in 1967, is a perfect example of freedom of thought not subservient to official dogma:

"Mr. and Mrs. Gauquelin have presented, both at Rutgers University and here in Italy, some surprising correlations between the time of birth and the positions of the moon and certain planets in their diurnal motions. Their results, which are the fruit of a strictly scientific and extremely extensive study, have withstood the most critical reviews. However, these statistically proven relationships, which are in no way connected with dogmatic astrological theories, frequently arouse a priori reactions which I must term 'allergic.' . . .

"Would it not be more worthwhile for the advancement of our knowledge to discover an explanation for these unusual relationships and to test new working hypotheses than to reject these facts a priori out of sheer 'allergy to the planets'? It is time for the twentieth century to solve these mysteries and the problems they incite and to examine both the beliefs transmitted from antiquity and the intolerance which these beliefs have instigated.

"Science can only progress cautiously, but this progress must occur in an atmosphere characterized by freedom of thought and the acceptance of scientifically established facts."

EPILOGUE

Pilgrimage to Sumer

THE ROAD TO UR is a difficult one. The slow train from
Baghdad deposits the traveler in the middle of the night
in the little village of Nasiriya. Then, in the morning, he
continues on into the desert by vehicle. On this winter
day, my wife and I were the only visitors. Low on the
horizon, the sun's shadows were lengthening. The Arab
driver at the wheel of his Land Rover was having trouble
avoiding the potholes. Far away in the yellow plain, a
Bedouin was slowly leading his camels to drink from the
waters of the Euphrates several kilometers away. Four
thousand years ago, when Ur was a flourishing city, the
river washed the sand with its muddy waters. But now it
has altered its course. The Euphrates no longer flows here
and Ur is in the desert. Suddenly, at the end of the road,
we saw ahead of us what we had come to see: the ziggurat
of Ur, a tower, formed of a succession of terraces, still
massive and ready to defend itself against all storms. It
gradually loomed larger as we approached—one of the
oldest observatories in the world, which was also a temple

where Sin, the moon god and lord of the city, cast the anchor in his sacred bark.

It was at Sumer that it all began. Here were born not only astrology but also the sciences and religions on which our Western civilization is founded. Here were Mesopotamia, the Garden of Eden, Abraham's homeland, Sumer, the country of the flood. Later Babylon was founded here with its tower formed of seven terraces almost touching the sky, and also Nineveh, Nimrud, and Ashur, and so many other cities which today lie buried under the sand. The entire origins of our civilization are in this abandoned corner of the earth, where the only life today flows silently under the desert through the oil pipelines. Sumer's blood is now nothing but petroleum.

We climbed the steep central flight of stairs of the tower. In fact, they are so steep that it is impossible to see the top of the tower while climbing. The stairway seems to lead to the sky. On top of the ziggurat of Ur, it is as though time had been suspended. One can almost see the astrologer-preacher in his white robe climbing slowly up to the top to take his turn at the ritual guard. For the stars must be under constant surveillance.

The tower is the only elevated area in the center of the completely flat plain. In the south, facing the sun, another prominence can be distinguished on the horizon. This is the remains of the ziggurat of Eridu, about twenty kilometers away. It is another Sumerian landmark which the armed Bedouin pointed out to us in faltering English as he accompanied us to the top of the tower. He is the sole guardian of this Mount Palomar of bricks—bricks which are trampled underfoot, some of which still bear the cuneiform seal left by the architect who had them placed there. A moving testimony.

On that day, the sky was clear and we could even see the moon shining feebly in the clarity of the day. We wanted to wait for the sun to set, to watch Venus-Ishtar setting over the horizon and the god Marduk rising, led by the chariot of the planet Jupiter. A clay tablet states: "If a child is born when Jupiter is rising, his life will be happy, he will become rich, and he will live for many years." Vain predictions which "serious" posterity has discarded with a wave of the hand—an impetuous gesture, or at least an imprudent one. The science of the Sumerians, like that of the Chaldeans, is not all vain words. The master astronomer from Sippar, north of Babylon, calculated very accurately the length of a lunar month down to the second. Did this prestigious man who pioneered great astronomical discoveries actually believe that the moon was a god? We will never know, because nothing is known about him. But this does not matter. Nor does it matter if the astrological priests of Mesopotamia considered the planets the dwelling places of supernatural beings. They had the feeling of an important relationship: these heavenly bodies were in some manner able to influence man.

Mesopotamia dotted with ziggurats scattered around the landscape; but also pyramids of Egypt or Mexico, the minarets in the Orient, cathedrals in our cities, steeples in country villages, rockets pointed toward the sky ready to be fired to the planets: the same question is always asked, but the answer is slow to be found. It is never a complete answer and sometimes it is even deceptive. Our pilgrimage to Sumer was not to gaze with wide-eyed admiration, searching vainly for a past which has become embroiled with magic and forever lost. We were trying to comprehend and state the relativity of what is called Knowledge.

Contemporary researchers, take care! Do not hastily reject what two thousand years of nights of watching the stars have produced. We are not asking you to believe in astrology, but to accept the idea that the influence of the stars can be studied scientifically, like astronomy.

The distance separating the Chaldean "god-lamps" from what modern scientists now call the "planet-clocks" is immeasurable. Yes, it is truly immeasurable; we cannot measure it: four thousand years, but these eras may only be a few steps apart . . . steps which lead the visitor to the top of the multistoried tower. Who would like to climb them with us?

APPENDIX

Questionnaire: What Would Your Planetary Type Be?

As GASTON BERGER wrote: "Characterology can shed some interesting light on the lives and characters of historical figures. But it aims primarily to help living people learn more about themselves and if not 'modify' their characters, at least understand them. Moreover, it is by being in permanent contact with human nature and studying the emotions, ideas, and behavior of as many different people as possible that psychology can broaden its comprehension of individuals and gradually perfect its methods of study." *(Traité pratique d'analyse du caractère.)*

This leads us to the question of whether the planetary typology we established in our study of celebrities can be used as the basis for diagnosing the temperament of every individual, famous or anonymous, merely by knowing his time of birth. We have described Mars temperament, which is often manifested when this planet had just crossed the horizon or the meridian at the moment of birth. If an ordinary person, not destined to become famous, is born under this position of Mars, can we conclude that he has a very strong chance of possessing the type of personality described as a Mars temperament? The answer is yes, probably, although this is only a statistical probability, of course. Moreover, this statistical probability may not be as pronounced in the average man as in successful people whose characterological tendencies are no doubt stronger, more defined, and therefore easier to describe.

From a practical point of view, this is a potentially very valuable tool for use in practical psychology to diagnose the basic tendencies of individuals. But this statistical tool has yet to be perfected, and this will require comprehensive investigations of large numbers of people.

The questionnaire we are publishing here is not a diagnostic tool, but an experimental questionnaire. By correlating the subjects' answers and the position of the planets at the time of their births, we hope to be able to extend its use for more functional purposes. We would be grateful if the readers of this book would answer the questions and give the questionnaire to their friends. The answers may be sent to our Laboratory. (More detailed instructions are given on the answer sheet.) Thank you for your cooperation.

How to Answer the Questionnaire

There are forty questions, ten relating to the planet Mars, ten to Saturn, ten to Jupiter, and ten to the moon. The questions have been mixed up.

There are three possible ways of answering each question: A, B, and C:

A means yes.

B means neither yes nor no.

C means no.

For every question, circle one letter as your answer.

For example, the first question states:

"You have great powers of determination and you are stimulated by even a difficult task."

If you put a circle around A, you are answering yes and you feel that this statement applies to you.

If you circle B, you are answering neither yes nor no, which means that sometimes you act and feel this way and other times you do not.

If you circle C, you are answering no; this statement does not apply to your character.

Try to be as accurate and honest with yourself as possible. To ensure greater objectivity, ask your relatives or friends to answer the questions for you.

QUESTIONNAIRE	YES	NEITHER YES NOR NO	NO
1. You have great powers of determination and you are stimulated even by a difficult task.	A	B	C
2. You have many friends and are well liked by them.	A	B	C
3. Do people say about you: "He is poised and relaxed"?	A	B	C
4. Do people feel that your behavior is cold and distant?	A	B	C
5. Are you told that you are easily influenced, agreeing with whoever is speaking?	A	B	C
6. You are aggressive and competitive.	A	B	C
7. You are not talkative and do not gesticulate a great deal when you talk.	A	B	C
8. Are you considered witty in a sarcastic or bantering way?	A	B	C
9. People find you obliging, devoted, and even indulgent.	A	B	C
10. Are you outgoing? Are you a likable person on first acquaintance? Do you have charm?	A	B	C
11. You are frank and loyal, but this frankness is occasionally forthright.	A	B	C
12. You seem modest and even shy.	A	B	C
13. You have a greater than average resistance to physical and psychological fatigue.	A	B	C
14. Conscientiousness, scruples, and earnestness are virtues which are often applied to you.	A	B	C
15. You have a cheerful, optimistic nature.	A	B	C
16. You are absent-minded and disorganized by nature.	A	B	C
17. You love your independence and hate to be contradicted.	A	B	C
18. You lack self-confidence and have a desire to withdraw and pass unnoticed.	A	B	C
19. Imagination and daydreaming play an important part in your life.	A	B	C
20. You are active and efficient in everything you undertake.	A	B	C

QUESTIONNAIRE	YES	NEITHER YES NOR NO	NO
21. You have good self-control even in difficult situations.	A	B	C
22. You believe that tolerance is one of the greatest human attributes.	A	B	C
23. You really want to be successful. You are ambitious and want to become famous.	A	B	C
24. The simplicity and dignity with which you conduct your life are often praised by people who know you.	A	B	C
25. You have a sense of leadership which you impose on others.	A	B	C
26. You enjoy a worldly life, following current fashions.	A	B	C
27. You have a distinct aversion to daydreaming, inaction, and even resting.	A	B	C
28. You weigh the pros and cons carefully before making a decision.	A	B	C
29. Tenacity and stubbornness in all matters are characteristic of your behavior.	A	B	C
30. Your friends think you are friendly, charming, and good company.	A	B	C
31. You know how to take advantage of good opportunities when they arise.	A	B	C
32. You are diligent and meticulous in everything you undertake.	A	B	C
33. You tend to be naïve and your whims are sometimes rather childish.	A	B	C
34. Your aggressiveness is shown in sudden outbursts of anger, but you do not bear grudges.	A	B	C
35. You do not enjoy social gatherings and feel ill at ease at such functions.	A	B	C
36. You dress fashionably and with a trace of originality.	A	B	C
37. You dislike detailed, minute tasks.	A	B	C
38. You are known for your courage, dynamism, and enterprising nature.	A	B	C
39. You become angry if someone resists your wishes.	A	B	C
40. You tend to be pessimistic and do not take advantage of worthwhile opportunities.	A	B	C

(Tabulate your answers on the next page)

Tabulation Sheet

The questions have been reorganized below into categories representing Mars, Jupiter, Saturn, and the moon. Put a cross in the column corresponding to your answer for each question. Then add the total number of answers per column. Thus you will have a score for each of the categories.

Mars Questions NO	Your Answer A	B	C	Jupiter Questions NO	Your Answer A	B	C
1				3			
6				8			
11				10			
13				15			
20				17			
21				23			
27				25			
29				31			
34				36			
38				39			
Mars score:				Jupiter score:			

Saturn Questions NO	Your Answer A	B	C	Moon Questions NO	Your Answer A	B	C
4				2			
7				5			
12				9			
14				16			
18				19			
24				22			
28				26			
32				30			
35				33			
40				37			
Saturn score:				Moon score:			

Answer Sheet

We suggest that you answer the following questions on a separate piece of paper so as not to tear this page out of your book. Or it is even a good idea to make a photocopy of this page and write your answers on the copy. If several persons have answered the questionnaire, each will require a separate answer sheet.

Male or Female:

Your birth data:
Place, day, month, year, time (please state if you were born A.M. or P.M.)

Your scores in the questionnaire (give the number of answers you stated for each planet and each column, A, B, or C).

Mars score
Jupiter score
Saturn score
Moon score

Very important: Put a circle around the letter or letters which apply to you, in the following questions:
A—Your birth was completely natural.
B—Your birth necessitated a Caesarean section or the use of forceps.
C—Your mother was given drugs to accelerate or retard delivery.
D—Your birth was induced—i.e., your mother was given medication so that you would be born at a certain prearranged time.

These questions are extremely important for persons under thirty years of age. If you are unable to answer them, ask the older members of your family for assistance.
Send your answer sheet to:

Dr. Michel Gauquelin
Director
Laboratory for the Study of the Relationships Between
    Cosmic and Psychophysiological Rhythms
8, rue Amyot Paris (5)
France

You may give your name and address or remain anonymous, whichever you prefer.

Thank you for your cooperation.

Notes and Comments

Chapter One—Is the Universe Astrological?

1. On consumer astrology, read Michel Gauquelin, *Songes et mensonges de l'astrologie;* (Machette, Paris 1969); *"L'astrologue paré de l'IBM"* (The Astrologer with an IMB Computer), *Science et Vie,* no. 611 (August 1968), pp. 80–89 (this article has been translated into English in *Aquarian Agent,* New York, May 1970); *"Analyse logique et psychologique de Madame Soleil"* (Logical and Psychological Analysis of Madame Sun), *Science et Vie,* no. 644 (May 1971), pp. 76–84.

2. Jean Porte, preface to *Méthodes pour étudier la répartition des astres dans le mouvement diurne,* by F. and M. Gauquelin, Paris, 1957.

3. Claude Bernard, *Introduction à l'étude de la médecine expérimentale,* Paris, 1856.

4. *L'Origine de la vie* (The Origin of Life), symposium, Pergamon Press, 1960.

5. Fred Hoyle, *Aux Frontières de l'astronomie,* Buchet-Chastel, 1963.

6. On the new science of cosmic influences: M. Gauquelin, *The Scientific Basis of Astrology,* Stein and Day, 1969, part III, "A New Science of Cosmic Influences," pp. 157–222; *The Cosmic Clocks,* Avon Books, 1969, part II, pp. 97–200 (with 200 references). In addition, two basic scientific books are worth consulting: G. Piccardi, *The Chemical Basis of Medical Climatology,* Ch. Thomas, Springfield, Ill., 1962; Fr. A. Brown, Jr., and John D. Palmer, *The Biological Clock: Two Views,* Academic Press, New York, 1970. We also suggest reading the pro-

ceedings of *The First and Second International Symposia on the Relationships Between Solar and Terrestrial Phenomena in Chemico-Physics and Biology,* University of Brussels, 1958 and 1968, Presses Académiques Européennes, Brussels.

7. Let us give an example of the disdain with which pop astrology treats its clients. Not everyone knows the hour of his birth, but this fact could mean a loss of clientele for the astrologer. So, in New York the clients of an electronic horoscope, are given a blue order form bearing the following statement: "Time of birth . . . (if unknown, we will use 12 noon of birth date." In another advertisement card (this one is yellow!), we find: "Time of birth . . . (if no time is given we will use 6 A.M.)." Thus, they not only agree to give a horoscope without knowing the hour of birth, but they even resort to choosing an hour at random!

8. Franz Boll, *Sternkunde des Altertums,* Koehler and Amelang, Leipzig, 1950.

9. On the history of astrology, read Bouché-Leclercq, *L'Astrologie grecque,* Paris, 1899; M. Gauquelin, *The Scientific Basis of Astrology,* Stein and Day, New York, 1969, part II, pp. 59–147; *The Cosmic Clocks,* Avon, New York, 1969, pp. 25–65.

Chapter Two—The Return of the Planets

1. S. K. Runkorn, preface to the collection *Magnetism and the. Cosmos,* Oliver and Boyd, London, 1967. This work is highly recommended for its presentation of the modern vision which astrophysicists have of the cosmos.

2. K.L. Franklin, "Radio Waves from Jupiter," *Scientific American,* vol. 211, no. 1, July 1964, pp. 34–49. This is the most interesting article relating the strange discovery of radio emissions from Jupiter. The most detailed article on this subject is J. A. Roberts, "Radio Emission from the Planets," *Planets Space Science,* 11, No. 3, 221, 1963.

3. A. Smith, G. Lebo, T. Carr, "Morphology of Jupiter's Decametric Radio Sources," *Magnetism and the Cosmos,* Oliver and Boyd, London, 1967, p. 318.

4. E. K. Bigg, "Influence of the Satellite Io on Jupiter's Decametric Emission," *Nature,* 203, p. 1008, 1964.

5. M. Trellis, *Marée solaire d'origine planétaire: Sur une relation possible entre l'aire des taches solaires et la position des planètes: Influence de la configuration du système solaire sur la naissance des centres d'activité* (Solar Tide of Planetary Origin: On a Possible Relationship Between the Area of Sunspots and the Position of the Planets: Influence of the Solar System's Configuration on the Development of Activity Centers); *Compte Rendus de l'Académie des Sciences,* vol. 262, pp. 221–24; 312–15; 376–77, January 1966.

6. J. H. Nelson, "Shortwave Radio Propagation Correlation with

Planetary Position," *RCA Review,* vol. 12, no. 1, p. 26, 1951.

7. N. F. Ness, "The Earth's Magnetic Tail," *Journal of Geophysical Research,* vol. 70, no. 13, 2989, 1965.

8. N. F. Ness, "Initial Results of the I.M.P.1. Magnetic Field Experiment," *Journal of Geophysical Research,* 69, 3566, 1964.

9. J. A. Jacobs and G. Atkinson, "Planetary Modulation of Geomagnetic Activity, *Magnetism and the Cosmos,* Oliver and Boyd, London, 1967, p. 402.

10. J. Houtgast and A. Van Sluiters, "The Geomagnetic Activity Around Conjunction and Opposition of Planets," *Magnetism and the Cosmos,* Oliver and Boyd, London, 1967, p. 399.

11. E. K. Bigg, "Lunar and Planetary Influences on Geomagnetic Disturbance," *Journal of Geophysical Research,* 68, 4099, 1963.

First Interlude—Louis XIV, the "Sun King"

1. Louis XIV: The biographical quotations are all taken from the work *La France de Louis XIV,* written under the direction of Robert Philippe, C.A.L. Paris, 1970, pp. 57, 103, 204, 205.

Chapter Three—The Gold Nugget

1. On the theoretical problems posed by the diurnal division into sectors, refer to F. and M. Gauquelin, *Méthodes pour étudier la répartition des astres dans le mouvement diurne,* Paris, 1957, part 2: "Division of the Diurnal Movement Into Sectors," pp. 28–55; M. Gauquelin, *Les Hommes et les astres,* Paris, Denoel, 1960, pp. 240–42; M. Gauquelin, "Methodological Model Analysing Possible Extraterrestrial Effects on the Daily Cycle of Birth," *Journal of Interdisciplinary Cycle Research,* 2, 2, 1971, pp. 219–25.

2. On the problem of the probability of statistical results, read *Les Hommes et les astres, op. cit.,* pp. 249–51. In addition, all specific works on statistics contain formulas for calculating the probability of deviations between observed and expected frequencies.

3. M. and F. Gauquelin, *Profession-Heredity,* results of series A and B. Laboratory for the Study of Relationships Between Cosmic and Psychophysiological Rhythms, Paris, 1972.

4. This experiment has been described in detail in our preceding works and originally in *l'Influence des Astres,* Le Dauphin, Paris, 1955, *"Analyse détaillée de la statistique de 576 médecins notables,"* pp. 104–23, and *"Étude sur nouveau groupe de 508 médecins notables,"* pp. 124–32.

Chapter Four—The Stars and Success

1. On the history of the registry office, see *Les Hommes et les astres,* *op. cit.,* pp. 35–41; on the accuracy of the registry office information, read F. Gauquelin, "Terrestrial Modulations of the Daily Cycle of Birth," *Journal of Interdisciplinary Cycle Research,* 2, 2, 1971, pp. 211–17; J. Reverchon, "Le Temps de la naissance selon l'état-civil," *Almanach Chacornac,* 1967, Paris, Editions Traditionnelles, pp. 85–94.

2. We consulted more than two hundred dictionaries, biographical works, and various lists to gather these births.

3. *Birth and Planetary Data Gathered Since 1949* by M. and F. Gauquelin: Series A, Vols. 1–6, Laboratory for the Study of Relationships Between Cosmic and Psychophysiological Rhythms, Paris, 1970–71. The text of each volume is in two languages, French and English. The works contain a summary of the method used; the family name, first name, date, hour, and place of birth of the subjects studied; the position at their births of the moon, Venus, Mars, Jupiter, and Saturn in one of the thirty-six sectors of the diurnal movement; and the extent of geomagnetic disturbance on the day of birth.

4. All the figures quoted were taken from M. and F. Gauquelin, *Profession-Heredity, op. cit.,* Paris, 1972.

5. Regarding the estimation of theoretical frequencies and the exact astronomical definition of the areas described as "after the horizon" and "after the meridian," read F. and M. Gauquelin, *Méthodes pour étudier la répartition des astres dans le mouvement diurne, op. cit.,* part 3: "Le Calcul de l'espérance mathématique," pp. 56–89; M. Gauquelin, *Les Hommes et les astres, op. cit.,* pp. 242–47; F. Gauquelin, "L'élimination des artefacts dans le problème des relations entre phénomènes solaires et terrestres dans les sciences de la vie: Exemple du rythme nycthéméral des naissances," *2nd Symposium of Solar-Terrestrial Relationships,* September 1–7, 1968, University of Brussels.

6. The moon also appears very frequently at the birth of politicians, but the results are not definitive and have yet to be confirmed.

7. The moon is also quite infrequent in these areas for sports champions and soldiers, but this is not really significant. The same is true for Jupiter and painters.

8. "Ideal" frequency curve: cf. *Les Hommes et les astres, op. cit.,* pp. 194–96.

9. *Ibid.,* p. 196.

10. The details concerning the professional control groups can be found in *Les Hommes et les astres,* pp. 67–132.

11. For the leaders of military bands, cf. *ibid.,* pp. 129–30.

Chapter Five—Success and Character

1. This figure was calculated in France by Alain Girard and confirmed in the U.S.A.

2. Alain Girard, *La Réussite sociale*, Presses Universitaires de France, 1967, Paris, p. 116.

3. Claude Lévy-Leboyer, *"Les déterminants de la supériorité"* in *La Réussite sociale*, Presses Universitaires de France, 1961, p. 47.

4. Anne Roe, "A Psychological Study of Eminent Physical Scientists," *Genetic Psychology Monographs*, 1951, a, 43, 121–239, quoted by D. E. Super.

5. For the complete details and results of this questionnaire, see our article *"Image caractérielle des qualités favorables·à la réussite professionnelle* (Characterological Picture of the Qualities Conducive to Professional Success), *La Caractérologie*, 11, pp. 49–63, Presses Universitaires de France, 1970.

Second Interlude: Four Portraits of Men of the Theater

1. Biographical notes taken from J.-L. Barrault's file, which is number Rt 5759 in the Arsenal Library.

2. Claude Roy, *Jean Vilar*, Seghers, 1968.

3. Biography: Arsenal Number: R. supp. 5483.

4. Biography: Arsenal Number: Ro 14662.

Chapter Six—Planets and Characters

1. It is obvious that illustrative examples are justifiable only if they have been preceded by a statistical study which has proved the reliability of a law of which the examples are nothing more than an illustration. All the examples given in this book follow this basic principle. This does not mean, however, that *every* individual has a character corresponding to his birth planet. There are some exceptions. But, in actual fact, there are not many.

2. For further information of the methodology of biographical studies and the value of character traits as a basis for the research, read M. Gauquelin, "Specific sensitivity of hereditary origin to exogenous factors in relation to time of birth; its importance in Psychology." *Second International Symposium on the Relationships Between Solar and Terrestrial Phenomena*, September 1–7, 1968, University of Brussels; M. Gauquelin, *"Saggio di evidenziazione di una componente temperamentale nell'effetto planetario dell'eredità,"* Minerva Medica,

1969, 60 (31):1499–1500; M. Gauquelin, *"Essai de mise en évidence et de description d'une composante tempéramentale dans l'effet planétaire en hérédité"* (Attempt to Demonstrate and Describe a Temperamental Component in the Planetary Effect in Heredity), *Relazioni del XVIe convegno della Salute,* Ferrara, May 24–25, 1969, 221–31, 1969; M. and F. Gauquelin, *"Planètes et traits de caractère, esquisse méthodologique pour la mise en évidence d'une composante tempéramentale dans l'effet planétaire d'hérédité* (Planets and Character Traits, Methodological Outline for the Demonstration of a Temperamental Component in the Planetary Effect of Heredity), *Zeitschrift für Grenzgebiete der Psychologie,* 1972, 1:12–36. Finally, each of the volumes published by our Laboratory on this subject (Series C: *Planètes et Tempérament)* contains a long methodological introduction. Presently published: Vol. 2, *Sports Champions ;* Vol. 3, *Actors;* Vol. 4, *Scientists* (1973). The biographical references used are listed in detail in each of these works.

    3. *L'Athlège,* ed. Kleber, Paris, 1949, pp. 323–24.

Chapter Seven—The Mars Temperament and Sports Champions

    1. This is a condensation of the study "What Makes Champions Win?" which was published in the journal *Psychologie,* no. 18, July 1971, pp. 25–30. On the psychology of sport, read Michel Bouet, *Signification du sport* and *Les Motivations des sportifs,* Editions Universitaires, Paris, 1968 and 1969, and the studies published in *The International Journal of Sport Psychology,* Rome.

    2. Dr. Cappon, *Le Sport,* Geigy documentation, 1968. This statement by Dr. Cappon is extremely interesting: In our studies, greater numbers of champions, military leaders and the big captains of industry are born after Mars has passed the horizon and reached the meridian.

    3. *Football Magazine,* No. 45.

    4. On Sheldon, see our chapter XIII, "Planetary Types and Modern Psychology."

    5. M. Bouet, *op. cit.,* p. 53.

    6. L'Athlyge, *op. cit.,* p. 324.

    7. L'Athlège, *op. cit.,* p. 267.

    8. All the numerical data can be found in Volume 2 of Series C published by our Laboratory: *Planète et psychologie des champions de sports* (1973). To give an idea of the comprehensiveness of the results, here is an example concerning only two character traits: "courageous" and "self-willed." We found 149 champions described as having either of these two traits. Moreover, eighty-five of these champions were born when Mars was in one of the four sectors after the horizon or the

meridian. The theoretical frequency is 49.7 and the deviation, +35.5. The critical ratio is 6.5, probability less than 0.000,000,1 (cf. vol. 2, Series C, *op. cit.*).

9. Raymond Huttier, *L'Athlège, op. cit.*, p. 160; G. Berretrot, *But-Club*, no. 228; Paul Ruinart, *But*, no. 249.

10. William F. Straub, "Personality Traits of College Football Players Who Participated at Different Levels of Competition," *International Journal of Sport Psychology*, 2, no. 1, 1971, pp. 31–41.

Chapter Eight—The Jupiter Temperament and Actors

1. For further information on the methods and results discussed in this chapter, refer to our Laboratory publication, Series C, vol. 3, *Planètes et psychologie de l'acteur* (1973).
2. AndréVilliers, *La Psychologie du comédien*, ed. Odette Lieutier, Paris, 1947.
3. Lugné-Poe: *"Le comédien ou l'excommunié,"* Comoedia, October 22, 1933. The portrait of Jules Berry will be described later in the book.
4. André Villiers, *La Psychologie du comédien, op. cit.*
5. Louis Jouvet, *Supplément au paradoxe sur le comédien*, p. 31.
6. Her idea of happiness is very similar to Jean Vilar's, another "modest" actor who was born after the culmination of Saturn and whose character has been described in the Second Interlude of this book.
7. Marcia Moore and Mark Douglas, *Astrology*, Arcane Publications, pp. 658, 662.
8. Remember that Jules Berry was born after Jupiter had reached its culmination. This was not the case with Ruggeri, or Miss Duse.
9. André Villiers, *La Psychologie du comédien, op. cit.*, p. 280.
10. Felix Larcher, *Revue d'art dramatique*, September 15, 1886.
11. La Bruyére, *Caractères*, Oeuvre II, p. 32.

Chapter Nine—The Saturn Temperament and Scientists

1. M. Gauquelin, *La Caractérologie*, Presses Universitaires de France, *art. cit.*, pp. 55, 56.
2. For further information on the methods and results discussed in this chapter, refer to our Laboratory publication, Series C, vol. 4, *Planètes et psychologie de l'homme de science*, 1973.

3. Edouard Rist, *Vingt-cinq portraits de médecins français*, Masson ed. Paris 1955, pp. 73–80.
4. S. Jonas, *100 portraits de médecins illustres*, Masson, 1960; P. Legendre, *Charles Bouchard et son temps*.
5. These two anecdotes are taken from the article "Einstein in a Jovial Mood." *Reader's Digest*, October 1972.
6. Alfred Rouxeau, *Allocution pour le monument à Maisonneuve*, 1901.
7. R. Courrier, *René Maire, notice biographique*, Academy of Sciences.
8. *Football Magazine*, no. 22, confidential tape-recorded interview.

Chapter Ten—The Lunar Temperament and Writers

1. For further information on the methods and results discussed in this chapter, refer to our Laboratory publications, Series C, vol. 5: *Planètes et psychologie de l'écrivain*, 1973.
2. *Dictionnaire biographique des auteurs*, ed. Laffont and Bompiani, 1964; *Dictionnaire de la littérature française contemporaine*, by André Bourin and Jean Rousselot, Larousse, 1966.
3. *Dictionnaire des comédiens français* by Lyonet.
4. Jean Rousselot, *Dictionnaire de la poésie française contemporaine*, Larousse, 1968.
5. See the index of vol. 6, Series A, of our Laboratory publication, pp. 37–55, "Writers Classified by Literary Genre." For the results according to literary genre: *Les Hommes et les astres, op. cit.*, p. 138–39.
6. *Dictionnaire des sports*, p. 61; *Le Miroir des sports*, no. 238; *But-Club*, no. 216.
7. *Sport et vie*, no. 14.
8. *Miroir des sports*, no. 812.
9. Arnaud Denjoy, *H. Lebesgue* (obituary notice), Academy of Sciences, 1941.

Chapter Eleven—The Diagnosis of Temperament

1. This is the provisional list of common traits appearing in both the Mars and Jupiter lists: Absolute, aggressive, ardent, bold, brave, leadership, quick-tempered, hot-headed, enthusiastic, lively, excitable, excessive, frank, audacious, heroic, immoderate, impatient, impetuous, pitiless, assertive, impulsive, independent, uncontrollable, biting,

personality, rash, terrible, sharp, vindictive, vivacious. Great soldiers are born more often than ordinary people after Mars *or* Jupiter has reached the horizon or the meridian. The list of common traits between Mars and Jupiter provides an excellent description of the military temperament.

Chapter Twelve—The Planet with a Thousand Faces

1. A planetary type comprises a large family. When we have finished our biographical investigations, we shall synthesize our observations in a book on each planetary type. This chapter is an indication of the way in which these books will be written. But here we are dealing with only a few of the problems posed by the diversity of the types. There are many other problems. Here are some of the questions we hope to be able to answer in the future:

1) What happens when a person is born when two or more planets are just after the horizon or the meridian at the time of birth?

2) Our observations show that after the setting or the lower culmination of a given planet, it is not as reliable an indication of the subject's temperament as it is after the rise or at the upper culmination. Why?

3) In addition, the birth planet does not always correspond to the subject's temperament. What is the explanation for these exceptions to the general rule?

4) Why is there such diversity for one and the same type? For example, the Jupiter types range from entertainers to tyrants.

These questions and many others are presently being studied statistically in our Laboratory and we will be publishing detailed reports on them.

2. *France-Soir*, December 9, 1947, *L'Ordre, Combat*, same date, *L'Ordre*, September 7, 1946.

3. Jean François Genest, *La France de la Troisième Règublique*, C.A.L., 1971, p. 203; Joseph de Bonnafos, *Historia*, special edition, no. 19, pp. 149-51.

4. *France-Soir*, April 24, 1970.

5. Louis Perche, *Alfred Jarry, Classique du XXe*, Editions Universitaires, 1965.

6. Jacques Lorcey, *Sacha Guitry*, La Table Ronde, 1971, pp. 119-21.

7. These results of Jupiter observed at the births of 1116 institutionalized alcoholics are part of a statistical study covering more than 6000 psychiatric patients (schizophrenics, manic-depressives, raving and unbalanced patients, etc.), the results of which will be published soon by our Laboratory under the title *Planètes et maladies mentales, une enquête statistique* (Planets and Mental Illnesses, a Statistical

Study). We also hope to publish the 6000 birth and planetary coordinates in conjunction with this publication. One of the important conclusions of this study will probably be that planetary types seem solely related to *normal psychology* and do not relate to *pathological psychology* and psychoses in particular. This important restriction of the field of planetary psychology seems determined by the very disappointing results recorded at the births of subjects suffering from mental disorders.

8. M. and F. Gauquelin: *Profession-Heredity, op. cit.,* 1972.
9. *La Revue Aérienne,* July 25, 1912.
10. Michel Lhospice, *Match pour La Manche,* Denoel, 1964, pp. 22, 84, 89, 292.
11. Jacques Mortane, *Hélène Boucher,* Plon, 1936.
12. Jupiter and the Third Reich: cf. *Les Hommes et les Astres, op. cit.,* pp. 112–14.
13. André Brissaud, *Historia,* special edition, no. 20, p. 69.
14. André Brissaud, *op. cit.,* pp. 74–76.
15. M. and F. Gauquelin, *La Psychologie au XXe siècle,* Editions Sociales Françaises, 1963, pp. 166–67.
16. The portrait of Louis XIV (see "First Interlude"). Nicolas Fouquet was born, according to the chroniclers of that era, on January 24, 1615, at 5:15 A.M. in Paris. Jupiter was at its culmination.

Chapter Thirteen—Planetary Types and Modern Psychology

1. For the methods of modern characterology, read M. Gauquelin, *Connaître les autres,* Denoel, 1970.
2. C. G. Jung, *Psychological Types,* 1950, pp. 341–44.
3. W. Sheldon, *The Varieties of Human Physique,* Harper, New York, 1940, and *The Varieties of Temperament,* Harper, New York, 1942.
4. Table taken from J. Nuttin, *La Structure de la personnalité,* Presses Universitaires de France, 1965, p. 189.
5. Dr. Escoffier-Lambiotte, *"Vers une biochimie du comportement"* (The Biochemistry of Behavior), *Le Monde,* June 2, 1971.
6. On this topic, also read Roger J. Williams, *Biochemical Individuality,* John Wiley, New York, 1963.
7. The development of research on the biochemistry of behavior will perhaps explain an important point: the same planetary factor seems represented with varying intensity among the individuals. For example, there seem to be strong Mars types and weak Mars types. Will every planetary factor have to be related to Sheldon's definition of components of varying intensity rather than to a traditional fixed type? Future research will enable us to answer this question but the concept

of planetary components of varying intensities seems more in accordance with our present observations than the concept of a traditional type.

Third Interlude—"Like Father, Like Son"

1. On the heredity of temperamental predispositions: E. Kretschmer, *Körperbau und Character*, Springer, Berlin, 25th ed., 1967.
2. J. Nuttin, *La Structure de la personnalité*, *op. cit.*, p. 202.
3. *Les Ecoutes*, June 7, 1925, article written by P.L.; Jacques Lorcey, *Sacha Guitry*, *op. cit.*, pp. 17–18, 52.
4. Jacques Lorcey, *op. cit.*, pp. 323–44, pp. 34, 35, 42.

Chapter Fourteen—Cosmic Genetics

1. Professor M. Lamy, *Tempérament et prédisposition aux maladies*, Hachette, p. 78.
2. Manfred Curry, *Bioklimatik*, 2 vols., Riederau, 1946.
3. G. Piccardi, preface to our work *L'Hérédité planétaire*, Denoel, 1966, p. 17.
4. Michel Gauquelin, *L'Hérédité planétaire*, *op. cit.*, pp. 87–88.
5. *Birth and Planetary Data Gathered Since 1949*, by M. and F. Gauquelin: Series B, vols. 1–6, Laboratory for the Study of Relationships Between Cosmic and Psychophysiological Rhythms, Paris, 1970. For a summary of the results and statistical method: *Profession-Heredity*, *op. cit.*, Paris, 1972.
6. On the effects of planetary heredity in general, the work to consult is M. Gauquelin, *L'Hérédité planétaire*, Denoel, Paris, 1966. It contains all the methodological data and all the statistics gathered in the course of our research.
7. On the distance diagonal mass effect, read *L'Hérédité planétaire*, *op. cit.*, pp. 97–100; M. Gauquelin: *"L'Effet planétaire d'hérédité en fonction de la distance de Vénus et de Mars a la terre,"* C.A., 1968, 136, pp. 561–569; M. Gauquelin: *"L'Effet planétaire dans les secteurs du coucher et de la culmination inférieure*, C.A., 1968, 134, pp. 451–58.
8. On the planetary effect between brothers and sisters, see *L'Hérédité planétaire*, *op. cit.*, pp. 126, 203, 212 (table).
9. On the planetary effect and genetic laws, see *L'Hérédité planétaire*, *op. cit.*, pp. 117–27.

Chapter Fifteen—The Baby's Role in Timing Birth

1. Based on the fact that all the fetal material has the same genetic makeup as the fetus, a revolutionary technique called amniocentesis has been developed. With this procedure, the chromosomal structure of the future child can be learned during the third month of pregnancy. Using a syringe, the doctor removes a few drops of the amniotic fluid filling the sac surrounding the fetus. The fetal cells floating in this fluid are examined. Thus the sex of the child can be determined, and possible chromosomal aberrations, like those causing mongolism, can be found. Professor Serr of the Tel Hashomer Hospital in Israel, who developed this method, has predicted that one day we will practice not only fetal medicine, but even fetal psychiatry. These new perspectives are indirectly important for our work. The fetal material has the same heredity as the fetus itself. By proving the importance of this fetal material in parturition, we can accept the idea that through this intermediary, the fetus helps choose the moment of its birth. (International Congress on Human Genetics, Paris, September 1971).

2. A. Csapo, "Function and Regulation of the Myometrium," *Annals of the New York Academy of Science*, 75, 2, p. 803, 1959.

3. Csapo, *ibid.*, p. 807.

4. Dr. G. C. Liggins, "The Fetal Role in the Initiation of Parturition in the Ewe," *Foetal Autonomy*, Ciba Foundation, Churchill ed., London, 1969, pp. 218–44. We recommend reading all the material in *Foetal Autonomy*, which is like a reference book on this interesting topic.

5. Dr. G. S. Dawes, *Foetal Autonomy, op. cit.*, p. 1.

6. J. Malek, "Characteristics of the Daily Rhythm of Menstruation and Labor," *Annals of the New York Academy of Science*, 1962, 98, 4, pp. 1042–55.

7. F. Gauquelin, "The Hour of Birth," *Population*, 1959, 4, p. 683; on the hour of birth, see *Le Concours médical*, 1960, 25, p. 3241, and 26, p. 3371. The elimination of artifacts in the problem of relationships between solar and terrestrial phenomena: "Example of the Diurnal Rhythm of Births," *Second International Symposium on Solar Terrestrial Relationships*, September 1–7, 1969, University of Brussels, "Terrestrial Modulations of the Daily Cycle of Birth," *Journal of International Cycle Research*, vol. 2. no. 2, 1971, pp. 211–17.

8. On the question of "fixed-date" births, read the interesting report in the collective work *Induction of Labor*, Macmillan, New York, 1965.

9. Claude Sureau and Jacques Chavinié, "*Causes et conséquences de l'activité contractile de l'utérus,*" *Progrès récents en Obstétrique*, Flammarion, 1970, pp. 78–9.

Chapter Sixteen—Planetary Effect and Parturition by Appointment

1. On the important question of the modification or disappearance of the planetary effect with the introduction of modern medical methods, read *L'Hérédité planétaire, op. cit.*, "*Rôle des conditions de l'accouchement,*" pp. 107–17; M. and F. Gauquelin, "Incidence of Parturition Conditions and Possible Role of the Full-term Fetus on the Planetary Effect in Heredity." *Relazioni del XV convegno della salute,* Ferrara, 1968, pp. 179–87. M. Gauquelin, "Die planetare Heredität," *Zeitschrift für Parapsychologie und Grenzgebiete der Psychologie,* 5, 168, 1961.

2. H. Vignes, *Les Douleurs de l'Accouchement,* Masson, Paris, 1951, pp. 162–3.

3. A study conducted on sports champions seems to confirm a diminution of the planetary effect in time. Likewise, champions born *since 1930* are not born as often when Mars is passing the horizon or the meridian as those born *before 1930.*

4. Perhaps one day we will be able to diagnose the planetary type to which an individual belongs from knowing his biochemical makeup. Then it will not be necessary to know the person's time of birth or the stellar configuration at the time of his birth. The diagnosis of astronomical temperament would become a biochemical matter. But as long as man and the solar system stay as they have been for thousands of years, the time of natural birth will always be, at least potentially, a valuable indication of the child's temperament.

Chapter Seventeen—The Sun: Heart of Planetary Influences

1. On living creatures and the magnetic field: M. Gauquelin, "*Effets biologiques des champs magnétiques,*" *Année biologique,* 1966, 5, pp. 595–611; M. F. Barnothy, *Biological Effects of Magnetic Fields,* vols. 1 and 2, Plenum Press, 1965 and 1969; Fr. A. Brown and J. D. Palmer, *The Biological Clock, op. cit.*; H. Friedman, R. Becker, C. Bachman, "Geomagnetic Parameters and Psychiatric Hospital Admissions," *Nature,* 1963, 626, p. 200; W. Cyran, *Geburtshilfe und Frauenheilkunde,* 1950, 10, p. 667; H. L. Yeagley, *Journal of Applied Physics,* 1947, 18, p. 1035.

2. L. G. Johnson, "Diurnal Patterns of Metabolic Variations on Chick Embryos," *Biological Bulletin,* 131, no. 2, 1966, p. 308.

3. Fr. A. Brown, *The Biological Clock, op. cit.,* pp. 36–38.

4. G. Piccardi, *The Chemical Basis of Medical Climatology, op. cit.*

5. R. Wever: "*The Influence of Weak Electromagnetic Fields on*

Circadian Rhythms in Man," Zeitschrift für Vergleichende Physiologie, 56, 1967, pp. 111–28.

6. The fact that the planet has two major periods of influence after its rise and its upper culmination is a strange and unexplained fact today. But perhaps this question will be answered in the future. Some phenomena in nature have also been shown to follow a similar rhythm. For example, Thomas J. Herron has shown that the diurnal activity of geomagnetic micropulsations has two peak activity periods between 6 and 8 A.M. (after the sun has risen) and between 12 noon and 3 P.M. (after the sun has reached the highest point in its path across the sky). It is possible that all this recent research into geomagnetic micropulsations will have a special bearing on our own work. (Thomas J. Herron, "Phase Characteristics of Geomagnetic Micropulsations," *Journal of Physical Research,* 71, no. 3, 1966.)

7. H. König and F. Ankermüller, *Naturwissenschaft,* 21, 1960, p. 483.

8. J. R. Hamer, *Biological Entrainment of the Human Brain by Low Frequency Radiation,* thesis (Northrop Space Lab.), 1967.

Fourth Interlude—The Woman in the Moone, An Astrological Comedy

1. Johnstone Parr, *Tamburlaine's Malady and Other Essays on Astrology in Elizabethan Drama,* University of Alabama Press, 1953, pp. 38–48.

2. All the quotations by ancient astrologers have been taken from J. Parr's book, *op. cit.* In the notes of his book, there are very exact references for the passages quoted.

Chapter Eighteen—Neo-astrology?

1. M. Rutten, *La Science des Chaldéens,* Presses Universitaires de France, 1960.

2. A. Sachs, "Babylonian Horoscopes," *Journal of Cuneiform Studies,* vol. 6, no. 2, 1952, 49.

3. From Lawrence Babb, *The Elizabethan Malady,* quoted in *Cycles.* This doctrine is also expressed in the works by N. Culpeper, *Astrological Judgement of Diseases* (early seventeenth century).

4. H. Selva, *La Théorie des déterminations astrologiques de Morin de Villefranche,* Bodin, Paris, no date, pp. 210–11.

5. In reference to sculptors, see *L'Influence des astres, op. cit.,* pp. 238, 241.

6. Dal Lee, *Dictionary of Astrology,* Paperback Library, New

York, 1968, pp. 157–58.

7. *New Webster Dictionary*, international edition, 1969.

8. J. A. West and J. G. Toonder, *The Case for Astrology*, Coward-McCann, New York, 1970, p. 164.

9. J. Porte, preface to the work by F. and M. Gauquelin, *Méthodes pour étudier la répartition des astres dans le mouvement diurne*, Paris, 1957, p. vi.

10. *Le Courrier rationaliste*, January 1970, p. 29.

11. We should add worldwide astrology, predictions of the events on our globe by consulting the stars. This form of astrology is very popular today. For a detailed account of this mundane astrology, read the work by Jacques Reverchon, *Value of the Astrological Judgments and Forecasts*, Paris 1971); also our work *Songes et mensonges de l'astrologie*, Hachette, 1969, Chapter VII: *"Nostradamus d'hier et d'aujourd'hui,"* pp. 197–222.

Chapter Nineteen—The Three Astrological Roulette Wheels

1. On the statistical analysis of the three astrological roulette wheels, see M. Gauquelin, *L'Influence des astres, étude critique et expérimentale*, Le Dauphin, Paris, 1955. A more complete survey is being prepared for publication by our Laboratory. Also refer to Paul Couderc, *L'Astrologie*, Presses Universitaires de France, 1951, and J. Allen Hynek, who several years ago studied the birth dates of scientists listed in *American Men of Science*, but obtained no results to confirm astrological theories.

2. Dal Lee, *Dictionary of Astrology, op. cit.*, pp. 66, 78.

3. This statement was one the astrologer Paul Choisnard tried vainly to have accepted on the basis of his statistical studies. All the details on the refutation of this law can be found in *The Scientific Basis of Astrology, op. cit.*, pp. 139–40.

4. Our observations do not concur with the unorthodox delineation of the twelve houses which is practiced by some astrologers. For example, there is the *Modus Aequalis*, in which each house is represented by a part of the zodiac, invariably equal to 30°, without taking into account the inclination of the ecliptic over the celestial equator. There is also the example of a French astrologer who has altered the numbering of the twelve houses. Each house number has been advanced one slot in the direction of the diurnal motion: thus the eleventh house becomes the twelfth house, the tenth house becomes the eleventh, the ninth house becomes the tenth, etc. (L. Lasson, *Ceux qui nous guident*, Debresse, 1946, pp. 147–48).

5. Quoted by A. and S. Strauss, *Die Astrologie des Johannes Kepler*, Berlin, 1926, p. 173.

6. P. Choisnard, *Le Loi d'hérédité astral*, Chacornac, 1919, Paris.

7. On the verification and criticism of astral heredity in an astrological sense, read: *L'Influence des astres, op. cit.*, 1955, astral heredity according to Choisnard, pp. 28–31; astral heredity according to Krafft, pp. 40–43.

8. M. Gauquelin: Astral heredity, *Cahiers astrologiques*, May–June, 1962, pp. 132–43.

Chapter Twenty—The Scientific Shock

1. Damon Knight, *Charles Fort, Prophet of the Unexplained*, Gollancz, London, 1971, p. 128, quoting Thomas S. Kuhn, *The Structure of the Scientific Revolution*, University of Chicago Press, 1962.

2. See M. Gauquelin, *Le Dossier des Influences Cosmiques*, Denoël, Paris, 1973.

3. Its entire title is "Belgain Committee for the Scientific Study of So-Called Paranormal Phenomena."

4. For a detailed report, see: M. Gauquelin, "Possible Planetary Effects at the Time of Birth of 'Successful' Professionals: An Experimental Control," *Journal of Interdisciplinary Cycle Research*, vol. 3, nos. 3 and 4, 1972, pp. 381–389.

Afterword
THE PLANETARY FACTORS IN PERSONALITY

SUMMARY

Some years ago, we devised a statistical approach to the problem of the planetary factors in personality: the character-traits method.[1] The character-traits of sports champions, scientists, actors, and writers were gathered from biographical documents. Each character-trait was then compared with the positions of the planets during their diurnal movement, at the time of birth of the studied individuals. Whatever the profession, a constant relationship was observed between a given planet and given character-traits. Correlations appeared between:

> Mars and the typical personality of sports champions
> Saturn and the typical personality of men of science
> Jupiter and the typical personality of actors
> The Moon and the typical personality of writers[2]

This method permitted us to discover a significant relationship between planetary positions at birth and personality types.[3] The planetary factors of personality Mars, Jupiter, Saturn and the Moon can therefore now be accurately described.

AIM OF THE PRESENT STUDY

Until now, however, our research remained incomplete. Each planetary temperament has been described through notabilities pertaining to one specific professional group only. It is necessary to demonstrate that the same character-traits are always correlated with the same planet, whatever the professional activity of the subjects. We will now prove it.

TABLE I   MARS

Subjects having the typical sports champion's personality traits.

12 SECTORS

sector	A) SPORTS CHAMPIONS (RECALL)			B) SCIENTISTS, ACTORS & WRITERS		
	obs	theo	dif	obs	theo	dif
1	558	403.6	+154.4	723	560.1	+162.9
2	75	84.4	- 9.4	481	597.4	-116.4
3	104	127.1	- 23.1	546	593.2	- 47.2
4	293	246.5	+ 46.5	712	574.0	+138.0
5	71	93.3	- 22.3	346	497.2	-151.2
6	128	166.2	- 38.2	780	677.6	+102.4
7	233	203.0	+ 30.0	512	453.1	+ 58.9
8	199	266.6	- 67.6	373	434.1	- 61.1
9	105	170.3	- 65.3	337	370.9	- 33.9
10	235	207.8	+ 27.2	745	636.3	+108.7
11	115	168.1	- 53.1	393	530.2	-137.2
12	183	162.1	+ 20.9	490	513.9	- 23.9
N	2299	2299	0	6438	6438	0

18 SECTORS

sector	A) SPORTS CHAMPIONS (RECALL)			B) SCIENTISTS, ACTORS & WRITERS		
	obs	theo	dif	obs	theo	dif
1	242	176.6	+ 65.4	277	239.6	+ 37.4
2	420	299.3	+120.7	588	462.6	+125.4
3	60	68.3	- 8.3	382	445.5	- 63.5
4	43	59.1	- 16.1	327	419.5	- 92.5
5	76	84.4	- 8.4	318	325.6	- 7.6
6	189	153.9	+ 35.1	494	366.1	+127.9
7	121	120.1	+ 0.9	341	368.6	- 27.6
8	54	65.8	- 11.8	223	336.6	-113.6
9	71	95.9	- 24.9	497	412.2	+ 84.8
10	119	129.0	- 10.0	497	461.8	+ 35.2
11	171	144.2	+ 26.8	298	256.7	+ 41.3
12	148	186.2	- 38.2	245	250.9	- 5.9
13	85	140.1	- 55.1	266	321.2	- 55.2
14	71	110.4	- 39.4	199	232.9	- 33.9
15	165	141.2	+ 23.8	572	461.7	+110.3
16	91	90.7	+ 0.3	366	426.7	- 60.7
17	94	143.9	- 49.9	200	278.0	- 78.0
18	79	89.9	- 10.9	348	371.8	- 23.8
N	2299	2299	0	6438	6438	0

THE MARS FACTOR IN PERSONALITY

A character-traits list describing the sports champions' typical personality is reproduced hereafter. In a preceding volume[2] we demonstrated that the champions to whom their biographers had attributed one or several traits of this list, were born more often than the whole champions set when the planet Mars had just passed the horizon or the meridian (see Table 1A).

We then checked for these traits in the catalogues of scientists, actors and writers.[2] We studied the Mars distribution among scientists, actors and writers to whom these traits had been attributed.

The catalogues of these three groups contained a total of 46,125 units, i.e. a trait attributed to a person (of course a trait was often attributed to several persons, or described several times the same person). Among these 46,125 units, 6438 were traits of the list "typical personality of the champions." Table I B gives the 12 and 18 sectors distributions of Mars during its diurnal movement, at the birth hour of the scientists, actors and writers described with these traits.

The corresponding theoretical frequencies were obtained proportionally to the whole set of individuals in each of these three groups, according to the procedure detailed in our preceding publications.[2]

As one can read in Table I B, the scientists, actors and writers described by the "champion's typical personality" traits are significantly more often born with Mars situated in the sectors following the horizon and the meridian than the whole set of individuals in these three groups.

This new distribution of Mars is positively correlated with the Mars distribution previously observed with the sports champions described by the same traits (Table I A). The Pearson correlation coefficient (r) gives following values: on the 12 sectors distributions, $r = 0.68$, probability $< .02$; on the 18 sectors distribution, $r = 0.59$, probability $< .01$.

We can therefore assume that the relationship between the diurnal position of Mars and a definite psychological temperament is not a feature of the champions only; it appears as well with individuals belonging to groups specialized in other activities such as scientists, actors and writers. This replication is an important confirmation of the existence of a Mars factor in personality.

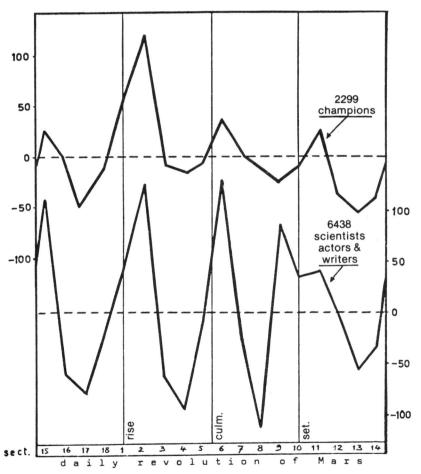

Figure 1: *Mars and the champions' typical personality traits*

TABLE II   JUPITER

Subjects having the typical actor's personality traits.

12 SECTORS

sector	A) ACTORS (RECALL) obs	theo	dif	B) CHAMPIONS, SCIENTISTS & WRITERS obs	theo	dif
1	1144	801.4	+342.6	731	683.0	+ 48.0
2	329	606.8	-277.8	469	578.3	-109.3
3	431	503.5	- 72.5	741	712.8	+ 28.2
4	1509	931.8	+577.2	938	724.4	+213.6
5	612	639.5	- 27.5	616	613.1	+ 2.9
6	267	412.1	-145.1	459	415.1	+ 43.9
7	389	402.3	- 13.3	965	919.4	+ 45.6
8	203	308.5	-105.5	537	631.8	- 94.8
9	269	540.8	-271.8	615	741.9	-126.9
10	610	541.2	+ 68.8	880	885.1	- 5.1
11	185	177.7	+ 7.3	576	696.5	-120.5
12	384	466.4	- 82.4	1140	1065.6	+ 74.4
N	6332	6332	0	8667	8667	0

18 SECTORS

sector	A) ACTORS (RECALL) obs	theo	dif	B) CHAMPIONS, SCIENTISTS & WRITERS obs	theo	dif
1	706	541.9	+164.1	828	673.1	+154.9
2	577	381.1	+195.9	454	461.2	- 7.2
3	250	327.5	- 77.5	266	333.3	- 67.3
4	156	427.3	-271.3	335	419.1	- 84.1
5	354	355.4	- 1.4	609	538.7	+ 70.3
6	1054	664.6	+389.4	527	433.1	+ 93.9
7	645	465.4	+179.6	642	500.8	+141.2
8	422	441.4	- 19.4	385	403.8	- 18.8
9	156	289.4	-133.4	298	258.8	+ 39.2
10	229	236.9	- 7.9	496	515.6	- 19.6
11	271	288.0	- 17.0	630	559.9	+ 70.1
12	125	152.7	- 27.7	387	452.1	- 65.1
13	224	472.1	-248.1	383	470.3	- 87.3
14	123	224.6	-101.6	382	451.3	- 69.3
15	466	430.1	+ 35.9	619	605.0	+ 14.0
16	221	186.9	+ 34.1	440	503.0	- 63.0
17	108	101.9	+ 6.1	397	473.7	- 76.7
18	245	344.8	- 99.8	589	614.2	- 25.2
N	6332	6332	0	8667	8667	0

THE JUPITER FACTOR IN PERSONALITY

A character-trait list describing the actors' typical personality is reproduced hereafter. Previously we demonstrated that the actors to whom their biographers had attributed one or several traits of this list, were born more often than the whole actors set when the planet Jupiter had just passed the horizon or the meridian (see Table II A).

We then checked for these traits in the catalogues of sport champions, scientists and writers.[2] We studied the Jupiter distribution among sports champions, scientists and writers to whom these traits had been attributed.

Among the 34,349 traits of these three catalogues, 8667 belonged to the "typical personality of the actor." Table II B gives the 12 and 18 sectors distributions of Jupiter during its diurnal movement at the birth hour of the champions, scientists and writers described with these traits. The corresponding theoretical frequencies were obtained proportionally to the whole set of individuals in these three groups. As one can read in Table II B, champions, scientists and writers described by the "actors' typical personality" traits are significantly more often born with Jupiter situated in the sectors following the horizon and the meridian than the whole set of individuals in these three groups.

This new distribution of Jupiter is correlated with the Jupiter distribution previously observed with the actors described by the same traits (see Table II A). The Pearson correlation coefficient (r) gives following values: with the 12 sectors distribution, $r = 0.74$, probability $< .01$, with the 18 sectors distribution, $r = 0.78$, probability $< .01$.

We can therefore assume that the relationship between the diurnal position of Jupiter and a definite psychological temperament is not just a feature of the actors group; it appears with individuals belonging to groups as different as sports champions, scientists and writers. The existence of a Jupiter factor in personality is confirmed by these results.

Figure 2 visually shows the striking resemblance between these two distributions of Jupiter.

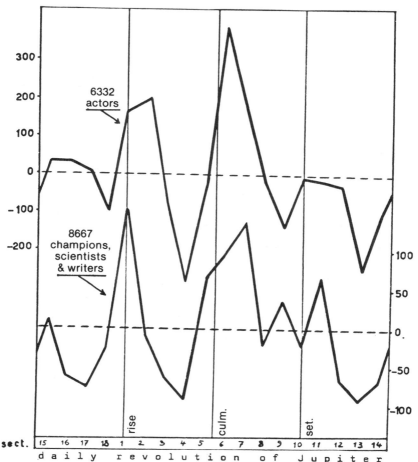

Figure 2: *Jupiter and the actors' typical personality traits*

Abscissa: the diurnal movement of Jupiter divided in 18 sectors.
Ordinate: differences between actual and theoretical frequencies.

Both curves show the same pattern: maximum of births when Jupiter has just passed the horizon and the meridian, in particular after its rise and its upper culmination (r = 0.78 P < 0.01).

TABLE III   SATURN

Subjects belonging to the typical science personality traits.

12 SECTORS

sector	A) SCIENTISTS (RECALL)			B) CHAMPIONS, SCIENTISTS & WRITERS		
	obs	theo	dif	obs	theo	dif
1	486	388.9	+ 97.1	950	671.5	+278.5
2	124	154.6	- 30.6	801	928.6	-127.6
3	387	427.2	- 40.2	976	992.6	- 16.6
4	474	364.4	+109.6	1043	695.9	+347.1
5	148	187.9	- 39.9	1014	1080.7	- 66.7
6	173	157.0	+ 16.0	618	611.1	+ 6.9
7	272	350.9	- 78.9	906	797.5	+108.5
8	181	200.3	- 19.3	516	629.9	-113.9
9	315	277.6	+ 37.4	442	604.8	-162.8
10	119	137.5	- 18.5	753	893.9	-140.9
11	327	303.5	+ 23.5	772	766.9	+ 5.1
12	203	259.2	- 56.2	687	804.6	-117.6
N	3209	3209	0	9478	9478	0

18 SECTORS

sector	A) SCIENTISTS (RECALL)			B) CHAMPIONS, SCIENTISTS & WRITERS		
	obs	theo	dif	obs	theo	dif
1	217	198.0	+ 19.0	379	307.1	+ 71.9
2	340	243.7	+ 96.3	800	537.2	+262.8
3	116	143.2	- 27.2	583	686.8	-103.8
4	87	109.9	- 22.9	497	551.2	- 54.2
5	308	328.7	- 20.7	697	683.6	+ 13.4
6	388	302.2	+ 85.8	751	479.0	+272.0
7	126	105.5	+ 20.5	764	643.0	+121.0
8	108	144.5	- 36.5	542	654.6	-112.6
9	96	91.4	+ 4.6	359	337.0	+ 22.0
10	162	167.1	- 5.1	698	610.6	+ 87.4
11	187	249.4	- 62.4	467	461.1	+ 5.9
12	89	112.6	- 23.6	345	432.8	- 87.8
13	182	161.0	+ 21.0	338	462.5	-124.5
14	225	204.4	+ 20.6	275	339.4	- 64.4
15	70	102.9	- 32.9	474	493.4	- 19.4
16	132	129.7	+ 2.3	417	571.3	-154.3
17	244	208.4	+ 35.6	634	595.7	+ 38.3
18	132	206.4	- 74.4	458	631.7	-173.7
N	3209	3209	0	9478	9478	0

THE SATURN FACTOR IN PERSONALITY

A character-trait list describing the scientists' typical personality is reproduced hereafter. Previously we demonstrated that the scientists to whom their biographers had attributed one or several traits of this list, were born more often than the whole scientists set when the planet Saturn had just passed the horizon or the meridian (see Table III A).

We then checked for these traits in the catalogues of sport champions, actors and writers.[2] We studied the Saturn distribution among sports champions, actors and writers to whom these traits had been attributed.

Among the 42,762 traits of these three catalogues, 9478 belonged to the "typical personality of the scientist." Table II B gives the 12 and 18 sectors distributions of Saturn during its diurnal movement at the birth hour of the champions, actors and writers described with these traits. The corresponding theoretical frequencies were obtained proportionally to the whole set of individuals in these three groups. As one can read in Table III B, champions, actors and writers described by the "scientists' typical personality" traits are significantly more often born with Saturn situated in the sectors following the horizon and the meridian than the whole set of individuals in these three groups.

This new distribution of Saturn is correlated with the previous Saturn distribution observed with the scientists described by the same traits (see Table III A). The Pearson correlation coefficient (r) gives following values: with the 12 sectors distribution, $r = 0.64$, probability $< .02$, with the 18 sectors distribution, $r = 0.74$, probability $< .01$.

We can therefore assume that the relationship between the diurnal position of Saturn and a definite psychological temperament is not only a feature of the scientists group; it also appears with individuals belonging to groups as different as sports champions, actors and writers. These results are an important confirmation of the Saturn factor in personality.

Figure 3 visually shows the striking resemblance between these two distributions of Saturn.

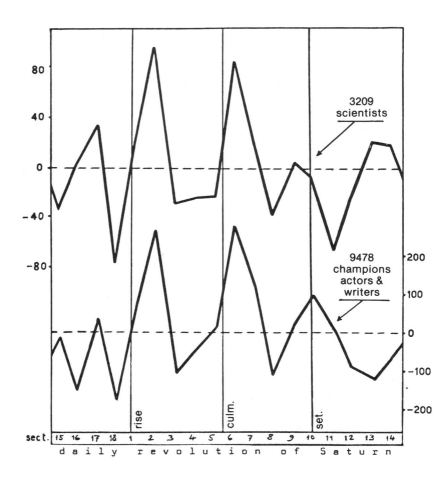

Figure 3: *Saturn and the scientists' typical personality traits*

Abscissa: the diurnal movement of Saturn divided in 18 sectors.
Ordinate: differences between actual and theoretical frequencies.
Both curves show the same pattern: maximum of births when Saturn has just passed the rise and the upper culmination (r = 0.74 P < 0.01).

TABLE IV   MOON

Subjects having the typical writer's personality traits.

12 SECTORS

sector	A) WRITERS (RECALL) obs	theo	dif	B) CHAMPIONS, SCIENTISTS & ACTORS obs	theo	dif
1	776	546.4	+229.6	704	568.8	+135.2
2	131	197.5	- 66.5	343	380.4	- 37.4
3	389	364.1	+ 24.9	528	619.1	- 91.1
4	821	624.8	+196.2	427	377.6	+ 49.4
5	319	422.4	-103.4	289	280.0	+ 9.0
6	212	232.6	- 20.6	506	464.7	+ 41.3
7	361	327.8	+ 33.2	422	434.7	- 12.7
8	279	374.5	- 95.5	492	541.9	- 49.9
9	259	267.2	- 8.2	403	438.7	- 35.7
10	421	399.9	+ 21.1	516	527.5	- 11.5
11	265	345.0	- 80.0	501	505.9	- 4.9
12	274	404.8	-130.8	424	415.7	+ 8.3
N	4507	4507	0	5555	5555	0

18 SECTORS

sector	A) WRITERS (RECALL) obs	theo	dif	B) CHAMPIONS, SCIENTISTS & ACTORS obs	theo	dif
1	125	135.8	- 10.8	350	323.3	+ 26.7
2	753	528.9	+224.1	435	352.3	+ 82.7
3	106	124.4	- 18.4	267	268.8	- 1.8
4	176	215.7	- 39.7	313	455.7	-142.7
5	238	221.5	+ 16.5	291	275.0	+ 16.0
6	443	309.1	+133.9	283	243.2	+ 39.8
7	461	430.9	+ 30.1	263	253.1	+ 9.9
8	236	307.2	- 71.2	170	161.2	+ 8.8
9	152	172.6	- 20.6	303	277.2	+ 25.8
10	117	119.6	- 2.6	363	328.9	+ 34.1
11	304	268.2	+ 35.8	262	293.2	- 31.2
12	118	166.1	- 48.1	372	363.1	+ 8.9
13	204	268.0	- 64.0	243	312.7	- 69.7
14	216	207.7	+ 8.3	280	304.9	- 24.9
15	257	227.8	+ 29.2	332	301.6	+ 30.4
16	273	336.0	- 63.0	323	370.7	- 47.7
17	156	181.1	- 25.1	362	361.0	+ 1.0
18	172	286.4	-114.4	343	309.1	+ 33.9
N	4507	4507	0	5555	5555	0

THE MOON FACTOR IN PERSONALITY

A character-trait list describing the writers' typical personality is reproduced hereafter. Previously we demonstrated that the writers to whom their biographers had attributed one or several traits of this list, were born more often than the whole writers set when the Moon had just passed the horizon or the meridian (see Table IV A).

We then checked for these traits in the catalogues of sport champions, scientists and actors.[2] We studied the Moon distribution among sports champions, scientists and actors to whom these traits had been attributed.

Among the 33,691 traits of these three catalogues, 5555 belonged to the "typical personality of the actor." Table IV B gives the 12 and 18 sectors distributions of the Moon during its diurnal movement at the birth hour of the champions, scientists and actors described with these traits. The corresponding theoretical frequencies were obtained proportionally for the whole set of individuals in these three groups. As one can read in Table IV B, champions, scientists and actors described by the "writers' typical personality" traits are significantly more often born with the Moon situated in the sectors following the horizon and the meridian than the whole set of individuals in these three groups.

This new distribution of the Moon is correlated with the Moon distribution previously observed among writers described by the same traits (see Table IV A). The Pearson correlation coefficient (r) gives following values: with the 12 sectors distribution, $r = 0.60$, probability $< .05$, with the 18 sectors distribution, $r = 0.50$, probability $< .05$.

Therefore we can assume that relationships between the diurnal position of the Moon and a definite psychological temperament is not just a feature of writers; it appears with individuals belonging to the other groups as well. These results confirm the existence of a Moon factor in personality.

Figure 4 visually shows the striking resemblance between these two distributions of the Moon.

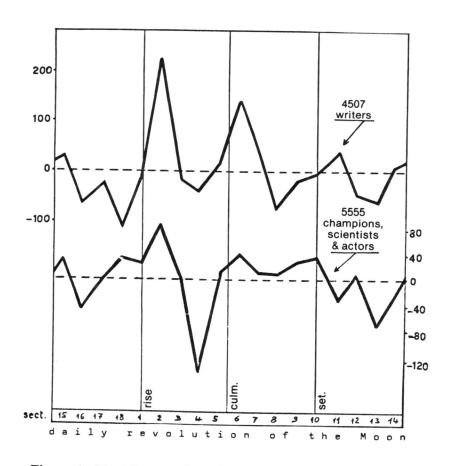

Figure 4: *The Moon and the writers' typical personality traits*

Abscissa: the diurnal movement of the Moon divided in 18 sectors.
Ordinate: differences between actual and theoretical frequencies.

Both curves show the same pattern: maximum of births when the Moon has just passed the rise and the upper culmination ($r = 0.50$ P < 0.05).

PROMINENCE OF HORIZON AND
MERIDIAN ZONES

With the character-traits method, we obtain planetary distributions that all follow the same patterns a maximum of births after the planet's crossing of the horizon and the meridian, particularly after its rise and after its upper culmination.

Figure 5 gives the sum of the positions of Mars, Jupiter, Saturn and the Moon for the 46,485 traits of our four lists. Table V gives their frequencies. Due to the great number of cases, the fluctuations due to chance are less important and the planetary effect appears more clearly in the diurnal movement. It is interesting to note how similar the character-traits and planetary positions are to the graphs obtained with the professional notabilities and with the experiment in heredity in which the planetary positions at the birth of parents and children were compared.[5]

TABLE V

Total of the preceding distributions of Mars, Jupiter, Saturn and the Moon (see Tables I to IV). (Here only the differences between actual and theoretical frequences are given)

12 SECTORS		18 SECTORS	
sector	difference	sector	difference
1	+ 1448	1	+ 529
2	− 775	2	+ 1101
3	− 238	3	− 368
4	+ 1678	4	− 724
5	− 399	5	+ 78
6	+ 7	6	+ 1178
7	+ 171	7	+ 476
8	− 608	8	− 375
9	− 667	9	− 3
10	+ 50	10	+ 112
11	− 360	11	+ 69
12	− 307	12	− 287
		13	− 683
		14	− 305
		15	+ 191
		16	− 352
		17	− 149
		18	− 488

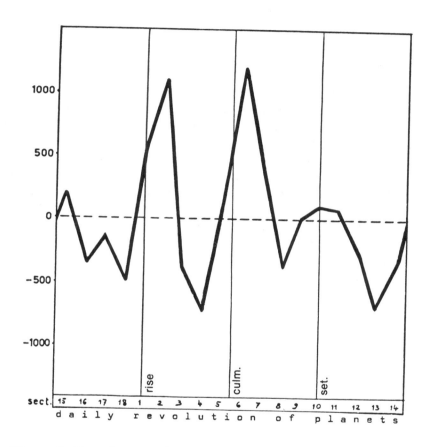

Figure 5: *Prominence of horizon-meridian zones*

Total distribution of Mars, Jupiter, Saturn and the Moon in the present study
(N = 46,485).

The whole distribution illustrates the prominence of the zones situated just
after horizon and meridian, principally after the rise and the upper culmination of the planets. This pattern was already observed in our previous studies
on notable professionals.[5]

CONCLUSION

The planetary factors of personality which relate to Mars, Jupiter, Saturn or the Moon can now be accurately described. Whatever the professional activity, definite character-traits appear in relation to the diurnal position of these planets at birth.

Whether these planetary factors appear in the personality of non-notable subjects remains to be discovered. We cannot apply the character-traits method on biographies, but we can use modern techniques of personality assessment such as tests and questionnaires in this search.

A large inquiry already has been initiated with the help of Hans J. Eysenck, of London University.[6] We are researching the answers of 2,000 persons to the Eysenck Personality Questionnaire (E.P.Q.), to analyze any correlations between the main factors of personality (introversion-extroversion, stability-instability, etc.) and the diurnal positions of Mars, Jupiter, Saturn and the Moon at birth. We await the results with anticipation.

LISTS OF CHARACTER TRAITS DESCRIBING THE MARS, JUPITER, SATURN AND MOON TEMPERAMENTS

Each of these lists is reprinted from a volume of the "Psychological Monographs" series.[2] Because these lists were established from biographical sources, the typical personality of the sports champion (Mars factor) is described with less traits than the typical personality of the actor (Jupiter factor) or the writer (Moon factor). The reason, of course, is that the sports vocabulary is poorer and more stereotyped than the vocabulary of the stage or literature specialist.

The temperamental descriptions published here are only a beginning. In order to be more objective, we have not modified these lists. In the future, our lists of traits representing the typical personality of sports champions, actors, scientists and writers will be enlarged in order to give better descriptions of the real Mars, Jupiter, Saturn and Moon factors in personality.

LIST OF CHARACTER TRAITS DESCRIBING
THE SPORTS' CHAMPION'S TYPICAL PERSONALITY*
(MARS FACTOR)

grasping	quick-tempered	sharp
strenuous	liveliness	obstinate
active	training hard	offensive
restless	enterprising	persistent
aggressive	quixotic	opponent
alert	exceptional	passionate
go-getter	excessive	piercing
animates	explosive	percussive
animated	fanatic	steadfast
harsh	fierce	personality
ardent	firm	fearless
audacious	ferocious	all of a piece
adventurous	feverish	pioneer
quarrelsome	dash	prowess
fighting	fervour	powerful
bellicose	charger	violent-tempered
boiling	full of strength	producer
an old salt	fiery	realistic
surly	frantic	redoubtable
brave (courageous)	winner	regular
brutal	hot-tempered	resistant
plodder	bold	takes risks
obstinate	peevish	robust
nut	heroic	rough
character(to have)	bad tempered	rugged
bad-tempered	immoderate	coolness
curt	impatient	dry
reckless	impetuous	solid
plenty of guts	pitiless	spontaneous
hardhitter	implacable	sure
choleric	imprudent	overcomes difficulties
combative	impulsive	rash
concentrated	incisive	temperamental
conqueror	independent	tenacious

*according to the alphabetical order of the French words

tough
courageous
resolute
plucky
resolute

determined
likes difficulty
direct
straight
hard
dynamic
efficacious
hot-headed
long-suffering
energetic
enthusiastic

undisciplined
intameable
unshakeable
indefatigable
inflexible
tireless
stiff-necked
intransigent
invincible
irascible
unconsidered
fighter
self-controlled
moral courage
mordant
goes at it
terrible

headstrong
stubborn
hard-working
turbulent
valiant
valorous
ripe old age
lively
vindictive
violent
virile
virulent
vitality
self-willed

LIST OF CHARACTER TRAITS DESCRIBING
THE ACTOR'S TYPICAL PERSONALITY*
(JUPITER FACTOR)

briskness
abundant gestures
engrossing
accent
vivavious
stinging
born actor
bustling
sense of business
attracts notice
provocative
enticing
ease (with)
alert
buoyant
cheerful
a good presence
haughty
ambitious
self-love
passing fancies
self-esteem
breadth
amusing
enjoys himself
tells anecdotes
animated
self-assurance
apostrophizes public
aptness
likes money
made man
thruster
ascendancy
assurance

bohemian
patter
enjoys life
buffoon
boiling point
not homely
quick-witted
full of fun
brilliant
dash
disagreement
acts with verve
boisterous
burlesque
drinker
a nut
pusher
receives at the
    coffee-house
street hawker
bad comrade
vulgar manners
capricious
bad tempered
caricaturist
caricatured
curt
categorical
talkative
caustic
rowdy
warm
variety singer
charming
sultry voice

condescending
lecturer
self-confident
non-conformist
conqueror
conscious of his value
pleased with himself
contestant
contrariness
controversy
convincing
defies conventions
good conversationalist
coquettish
cutting
courtesan
braggart
shouts
criticizes others
cruel
cyclone
cynical
noble lady
a dandy
overflowing
resourceful
relaxed
never discouraged
disdainful
perky
likes disguises
indelicate
cute
contentious
inordinate

astute	chief	spendthrift
attractive	smart	does not resign
alluring	lashing	detached
audacious	clown	disobliging
autocratic	droll	screamingly funny
authoritative	choleric	despot
authority	coloured	diatribe
superior manners	colossal	god-like
comely	comic	difficult person
adventurous	sense of command	arguer
greedy	commercial	fluent
gift of gab	gossip	diverting
mountebank	difficult to deal with	domineering
garrulous	communicative	Don Juan
wag	all-round actor	funny
strong	excessive	yapping
hard	exciting	glory-seeker
wishes to dazzle	exacting	scoffer
wild	expansive	waggish
makes a splash	explosive	gourmand
sparkling	expressive	greatness
crushing	exteriorized	seignorial
effervescent	extraordinary	grandiloquent
frightful	extravagant	grand
cheeky	exuberant	grimaces
selfish	mythomaniac	licentious
elan	facetious	unmannerly
elegant	facility	grotesque
bad pupil	fluency of speech	rawler
eloquent	fancy	skillful
excited	whimsical	bold
bright eye	fantastic	haughty
busybody	vain	ruddy complexion
emperor	joker	whinnying
bombast	outlandish	not hesitating
hot-headed	fascinating	happy
enchanter	ostentacious	hilarious
in debt	woman of the world	man of the world
dazzling	firm	hot human
hastiness	ferocious	good mood
pampered child	pride	not even-tempered

burning
coaxer
playful
has enemies
enormity
sorcerer
headstrong
enthusiastic
quick-tempered
liveliness
enterprising
invading
captivating
beaming face
prankish
wit
sparkling
astonishing
stunning
awake
exaggeration
stirring
exasperation
eccentric

indefatigable
independent
undisicplined
individualistic
not docile
untameable
not indulgent
inexhaustible
indefatigable
infernal
unfaithful
inflexible
exercises influence
unjust
tireless
inquisitive

full of strength
formidable
overwhelming
fiery
frank
blunt
free-lance
plays pranks
sows wild oats
humming
brisk
frivolous
banterer
humbug
cunning
gay
cheery
gallant
tells tall stories
skips
very elegant
bad manners
broad humour
scoffing
unfashionable
majestic
malicious
shrewd
very funny
massive
show-off
bad lot
backbiter
megalomaniac
leader
contemptuous
meridional
marvellous
not temperate
had numerous jobs
mimics

humorous
harum-scarum
hypnotizes
idol
imitator
immodest
impatient
imperious
impertinent
impetuous
pitiless
implacable
impolite
important
imposing
asserts himself
impressive
improviser
unchaste
impulsive
unappeased
outburst
incisive
improper

orator
organizer
proud
original
excesses
open
palpitating
paradoxical
goes on parade
talks a great deal
gets talked about
breaks his promise
patron
pedant
persuasive
sparkling

insistant
insolent
careless
insufferable
endless arguer
intemperate
self-seeking
intimidating
stiff-necked
intransigent
intriguer
inveighs
irascible
ironic
irradiating
irresistible
irreverent
irritable
gambler
sensualist
journalist
jovial
merry
legendary
nimble
likes liberty
unconventional
gleaming eye
likes luxury
Machiavellian
stage magician
magnetic
magnificent
protector
provocative
advertises himself
powerful
quarreler
Rabelaisian
story-teller
radiant
bantering

not minute
flashing eye
missions
mobile face
fashionable
modern
not modest
egotism
mundane
huge actor
likes display
mocking
mordant
witticism
skunk
saucy
hoaxer
mythic
chaffer
somnambulist
no nuance
obscene
obstinate
very busy
ogles
offers herself
olympian
easily offended
omnipotent
persistent
opportunist
opponent
optimistic
seductive
sprightly
sensational
makes a sensation
sensual
takes himself seriously
not serious
sex-appeal
lack of simplicity

frisky
phenomenon
prancing
spruce
piquant
clown
picturesque
jokes
pleases
likes amusement
full voice
polemist
not polite
political
pompous
popular
practical
engaging
presence
president
presumptuous
fine presence
quick
wondrous
pretentious
spontaneous
litigant
prodigious
prodigal
not deep
prompt
propagandist
prosperous
whirling
trenchant
agitation
triumphant
has triumphs
coarse
boon companion
tumultuous
turbulent

recriminative
rapacious
entrancing
radiant
radiance
likes to receive
redoubtable
cheering
has influential friends
noteworthy
attracts attention
widely known
quick at repartee
reputed
not reserved
not resigned
resplendent
resounding
demanding
rich
open to ridicule
fond of fun
ripostes
takes risks
rivalries
king, queen
outspoken
caty
foxy
grouser
against routine
rubicund face
gripping
over-familiarity
sarcastic
satanic
satiricial
savoir-faire
racy
scandalous

simulator
sociable
solemn
dreads solitude
sumptuous
loud voice
flares up easily
smiling
sovereign
speculates
witty
splendid
spontaneous
stimulating
not studious
stupefying
subjugates
successful
forces success
superb
superficial
haughtiness
self-assured
over-estimated
gets over difficulties
surprising
susceptible
sympathetic
synthetic mind
keeps above board
lack of tack
roisterer
teasing
rash
much temperament
tempestuous
terrible
strong-minded
theatrical
stentorial voice
crazes

tyrannical
go-getter
vanquisher
knows his merit
conceited
likes variety
star
vehement
crude speech
verve
loose living
lively
vindictive
vitality
vivifying
pleasure-seeker
fickle
volubility
voluptuous
vulgar
laughing

LIST OF CHARACTER TRAITS DESCRIBING THE SCIENTIST'S TYPICAL PERSONALITY (SATURN FACTOR)

abnegation	discouraged	uneasy
absorbed	deductive	grave
lack of ambition	delicate	skilful
analytical mind	has depressions	has habits
anguished	disillusioned	hesitating
anxious	disinterested	honest
apostle	sense of detail	does not seek honours
diligent	sense of duty	humble
not a thruster	dignified	immutable
ascetic	not a dilettante	impartial
assiduous	not diplomatic	impassive
attentive	not a director	impeccable
austere	discipline	impenetrable
intellectual curiosity	discreet	imperturbable
well advised	distant	does not improvise
patient work	well informed	uncomfortable
sincere	pained	ingenious
common sense	doubts himself	tireless
surly	soft	unquiet
good fellow	straight	unsociable
brief	fails	upright
handy	economical	intellectual reputation
horror of noise	listens	likes intimacy
calm	writes little	not intriguing
likes country life	unobtrusive	introverted
artless	good scholar	irreproachable
Cartesian	not bombastic	isolated
bachelor	enigmatic	jansenist
ragged professor	headstrong	judicious
classifier	equitable	likes justice
collector	erudite	labman
not commercial	esteemed	laborious
competent	narrow-minded	slow
concentrated	exact	limpid soul
concise	apologizes	logical
condensed	exemplary	distant

trustworthy
not confident
no confidences
eager for knowledge
conscientious
constant
continuity
good control
convinced
correct
timorous
critical sense
inqusitive mind

misanthropic
not fashionable
model
modest
mundane
moral
morose
naive
loves nature
natural
neglected
takes notes
objective
obscure
observant
obstinate
persistent
orderly
organized
not proud
not ostentatious
pacific
peaceful
pale
speaks little
likes the past
patient

experimenter
expert
no facility
weak voice
likes facts
starveling
likes family life
unsociable
faithful
fervour
freshness
cold
frugal
awkward
poor
pensive
seeks perfection
steadfast
persistent
pessimistic
prefers to walk
placid
non polemist
punctual
well balanced
precise
preoccupied
not pretentious
foreseeing
has principles
upright
deep
prudent
chaste
pure
qualified
stiff
reasoned
little gestures
rational
grim

loyal
lucid
mastership
clumsy
maniac
stony
early riser
meditative
distrustful
melancholy
temperate
methodical
meticulous
minute
does not like
   receptions
recluse
rectitude of
   judgment
meditative
reflective
regular
uncommunicative
reserved
resigned
respectful
retiring
lives in retirement
dreaming
rigid
rigorous
sagacious
wise
coolness
unsociable
learned
scrupulous
secret
selective
sensitive
serene

serious
silent
simple
sincere
sober
careful
solitary
hollow voice
strict
studious
not very successful

systematic
taciturn
retarded
technician
tenacious
loves native place
timid
timorous
tormented
hard-working
sad

embittered
valetudinary
not conceited
verifies everything
seeks the truth
virtuous
old bachelor
vigilant
travels little
true
zealous

LIST OF CHARACTER TRAITS REPRESENTING THE WRITERS' TYPICAL PERSONALITY (MOON FACTOR)

Lets himself go
abundant
acceptance
accessible
arranging
agreement
welcoming
adaptable
adhesion
admires the others
aerial
agility of mind
agreeable
not aggressive
helps others
asks for help
amiable
loving
loved
altruistic
ambivalent
amenity
amused
not analytical
loves animals
appeasing
harlequin
assent
poetic atmosphere
winning
moved
not attentive
considerate
authentic
not authoritative

bucolic
frequents bars
no calculator
good comrade
chameleon
street hawker
likes countrylife
artless
capricious
not caustic
changing
melodious poetry
songwriter
charitable
shimmering style
not a chief
chimerical
tries not to shock
great hearted
not coherent
in collaboration
sense of collectivity
not combative
communicative
communal
in communion
good companion
compassionate
obliging
complicity with others
pays compliments
understanding
not concentrated
conciliating
lecturer

easy going
overflowing
disconcerting
relaxed
defends others
delegate
canvassing
half-tone
dependant
spendthrift
disarming
relaxed
disordered
devoted
variegated
diffuse
dilettante
diplomatic
is a disciple
dispersed
available
not dissimulating
not distant
quiet hobby
absent minded
diverse
docile
not dogmatic
giver
dazzled
eclectic
listens to others
effusion
not selfish
elegiac

no authority
comely
hustler
stroller
playful
frequently dances
talkative
loves animals
bohemian
genuine
good hearted
simple good heart
good guy
happy
good nature
willingly
willingness
good form
enjoys life
always moving
playwright
good fellow

apologizes
not exacting
exotic
expansive
need to express
   himself
exteriorized
fabling
facetious
has facility
familiar
imagination
phantasmagoric
whimsical
likes the fantastic
fascinated
prolific

confessions
confiding in others
makes confidences
is the confident
no conflict
worth consulting
assent
consoler
contemplative
narrator
contradictory
convinced
conversationalist
changes faith
feeling of
   correspondence
cosmic sense
cosmopolitan
not courageous
flattering manners
credulous
not critical
believer
not cruel

hospitable
not hostile
human
humanist

idolizes someone
illogical
has illusions
picturesque style
lives in the imaginary
imaginative
impecunious
imprecise
impressionable
impressionist
unforeseeable
improvident

amazed
emotional
shows attention
sense of childhood
childish
not enigmatic
has no enemies
sensitive to
   surrounding
not envious
effusiveness
dispersed
epicurean
letter writer
wandering life
esoterism
mischievious
esteems others
astonished
scatterbrained
need to escape
evocative
not exact

youthful
carelessness
loves the language
languid

lightness
winning manner
liberal
limpid soul
not logical
likes playing
bright
lunar
lunatic
lyric
malicious
malleable

likes fairyhood
faithful
subtle
dawdler
flatterer
naive lover
flexible
floating
fluctuates
fluid
has fervour
abundance
likes folklore
not formal
freshness
very French
fraternal
eccentric
fusion
fleeing
gambolling
prankish
waster
awkward
kind
gentleman
weathercock
willingly
gracious
gratitude
in a group
likes to be guided
not stiff
no hatred
harmonic
risky
hasty
hesitating
not punctual
happy
unexpected

improvisor
impulsive
does not finish
unforeseen
uncertain
incoherent
importance of the
  unconscious
inconsistent
inconstant
irresolute
undefinable
indolent
uneven
unpunctual
infantile
susceptible to
  influence
ingenuous
innocent
difficult to catch
careless
inspired
unstable
instinctive
endless chatter
international
interpreter
likes to be interviewed
not intimidating
intimidated
intuitive
inventive
likes to be invited
irrational
unrealistic
unreal
irregular
never isolated
gushing
not jealous
fond of gardening
juggler

masuetude
harmless
not backbiting
likes meetings
melodic
at someone's mercy
memorialist
sense of the
  supernatural
not mean
not methodical
mimesis
likes mirages
mobile
fashionable
mundane
not mordant
no haughtiness
flabby
multifariousness
musical
not mysterious
mystical sense
naive
loves nature
natural
negligent
nomadic
nonchalant
no notes
expresses nuances
obedient
idle
dreamlike
undulating
opportunist
not opposing
not organized
not proud
oscillating
osmose
oblivious
open minded

pacific
pacifist
peaceful
needs peace
pantheistic

fluttering
paradoxical

paraphrase
shares
need to participate
passive
pastiche
pastoral
loves native place
not a thinker
perceptive
lost look
does not seek
perfection
pirouettes
pitying others
placid
wants to please
likes amusement
pluralism
poetical
not a polemist
political
polyglot
popular
populist
no preparation
lives in the
    present time
not pretentious
primary
primitive
spontaneous
near to others

not grudgebearing
reassuring
not rational
not realistic
not rebellious

receptive
becomes friends
    again
comforting
redundant
not reflective
relaxation
religious sense
widely known
not reserved
likes gatherings
dreaming
not rebel
not rigorous
romantic
romantic
against routine
against breaking off
moves in fashionable
    circles
satisfied
not sceptical
not scientific
scintillating
not scrupulous
not sectarian
easily seduced
open to sensations
sensitive
very sensitive
sensualism
sentimental
obliging
sociable
social action

superficial
superabundant
eager of sympathy
sympathetic
in sympathy with
    others
not systematic
desire to give
    evidence
temperate
tender
loves native place
tolerant
touching
busy-body
involved style
translator
tranquil
transparency
little working
not sad
troubadour
unifying
sense of the universal
utopian
vagabond
vaporous
varied
impulsive
venerates others
up-to-date
verbalism
changeable
loves life
not violent
virtuosity
visionary
receives many visitors
voluble
popularizer of
    knowledge

prodigal
not deep
prolific
prolix
rambler
propagandist
need of protection
proteus
likes his province
always in tune
puerile
pure
pusillanimous

not quarrelsome
quietude
rabelaisian
tells about himself
refined
refreshing
not a reasoner
socialist
solidarity
not solitary
solicits
solicitude
likes to go out

literary charm
carefree
supple
smiling
sense of remembrance
spiritualism
does not structure
not studious
stylist
submits to
subtle
singleness of mind

REFERENCES

1. Gauquelin, M. & F. (1972): Planeten und Charakterzuge. Z.f. Grenzgebiete der Psychologie, 14(1):12-36

2. Gauquelin, M. & F. (1973): The Mars Temperament and Sports Champions
Gauquelin, M. & F. (1974): The Saturn Temperament and Men of Science
Gauquelin, M. & F. (1974): The Jupiter Temperament and Actors
Gauquelin, M. & F. (1977): The Moon Temperament and Writers
Laboratoire d'etude des relations entre rhythmes cosmiques et psychophysiologiques, Paris.

3. Gauquelin, M.; Deloche, R.; Tanon, F. (1975): Temperamental significance of the planetary effect in heredity, methodology and results. J. Interdisipl. Cycle Research 6(1):60-70.

Gauquelin, M. (1975): Spheres of Influence. Psychology Today, London, number 7, pp. 20-27

4. Gauquelin, M. & F. (1972): Profession-Heredity, statistical results of Series A & B. Laboratoire d'etude des relations entre rhythmes cosmiques et psychophysiologiques, Paris.

5. Gauquelin, M. (1960): Les hommes et les astres
Gauquelin, M. (1966): L'heredite planetaire
Denoel, Paris

6. Eysenck, H.J. (1970): The Structure of Human Personality. Methuen, London

Eysenck, H.J. (1975): Planets, Stars and Personality. New Behavior, pp. 246-249

Eysenck, H.J. (1975): Les planetes, les etoiles et la personnalitie. Psychologie number 70, pp. 28-34

Eysenck, H.J., Gauquelin, M. & F. (to be published): Personality and Position of the Planets at Birth: an Empirical Study. British Journal of Social and Clinical Psychology.